READING CORINTHIANS

Charles H. Talbert

READING CORINTHIANS

A LITERARY AND THEOLOGICAL COMMENTARY ON 1 AND 2 CORINTHIANS

CROSSROAD · NEW YORK

1987

The Crossroad Publishing Company
370 Lexington Avenue, New York, N.Y. 10017

Printed in the United States of America

Library of Congress Cataloging in Publication Data

Talbert, Charles H.
Reading Corinthians

1. Bible. N.T.   Corinthians—Commentaries.
I. Bible.   N.T.   Corinthians, 1st.   English.   1987.
II. Bible.   N.T.   Corinthians, 2nd.   English.   1987.
III. Title.
BS2675.3.T34   1987   227'.206   86–23971
ISBN 0–8245–0804–1

Acknowledgments

Quotations from the Bible are taken from the Revised Standard Version or are by
the author unless otherwise specified. Quotations from the church fathers normally are from *The Ante-Nicene Fathers*. Citations from Greek and Roman
authors are usually from the Loeb Classical Library. Permission to use material
from the article "Paul's Understanding of the Holy Spirit: The Evidence of 1 Corinthians 12–14," *Perspectives in Religious Studies*, 11 (1984): 95–108, has gra-
ciously been granted by Mercer University Press.

To my family,
from whom I have learned
the meaning of inaugurated eschatology

CONTENTS

vii

PREFACE

That this volume was completed during the spring semester, 1986, was due to a Reynolds Research Fellowship from Wake Forest University and a grant from its Graduate Council. The research for the book was done largely in connection with my teaching of exegetical courses on the Corinthian correspondence over the past decade. The students at Wake Forest University who have taken these courses have served as a stimulus for my learning and deserve my sincere thanks. My thinking about many of the key issues was clarified by dialogue with my peers in the Catholic Biblical Association during two continuing seminars, one on 1 Corinthians in 1984 and the other on 2 Corinthians in 1985. Incentives for putting parts of the whole together were furnished by the opportunity to write an article for *Perspectives on the New Testament: Essays in Honor of Frank Stagg* (Macon, Ga.: Mercer University Press, 1985), by the invitation to produce a paper on Paul and the Covenants for a symposium on the New Testament and Judaism at the Southern Baptist Theological Seminary, April 1986, and by the privilege of giving the Sprinkle Lectures at Atlantic Christian College in March 1986. No contribution to this volume has been more significant than that of our family's dinnertime theological dialogues, which, over the past decade, have often focused on the issues raised by the Corinthian correspondence. To all of those who have assisted me in attempting to produce a book that I hope will introduce a reader with little or no knowledge of the biblical languages to the text itself, as opposed to literature about the text, I say thanks.

Pentecost, 1986

ABBREVIATIONS

ABR	*Australian Biblical Review*
AGD	W.F. Arndt, F.W. Gingrich, F.W. Danker, *A Greek-English Lexicon of the New Testament*, 2d ed. rev.; Chicago: University of Chicago Press, 1979.
AJP	*American Journal of Philology*
ATR	*Anglican Theological Review*
BA	*Biblical Archaeologist*
Barrett, *1 Corinthians*	C.K. Barrett, *The First Epistle to the Corinthians*, Harper's NT Commentaries; New York: Harper & Row, 1968.
Barrett, *2 Corinthians*	C.K. Barrett, *The Second Epistle to the Corinthians*, Harper's NT Commentaries; New York: Harper & Row, 1973.
Bib	*Biblica*
BTB	*Biblical Theology Bulletin*
BDF	F. Blass, A. Debrunner, R.W. Funk, *A Greek Grammar of the New Testament*, Chicago: University of Chicago Press, 1961.
Bultmann, *2 Corinthians*	Rudolf Bultmann, *The Second Letter to the Corinthians*, trans. R.A. Harrisville, Minneapolis: Augsburg, 1983.
CBQ	*Catholic Biblical Quarterly*
Furnish, *2 Corinthians*	Victor Paul Furnish, *2 Corinthians*, Anchor Bible; Garden City, N.Y.: Doubleday, 1984.
HDB	*Harper's Dictionary of the Bible*, ed. P.J. Achtemeier; San Francisco: Harper & Row, 1985.
HTR	*Harvard Theological Review*
IDB	*Interpreter's Dictionary of the Bible*, ed. George Buttrick; Nashville: Abingdon, 1962.

IDB Suppl	*The Interpreter's Dictionary of the Bible: Supplementary Volume*, ed. Keith Crim; Nashville: Abingdon, 1976.
Int	*Interpretation: A Journal of Bible and Theology*
JAAR	*Journal of the American Academy of Religion*
JBL	*Journal of Biblical Literature*
JJS	*Journal of Jewish Studies*
JR	*Journal of Religion*
JSNT	*Journal for the Study of the New Testament*
JTS	*Journal of Theological Studies*
NTS	*New Testament Studies*
NovT	*Novum Testamentum*
OJRS	*Ohio Journal of Religious Studies*
Plummer, *2 Corinthians*	Alfred Plummer, *A Critical and Exegetical Commentary on the Second Epistle of St. Paul to the Corinthians*, ICC; New York: Charles Scribner's Sons, 1915.
RB	*Revue Biblique*
TDNT	*Theological Dictionary of the New Testament*, 10 volumes, ed. G. Kittel; trans. G.W. Bromiley; Grand Rapids: Eerdmans, 1964–76.
TheolT	*Theology Today*
VigChr	*Vigiliae Christianae*
ZNW	*Zeitschrift für neutestamentliche Wissenschaft*

INTRODUCTION

L ike its predecessor, *Reading Luke* (New York: Crossroad, 1982), this volume does not follow the word-by-word, phrase-by-phrase, verse-by-verse method of traditional commentaries. Rather it is concerned to understand large thought units and their relationship to Pauline thought as a whole. The focus, moreover, is on a close reading of the text. Although the author's dialogue with the Corinthian correspondence is carried on in light of the history of interpretation, the commentary makes little reference to secondary literature. Its aim is not to direct one through the maze of scholarship but to make one feel at home in the biblical text itself. If one wants to use a traditional research commentary alongside this volume, one should consider Hans Conzelmann, *1 Corinthians*, Hermeneia (Philadelphia: Fortress, 1975), and Victor Paul Furnish, *2 Corinthians*, The Anchor Bible (Garden City, N.Y.: Doubleday, 1984). Throughout, this volume attempts to take to heart the advice of Clifford Geertz:

> A good interpretation of anything—a poem, a person, a history, a ritual, an institution, a society—takes us to the heart of that of which it is an interpretation. When it does not do that, but leads us instead somewhere else . . . it may have its intrinsic charms; but it is something else than what the task at hand . . . calls for. (*The Interpretation of Cultures* [New York: Basic Books, 1973], p. 18)

At the heart of the Corinthian correspondence are two things that demand attention: *what* is said and *how* it is said. Investigation into the mode of Pauline expression is facilitated by numerous directions of scholarship. (1) Recent research has paid renewed attention to the study of ancient letters (cf. *Semeia* 22[1981], where the entire issue is devoted to Studies in Ancient Letter Writing). Pseudo-Demetrius in *Epistolary Types* lists twenty-one types of letters: friendly, commendatory, blaming, reproachful, consoling, censorious, admonishing, threatening, vituperative, praising, advisory, supplicatory, inquiring, responding, allegorical, accounting, accusing, apologetic, congratulatory, ironic, thankful

(A.J. Malherbe, "Ancient Epistolary Theorists," *OJRS* 5[1977]:3–77). Paul's letters, like many other ancient epistles, were usually a mixture of such types. For example, in the places in 1 Corinthians where Paul responds to something in the Corinthians' letter to him, he is following a responding type; in 1 Cor 5 he is censorious; in 2 Cor 1:8–2:13 he is accounting; in 2 Cor 8–9 he is advisory; in 1 Cor 4 and 2 Cor 12–13 he is threatening; while in 2 Cor 2:14–6:10 he is apologetic.

(2) Recent New Testament study has also worked on the relevance of ancient rhetoric to the Pauline epistles (George A. Kennedy, *New Testament Interpretation through Rhetorical Criticism* [Chapel Hill, N.C.: University of North Carolina Press, 1984]). From such study one learns that 1 Corinthians is largely deliberative rhetoric; that is, it aims at effecting a decision about future action. 2 Cor 1–7 is mainly judicial rhetoric; that is, it seeks to bring about a judgment about events of the past. While 2 Cor 8–9 is deliberative, 2 Cor 10–13 is epideictic rhetoric; that is, it is the oratory of praise or blame, celebrating or condemning someone or something. In other words, just as the epistolary types are mixed in the Corinthian correspondence, so is the rhetoric.

(3) One of the features of the Corinthian correspondence noted for a long time and reemphasized by recent study is the use of quotations from the Corinthians, either from their letter to Paul or from the oral reports that had reached the apostle. These quotations function as a springboard for Paul's directives, for example, 6:12; 10:23; 6:13; 7:1; 8:1; 8:4, 8:5–6; 8:8; 11:2 (John C. Hurd, *The Origin of 1 Corinthians* [Macon, Ga.: Mercer University Press, new edition, 1983], pp. 65–74). Sometimes the quotations sound like the diatribe form of antiquity: for example, 2 Cor 10:10—"One says, 'His letters are weighty and strong, but his bodily presence is weak, and his speech of no account'" (cf. Epictetus 4.9.5–6: "And what do I lose? one says. Man, you used to be modest, and are no longer so; have you lost nothing?"). At other times, the remarks are not introduced by a recognizable phrase (like "one says") and must be recognized by their discontinuity with Paul's general stance and continuity with that of the Corinthians. This, of course, was also characteristic of the diatribe (George L. Kustas, *Diatribe in Ancient Rhetorical Theory* [Berkeley: Center for Hermeneutical Studies, 1976], p. 11). Apparently, just as Tertullian cited selections from Marcion before answering him, so Paul referred to Corinthian assertions before responding. Recognition of this fact is a major factor in a proper reading of the Corinthian correspondence.

(4) No close reading of the text is possible without an awareness of the ancient techniques of inclusion, or ring composition, and of chiasmus, or concentric patterning. In a culture that was oral, there was a need for some technique to signal the beginning and ending of a thought unit. Whereas in a literary culture such boundaries are designated by paragraphs, chapters, subheadings, or even enumeration, in an oral culture the signals had to be heard. It was customary to repeat key words, phrases, and ideas at the start and finish of a thought unit to indicate its boundaries. This we call inclusion, or ring composition. Sometimes the beginning and end of an excursus were so similar that modern scholars have contended that, if the excursus were taken out, the two edges would join naturally; hence the excursus is an interpolation. This is an improper inference. Josephus offers an illustration (*Antiquities* 18.5.2 §116,119). The paragraph is an excursus on the death of John the Baptist. It begins, "Now some of the Jews thought that the destruction of Herod's army came from God, and that very justly, as a punishment of what he did"; it ends, "Now the Jews had an opinion that the destruction of the army was sent as a punishment upon Herod, and a mark of God's displeasure." Similar examples are found in 1 Cor 12:31 and 14:1; in 2 Cor 11:1 and 16; and in 2 Cor 6:11–13 and 7:2. The function of such a framing technique was to mark the boundaries of a thought unit.

Another device used not only to signal the beginning and end of a thought unit but to indicate the arrangement within the unit was chiasmus, or concentric patterning. Stated abstractly, such an arrangement runs ABCB'A' or ABB'A'. It might involve asking several questions (ABC) and then answering them in reverse order (C'B'A'), as in 1 Cor 1:13 and 1:14–4:7. It might involve the organization of a paragraph as in 1 Cor 7:2–5, or the arrangement of a section as in 1 Cor 8–10, or the pattern of an entire letter as in 2 Cor 10–13. This technique was widespread in antiquity (John W. Welch, ed., *Chiasmus in Antiquity: Structures, Analyses, Exegesis* [Hildesheim: Gerstenberg, 1981]); it was also used extensively by Paul (John J. Collins, "Chiasmus, the 'ABA' Pattern and the Text of Paul," *Studiorum Paulinorum Congressus Internationalis Catholicus*, Analecta Biblica, 17 [Rome: Biblical Institute Press, 1963], pp. 575–84). Recognition of this principle of organization in the Corinthian correspondence often allows one to avoid the cliché that Paul's thought is disjointed when it does not seem to follow a linear line of argument. Recognition of these various modes of Pauline expression enables one to understand better *how* the apostle writes.

Each section of this commentary aims not only to explicate how Paul said what he did but above all to clarify *what* he said. Paul's Corinthian letters are religious documents. What this means is stated concisely by Jacob Neusner:

> Even though, through philology, we understand every word of a text, and, through history, we know just what happened in the event or time to which the text testifies, we still do not understand that text. A religious text serves not merely the purposes of philology or history. It demands its proper place as a statement of religion. Read as anything but a statement of religion, it is misunderstood. ("Judaism within the Disciplines of Religious Studies: Perspectives on Graduate Education," *CSR Bulletin* 14 [1983]: 143)

Some readers may wish to proceed at this point directly to the commentary's first section. Others will wish to know more about the background of 1 and 2 Corinthians, namely, about the city of Corinth, about the various letters to Corinth, and about Paul's opponents in Corinth. For such readers the following pages of the introduction are designed.

Corinth

The Corinth to which Paul came in the middle of the first century was a city with no old traditions. In 146 B.C. the old Greek city of Corinth was destroyed by the Roman consul Mummius. The walls and buildings were demolished and fire set to anything that would burn (Dio Cassius *Roman History* 21; Pausanius *Description of Greece* 7.16.7). The inhabitants who were not slain were sold into slavery (Dio Cassius 21). Many of its art treasures were sent to Italy (Strabo *Geography* 8.6.23). Cicero, who saw the destroyed city about 79–77 B.C., said scarcely a trace remained of it (*Tusculan Disputations* 3.53; *On the Agrarian Law* 2.87). In 44 B.C. Julius Caesar refounded Corinth as a Roman colony (Dio Cassius 143.50.3–5; Pausanias 2.1.2; 2.3.1). The Roman settlement was by poor freedmen for the most part (Strabo 8.6.23; Appian *History* 8.136), a fact lamented by the Greek Crinagoras (*Greek Anthology* 9.284). In 27 B.C. Augustus made Corinth the capital of the Roman province of Achaia and the residence of the governor (Dio Chrysostom *Oration* 37.8). Claudius, in A.D. 44, returned the control of Achaia and Macedonia to the Senate (Suetonius "Claudius" 35.3). Corinth remained the capital from which the proconsul sent out annually from Rome ruled.

Economically Corinth was a wealthy city. Its geographical location was no small reason for its prosperity. It was a maritime city with two harbors, one leading to Asia (Cenchraea), the other to Italy (Lechaeum). Profits were to be made from trade (Strabo *Geography* 8.6.20), from travel (Dio Chrysostom *Oration* 37.8.36; Philostratus *Life of Apollonius* 7.10), from banking (Plutarch *De Vitando Aere Alieno* 7), from bronze making (Pliny *Natural History* 34.1.6–8; Josephus *Life* 68; Pliny *Letters* 3.6), and from the Isthmian games held every two years (Pausanias 2.2.2; Dio Chrysostom 8.5–10; Aelius Aristides *Orations* 46.23) (Gerd Theissen, *The Social Setting of Pauline Christianity: Essays on Corinth* [Philadelphia: Fortress, 1982]; Jerome Murphy-O'Connor, *St. Paul's Corinth* [Wilmington, Del.: Michael Glazier, 1983]).

Religiously Corinth was a center of diversity. There were pagan cults of every stripe: Apollo, Athena, Poseidon, Hera, Aphrodite, Heracles, Jupiter Capitolinus, Asklepios, Isis and Serapis (Oscar Broneer, "Corinth," *BA* 14[1951]:77–96; D.E. Smith, "The Egyptian Cults at Corinth," *HTR* 70[1977]:201–31). Greek philosophers plied their wares as well (Dio Chrysostom *Oration* 8.5–10). There was a Jewish settlement in Corinth (Philo *Embassy to Gaius* 281). It is no surprise, therefore, to hear of a synagogue there (Acts 18:4) and to learn that an inscription reading "Synagogue of the Hebrews" has been found (*IDB*, 1:684). A Christian community in Corinth from the middle of the first century would have simply added to this diversity.

The Christian church in Corinth at the time of the correspondence with Paul was small. J. Murphy-O'Connor estimates about fifty persons (*St. Paul's Corinth*, pp. 156–57). It reflected a fair cross section of the urban society. Some of its members had social standing: Crispus (Acts 18:8; 1 Cor 1:14) was a synagogue ruler and had a house; Sosthenes (Acts 18:17; 1 Cor 1:1) was a synagogue ruler; Erastus (Rom 16:23) was the city treasurer; Gaius (Rom 16:23; 1 Cor 1:14) had a house large enough to accommodate the whole church; Stephanas (1 Cor 1:16; 16:15) had a house; some (1 Cor 6:1) had enough money to engage in legal proceedings. Most did not have such social standing (1 Cor 1:26–29; 11:22). Apparently the church was not poverty-stricken, because Paul presumed that all could make some contribution to the collection for the poor in Jerusalem (1 Cor 16:2; 2 Cor 8:1–6). The church was composed of both Jews and Gentiles (1 Cor 1:22–24). It was not composed exclusively of Christian households; 1 Cor 7:12–16 indicates some were married to unbelievers. As with other Pauline churches, the Corinthian community met in private houses (1 Cor 16:19; Rom 16:5; Philem 2; Col 4:15). A distinction must be made between "the church in the house of" and "the whole church." The former was the basic cell (cf. 1 Cor 16:19; Rom 16:5); the latter was the assembly of the various cells on occasion (Rom 16:23; 1 Cor 11:20; 14:23) (Wayne A. Meeks, *The First Urban Christians* [New Haven: Yale University Press, 1983]), pp. 75–76). One of these cells may have been the church in Cenchraea of which Phoebe was a deaconess (Rom 16:1).

According to Acts 18:12 Paul's initial visit to Corinth, during which time the church was established (1 Cor 15:1–2), coincided, in part, with the term of office of the Roman governor Gallio. It is the one fixed point in determining the approximate dates of the Corinthian correspondence. From an inscription found at Delphi it appears that Gallio probably became governor in July 51 and did not serve more than one year (Adolf Deissmann, *Paul* [New York: Harper & Brothers, 1957], Appendix I, "The Proconsulate of L. Junius Gallio"; J. Murphy-O'Connor, *St. Paul's Corinth*, pp. 141–52). If this is accurate, then, assuming Acts 18:11 (Paul stayed eighteen months), the apostle may have arrived in Corinth early in A.D. 50 and left late in A.D. 51. His stay in Ephesus may then have been A.D. 53–55 and his arrival in Corinth for the last time in 55 or 56. Although exactitude in dating is impossible, the probabilities are that Paul's dealings with Corinth took place in the first half of the fifties.

The Letters

Although the authenticity of the Corinthian letters is not questioned, the integrity is, especially of 2 Corinthians. The diversity of opinion is startling: e.g., (1) a three-letter hypothesis (2 Cor 6:14–7:1; 1 Cor; 2 Cor —so A. H. McNeile, *An Introduction to the Study of the New Testament*, 2d ed. [Oxford: Clarendon, 1953]; or 1 Cor; 2 Cor 1–9; 2 Cor 10–13—so C.K. Barrett, *2 Corinthians*; F.F. Bruce, *1 and 2 Corinthians* [Grand Rapids: Eerdmans, 1971]; Furnish, *2 Corinthians*); (2) a four-letter hypothesis (2 Cor 6:14–7:1; 1 Cor; 2 Cor 10–13; 2 Cor 1–9—so T.W. Manson, *Studies in the Gospels and Epistles*, ed. M. Black [Philadelphia: Westminster Press, 1962]); (3) a five-letter hypothesis (*a*. 1 Cor 10:1–23; 6:12–20; 11:2–34; 16:7, 8–9, 20–21; 2 Cor 6:14–7:1; *b*. 1 Cor 7; 8; 9; 10:24–11:1; 12; 13; 14; 15; 16:1–6, 15–19; *c*. 1 Cor 1:1–9; 1:10–6:11; 16:10–14, 22–23; *d*. 2 Cor 2:14–6:13; 7:2–4; 10–13; *e*. 2 Cor 1:1–2:13; 7:5–16; 9— so Johannes Weiss, *The History of Primitive Christianity*

[New York: Harper & Brothers, 1959], I/2); (4) a six-letter hypothesis (*a.* 2 Cor 6:14–7:1; 1 Cor 9:24–10:22; 6:12–20; 11:2–34; 15; 16:13–24; *b.* 1 Cor 1:1–6:11; 7:1–9:23; 10:23–11:1; 12:1–14:40; 16:1–12; *c.* 2 Cor 2:14–6:13; 7:2–4; *d.* 2 Cor 10:1–13:13; *e.* 2 Cor 9:1–15; *f.* 2 Cor 1:1–2:13; 7:5–8:24—so Walter Schmithals, *Gnosticism in Corinth* [Nashville: Abingdon, 1971]); (5) a nine-letter hypothesis (*a.* 1 Cor 11:2–34; *b.* 1 Cor 6:1–11; 2 Cor 6:14–7:1; 1 Cor 6:12–20; 9:24–10:22; 15:1–58; 16:13–24; *c.* 1 Cor 5:1–13; 7:1–8:13; 9:19–22; 10:23–11:1; 12:1–31a; 14:1c–40; 12:31b–13:13; 16:1–12; *d.* 1 Cor 1:1–4:21; *e.* 2 Cor 2:14–6:2; *f.* 1 Cor 9:1–18; 2 Cor 6:3–13; 7:2–4; *g.* 2 Cor 10:1–13:13; *h.* 2 Cor 9:1–15; *i.* 2 Cor 1:1–2:13; 7:5–8:24—so Walter Schmithals, "Die Korintherbriefe als Briefsammlung," *ZNW* 64[1973]:263–88). This sampling is representative but far from exhaustive.

There are still some who argue for the unity of both 1 and 2 Corinthians, for example, Phillip E. Hughes, *Paul's Second Epistle to the Corinthians* (Grand Rapids: Eerdmans, 1962) (the scheme of 2 Corinthians concerns Paul's itinerary relative to Corinth, viewed in its various aspects: past—the change of plan, chaps. 1–7; present—the sending of Titus and the brethren to complete the collection, chaps. 8–9; and future—the imminence of the apostle's arrival in Corinth, chaps. 10–13); A. M. G. Stephenson, " A Defense of the Integrity of 2 Corinthians," in *The Authorship and Integrity of the New Testament*, Theological Collections, 4 (London: SPCK, 1965).

This commentary works with the assumption that 1 Corinthians is a unity but that 2 Corinthians is composed of two separate letters: 2 Cor 10–13 and 2 Cor 1–9. Certain things in 2 Cor 10–13 seem to precede 2 Cor 1–9: for example, 12:11 precedes 3:1 and 5:12; 13:2 precedes 1:23; 13:10 precedes 2:3; 2:4; 2:9; 10:6 precedes 2:9; 7:15; also 11:3 is strange if written after the satisfaction expressed in chapters 1–7. These directional indicators cannot be reversed by the identification of Titus's visits in 2 Cor 8:6, 16–23 and 2 Cor 12:18. These are not the same visit. In 8:16–23 Titus is accompanied by two brethren; in 12:17–18 by one brother. It is further assumed by this commentary that 2 Cor 10–13 is the painful letter of 2 Cor 2:3–4, 9; 7:8, 12. The objection that the offense committed against Paul which occasioned the painful letter is not mentioned in 2 Cor 10–13 will not hold. The offense was perpetrated by an individual member of the Corinthian church (2:6; 7:12) but also involved sympathizers from the church at large (7:7–9, 12). 2 Cor 10–13 does respond to this matter, especially in 10:1–11 and 11:2–11 (Francis Watson, "2 Cor 10–13 and Paul's Painful Letter to the Corinthians," *JTS* 35[1984]:324–46).

The chronology of Paul's dealings with Corinth would look something like this.

1st visit to Corinth (echoed in 1 Cor 15:1–3; 4:15; cf. Acts 18)

   1st letter of Paul to Corinth (mentioned in 1 Cor 5:9–11), no longer extant
      Letter from Corinth to Paul (1 Cor 7:1, 25; 8:1; 12:1; 16:1, 12) and oral report to Paul by Chloe's people (1 Cor 1:11–12)

   2nd letter of Paul to Corinth (1 Corinthians), written from Ephesus (1 Cor 16:8) and delivered by Timothy (1 Cor 16:10; 4:17)

2nd visit of Paul to Corinth, the painful visit (2 Cor 2:1). This was not the visit projected in 1 Cor 16:1–9 to gather the collection but an additional visit. It was painful because someone at Corinth (2 Cor 2:5–8, 10; 7:12) challenged his authority. Instead of forcing a showdown, Paul withdrew to Macedonia and did not return to Corinth as promised (2 Cor 1:15–16, 23; 2:1).

   3rd letter of Paul to Corinth (2 Cor 2:3, 4, 9; 7:8, 12). This letter was in lieu of the promised visit (2 Cor 1:15, 16, 23). Its contents may be inferred from 2 Cor 1–7, which was written after the severe letter had done its work. (1) It dealt with the individual's challenge of Paul's apostolic authority and the community's implication in it (2 Cor 2:5–9; 7:12); (2) it included Paul's commendation of himself (2 Cor 3:1; 5:12). It is, in part, preserved in 2 Cor 10–13, which not only responds to the charges of the individual and his sympathizers (2 Cor 10:1–11; 11:2–15) but is also an exercise in inoffensive self-praise (2 Cor 11:1, 16–12:13). It also expresses concern about problems of behavior that remain uncorrected (2 Cor 12:21; 13:2). This letter was carried by Titus (2 Cor 7:13–14).
      After his visit to Corinth, Titus met Paul in Macedonia with news that the letter had done its work and the church had disciplined the offender (2 Cor 7:6–13a; 2:5–11).

   4th letter of Paul to Corinth (2 Cor 1–9), written from Macedonia and delivered by Titus (2 Cor 8:1–6, 17). This letter (1) rejoices in the settlement of the issue over the individual's challenge of Paul's authority (2 Cor 2:5–11; 7:6–13a); (2) gives the Corinthians a basis for answering those who boast in external appearances (2 Cor 5:12; so 2:14–7:5); (3) calls for correction of behavior that is not proper for Christians (2 Cor 6:14–7:1); and (4) urges completion of the collection in Corinth before Paul arrives (2 Cor 8–9).

3rd visit of Paul to Corinth. This visit fulfilled the purpose of the projected visit of 1 Cor 16:1–9 (cf. Rom 15:25–27). Also during this time Paul wrote Romans (Rom 16:23).

If it is proposed that 2 Cor 10–13 is a separate and earlier letter than 2 Cor 1–9, then the question arises as to why the two independent units were joined in the way that they are. There are two levels to any answer to such a question. First, the combination of the two parts into a whole most likely took place at the time when Paul's letters were collected, edited, and published (i.e., near A.D. 100). Second, two different explanations are offered for the principle of editorial activity. On the one hand, G. Bornkamm has argued that the placing of 2 Cor 10–13 last was done in line with a basic formal rule of early Christian edificatory literature: namely, that the warnings against false teachers are often expressed at the end of a writing or a fragment of a writing (e.g., Jude 17–19; 2 Pet 3:3–7; Heb 13:9; Rev 22:18–19; Didache 16; Matt 7:15–23, as the end of the Sermon on the Mount; Rom 16:17–20) ("The History of the Origin of the So-called Second Letter to the Corinthians," *NTS* 8[1962]:258–64). Behind the formal rule stands the acknowledged view that the appearance of false prophets was a sign of the last times. By placing 2 Cor 10–13 after 2 Cor 1–9 the editor was saying that Paul's opponents were false prophets. On the other hand, Furnish suggests that the principle may have been simply that of adding the shorter to the longer (*2 Corinthians*, p. 40). This was certainly one of the principles followed in the ancient arrangement of Paul's letters now reflected in our New Testaments (the shorter follows the longer, e.g., 1 Corinthians is shorter than Romans, 2 Corinthians is shorter than 1 Corinthians). Either explanation, singly or in conjunction with the other, offers a plausible, though unprovable, reason for the present shape of canonical 2 Corinthians.

Paul's Opponents

Preoccupation with the identity of Paul's opponents has characterized much of the research done on the Pauline epistles. Opinion has shifted from the position that the opponents are the same in both 1 Corinthians and 2 Corinthians (emissaries from Jerusalem, so F.C. Baur; Jewish-Christian Gnostics, so W. Schmithals) to that which regards them as different in the two letters (proto-gnostics in 1 Corinthians, Hellenistic-Jewish Christian itinerants in 2 Corinthians, so D. Georgi). (See John J. Gunther, *St. Paul's Opponents and Their Background* [Leiden: Brill, 1973], for a survey of options.) The research that has gone into production of this commentary has shown that in neither case can the problem be reduced to a single cause or set of opponents. In 1 Corinthians one finds a number of factors behind the problems: for example, overrealized eschatology (1 Cor 4; 7; 11; 15); the effects of social stratification (1 Cor 8–10; 11); misunderstanding of Paul's earlier letter (1 Cor 5); divisions due to allegiance to different leaders growing in part out of the scattered character of the various church groups or cells in Corinth; a carryover of Jewish norms that were contrary to Christian practice (e.g., 1 Cor 14:34–36). It is impossible to reduce all of the issues dealt with in 1 Corinthians to one cause like Gnosticism or overrealized eschatology.

The same is true for 2 Cor 10–13. The problems cannot be reduced to a single source, visiting apostles. On the painful visit to Corinth, Paul apparently did not discipline the arrogant Christians as he had said he would in 1 Cor 4:18–21. This lack of exercise of authority by Paul when present in Corinth caused one of the Corinthians to challenge his apostolic authority (2 Cor 10:1–11) and to make a depreciating comparison of Paul with the other apostles who had visited Corinth and who had acted with authority. This comparison used against Paul his unwillingness to accept money. Although the authoritative visitors had accepted funds, Paul did not. Either this showed his awareness of his lack of stature, or it revealed that he did not love the Corinthians, or it was a sign of his duplicity since he was absorbed with the collection (2 Cor 11:7–11; 12:16–17). As if to confirm the challenge to his authority, Paul withdrew to Macedonia and failed to return to Corinth as promised (2 Cor 1:15–16), prompting charges of vacillation on his part. What began with one individual's challenge grew as sympathizers joined his suspicions. The letter of tears (2 Cor 10–13) acknowledged that moral problems remained in Corinth (12:21; 13:2) and repeated the threats of 1 Cor 4:18–21 that such would be punished (2 Cor 12:21; 13:2–4; 10:11) when Paul came again. That he did not act decisively before was because he was waiting for the Corinthians themselves, as a group, to manifest their obedience, that is, their identification with his point of view (2 Cor 10:5–6). The letter also dealt with the disparaging comparison between Paul and the other apostles by an exercise in inoffensive self-praise (11:1, 16–12:13). In more than one place, Paul also tried to straighten out the misunderstandings about his attitude over accepting money (11:7–11; 12:16–18). 2 Cor 10–13, then, deals not only with problems posed by outsiders but even more so with that presented by a Corinthian individual and his sympathizers in the church.

2 Cor 1–9 likewise can be understood only in terms of multiple problems with no single cause. The letter begins with an attempt to dispel a bad impression of Paul created by his failure to return to Corinth from Macedonia as promised (1:15–18). It rejoices in the resolution of the issue of the individual's challenge to Paul's apostolic authority and the community's complicity in the matter (2:5–11; 7:8, 12). It offers the Corinthians the grounds for answering those who boast in external appearances (5:12, so 2 Cor 2:14–7:4 for the most part). It continues the appeal to some Corinthians to repent of their overidentification with the pagan culture (6:14–7:1). It finally appeals to the Corinthians for the completion of preparations for the collection before Paul's arrival (2 Cor 8–9). Even here an apologetic note is heard. The administrative procedure for the collection is to be circumspect (8:20–21). 2 Cor 1–9, then, is more than celebration over the resolution of the problems dealt with in 2 Cor 10–13. It continues the Pauline apology, though in muted terms, at the same time that it celebrates the official resolution of the crisis. Both apology and rejoicing serve the same end, that of the completion of the Corinthians' part in the collection.

1 Corinthians

SETTING THE RECORD STRAIGHT

PUTTING PREACHERS
IN THEIR PLACE

1 Corinthians 1–4

1 Cor 1:1–4:21 is the first large thought unit in the epistle. It consists of two of the components of the traditional Greek letter: (1) the letter introduction (1:1–9) and (2) the body of the letter (1:10–4:21). The first task attempted will be to trace the train of thought in this unit.

The traditional introduction of a Greek letter consisted of the formula A to B, greeting, followed by a prayer form. In 1 Cor 1:1–9 Paul has adapted this conventional opening for his own purposes: (*a*) Paul and Sosthenes (Acts 18:17), (*b*) to the church at Corinth, (*c*) grace and peace to you, (*d*) I give thanks to God for you. As in the introductions to his other letters, Paul uses the opening to introduce themes that will be crucial to his argument later. First, his apostolic calling is mentioned as basic to all that follows (1:1, "called by the will of God to be an apostle of Christ Jesus"; cf. 1 Cor 4:4, 15–16; chap. 9; 11:1; 14:37–38; 15:9–10; 2 Cor 2:17; 5:18, 20; 11:5; 12:12). Second, the Corinthian church's participation in the church universal is signaled as crucial (1:2, "called to be saints together with all those who in every place call on the name of our Lord"; cf. 11:16; 14:33; 16:1, 19). Third, there is the acknowledgment of the spiritual gifts bestowed on the Corinthians at their conversion (1:4 –7; cf. chaps. 12–14; 2 Cor 8:7). Fourth, an eschatological reservation accompanies Paul's talk about gifts (1:7–8, "you are not lacking in any spiritual gift, as you wait for the revealing of our Lord Jesus Christ; who will sustain you to the end, guiltless in the day of our Lord Jesus Christ"). The End remains a future hope (cf. 1 Cor 4:8–13; chap. 15). Having introduced his letter with the conventional form, adapted as needed, the apostle is ready to move to the body of the epistle.

The body of the letter begins with a request formula followed by the bases for the request (1:10–13). As in Philem 9–10, the request formula runs: "I appeal (*parakalō*) to you" (cf. 1 Pet 5:12; Heb 13:22; Acts 15:31). The content of the request is given in a threefold refrain: "that all of you

3

agree, that there be no dissensions among you, that you be united in the same mind." The bases for the request are two. In the first place, Chloe's people have reported to Paul that the Corinthians are quarreling about ministers (1:11–12). They either give their spiritual guides too great a status ("I belong to Paul"; "I belong to Apollos"; "I belong to Cephas") or no status at all ("I belong to Christ"). In the second place, the non-Christian character of this behavior reported to Paul is exposed by means of three rhetorical questions, each calling for a negative answer (v. 13): (1) Is Christ divided? (2) Was Paul crucified for you? (3) Were you baptized in the name of Paul?

The body of the letter continues with Paul's expanded answers to the three rhetorical questions (1:14–4:7), given in reverse order. Rhetorical question number three (Were you baptized in the name of Paul?) is answered first, in 1:14–16 (17). "I am thankful that I baptized only Crispus (Acts 18:8), Gaius (Rom 16:23), and the household of Stephanas (16:15), lest any should say that they were baptized in my name."

Rhetorical question number two (Was Paul crucified for you?) is answered next and at great length (1:17–3:4). This section falls into two self-contained parts: (1) 1:17–2:5 and (2) 2:6–3:4. The first, 1:17–2:5, is organized in a concentric pattern within an inclusion (1:17 and 2:1–5), with 1:23a, Christ crucified, as the center point.

    (a) The wise versus the foolish (1:18–20)
      (b) Preaching saves believers (1:21)
        (c) Jews demand signs and Greeks seek wisdom (1:22)
          (d) We preach Christ crucified (1:23a)
        (c') To Jews a stumbling block, to Greeks folly (1:23b)
      (b') Christ is power/wisdom to those called (1:24)
    (a') The wise/weak versus the foolish/strong (1:25–31)

In this self-contained unit Paul tells *what* he preached at Corinth, *how* he did it, and *why* he preached as he did. At the center of the chiasmus is *what* he preached: Christ crucified (1:23a). Judging from the context, the cross here does not refer to the death of Jesus as a sacrifice for sins (as in Rom 3:25–26), as a victory over the evil powers (as in Col 2:15), or as a revelation of God's love (as in Rom 5:8), but rather to Jesus' death to sin (as in Rom 6:10; he died rather than sin), in which believers are called to participate (e.g., Rom 6:3, 6–7, 10–11; Gal 2:20). 1 Cor 2:4 tells *how* this preaching was done: "my speech and my message were not in plausible words of wisdom, but in demonstration of Spirit and power." On the one hand, the persuasiveness of Paul's preaching did not rest in his oratorical skills (cf. 2 Cor 10:10, "his bodily presence is weak, and his speech of no account"). Contrast Socrates' description of the spell which the funeral orator's account of Athens's great past cast upon him: "as I listen, the spell falls upon me; I feel that I have become at the moment a greater, nobler, finer man, and this feeling persists for three or four days" (Plato *Menexenus* 235 A-C). On the other hand, his preaching was confirmed by a demonstration of the Spirit and power (cf. 1 Cor 1:5–6; Gal 3:1–5; 1 Thess 1:5). Apparently, in the founding of the Pauline churches, the Spirit would fall on those who were hearing the apostle preach very much as in the description of Peter's preaching to Cornelius in Acts 10 (vv. 44, 46, "While Peter was still saying this, the Holy Spirit fell on all who heard the word. . . . Then Peter declared, 'Can any one forbid water for baptizing these people who have received the Holy Spirit just as we have?'"). Since it was the Spirit's power rather than Paul's oratorical skill that convinced the converts, the Pauline Christians' faith would rest in the power of God instead of the wisdom of men (2:5). This is *why* he preached as he did.

The second self-contained part of 1:17–3:4 is 2:6–3:4, a section in which Paul explains *what* he did *not* teach the Corinthians, *how* he teaches such things when he does, and *why* he did *not* teach such matters at Corinth. In this regard, 2:6–3:4 corresponds loosely to 1:17–2:5, functioning as a contrast to the former section.

The first item of background information for understanding the issues of 2:6–3:4 lies in the Mediterranean belief that a philosopher taught both exoteric and esoteric doctrines. Plutarch clarifies the matter when speaking about Alexander the Great's teacher, Aristotle:

> It would appear . . . that Alexander not only received from his master his ethical and political doctrines, but also participated in those secret and more profound teachings which philosophers designate by the special terms "acroamatic" and "epoptic" and do not impart to many. ("Alexander" 7.3)

The Corinthians apparently regarded Paul's preaching of the cross as his exoteric doctrine and wanted to know why the apostle had not taught them the esoteric matters of the faith. By not imparting this wisdom, Paul had not been a faithful or trustworthy steward of the mysteries of God (4:2). The apostle, therefore, acknowledges that he does teach a secret and hidden wisdom of God among the mature (2:6–7).

A second item of background information is relevant here. In Mediterranean antiquity there were certain categories used for a person's progress
in the moral and spiritual arena (e.g., Philo *Allegorical Interpretation*
3.159; *On Husbandry* 165). There was the beginner (*ho archomenos*);
there was the one who was making progress (*ho prokoptōn*); and there
was the mature or perfect person (*ho teleios*). The terminology used by
the Corinthians and Paul for the first and third stages was (1) men of the
flesh (*sarkinois*), babes in Christ (*nēpiosis en Christō*), natural man (*psy-
chikos anthrōpos*); and (3) the mature (*teleios*), the spiritual man (*ho
pneumatikos*). Paul's practice is to teach this wisdom only to those in
stage three, to the mature or the spiritual.

Is it possible to discern of what this wisdom consists? V. 12b offers the
clue: "that we might understand the gifts bestowed on us by God." The
secret wisdom that Paul did not teach the Corinthians dealt with the
gifts of the Spirit. When he does impart this wisdom, *how* does he do it?
"We impart this in words not taught by human wisdom but taught by
the Spirit" (2:13). *Why* did Paul not teach this to the Corinthians? "I . . .
could not address you as spiritual men, but as men of the flesh, as babes
in Christ" (3:1). "For when one says, 'I belong to Paul,' and another, 'I
belong to Apollos,' are you not merely men?" (3:4) The presupposition
underlying Paul's argument is the common Greco-Roman epistemological
conviction: like is known by like (Plato *Protagoras* 337C–338A; *Timaeus*
45C; Philo *On the Change of Names* 6; Plotinus *Enneads* 4.5.7, 23–62;
1.6.9, 30–45). Since the Corinthians who acted as if they had not died to
sin were not spiritual, Paul could not teach them matters that are only
spiritually discerned.

Before he could make such a judgment about these Corinthians, Paul
had to confront a claim of theirs. They said, "The spiritual man judges
all things, but is himself judged by no one" (2:15), and quoted Isa 40:13
in support of their contention: "For who has known the mind of the Lord
so as to instruct him?" (A. C. Thiselton, "Realized Eschatology at Corinth," *NTS* 24[1978]:510–26). That this is a Corinthian assertion is supported by the fact that they try to judge Paul in 4:3–5; by the behavior in
1 Cor 5, where one is living in incest, judging all things for himself and
the community is proud of his freedom and refuses to judge him; by the
behavior in 1 Cor 6:1–11, where the Christians refuse to judge one another; and by the claims of 6:12–20, "all things are lawful for me" and
"every sin which a man commits is outside the body." In response to their
proof text, Paul says, "*We*, however, *have* the mind of Christ" (2:16).

And as one with the mind of Christ, the apostle pronounces those who are quarreling over the status of various ministers "men of the flesh" and "babes in Christ." To such the wisdom fit for the mature could not be given. They needed and need what Paul did preach, "Christ crucified"; that is, as he died to sin, so must we (Gal 2:20). Until one has died with Christ to sin, there is no possibility for his or her properly understanding the gifts. The gifts will rather be understood from the point of view of the sinful self that seeks only self-gratification and status. That is why Paul taught as he did.

Rhetorical question number one (Is Christ divided?) is answered last but at length in 3:5–4:7. This section also falls into two parts, 3:5–23 and 4:1–7, each dealing with the role of Christian missionaries. The first part, 3:5–23, argues that missionaries are but servants (*diakonoi*) with differing tasks assigned them by the Lord. This point is illustrated by two paragraphs, each with a different image of the church. In the first (3:6–9b), the church is spoken of in terms of the image of a field or garden. Paul planted; Apollos watered; God gave the increase. Paul and Apollos are equal, and each will have his reward. In the second paragraph (3:9c–15), the church is referred to in terms of the image of a building or house. Paul laid the foundation (only Jesus Christ); another builds on it; God will judge every man's products. If one's work is built on the foundation (Jesus), it survives the Last Judgment, and one will have a reward (cf. Testament of Abraham 13).

Whatever the tasks assigned various ministers, they are intended for the well-being of the church, not its destruction. This point is made in a third paragraph (3:16–17), where the church is conceived under the image of a temple: "Do you all not know that you are God's temple [*naos*] and that God's Spirit dwells in you" (3:16)? Here, as in 6:19 and 2 Cor 6:16, Paul uses for temple the term *naos*, not *hieron*. Whereas the LXX uses *hieron* to refer to the Jerusalem temple generally, it uses *naos* for the most sacred parts of the temple, either the Holy Place (1 Kings 6:17; 2 Chron 4:22; Ezek 8:16), or the porch or vestibule (1 Chron 28:11; 2 Chron 8:12), or the Holy of Holies (Ps 28:2). Paul's usage reflects that of his Bible. He regards the church as the most sacred portions of the temple, within which God's Spirit dwells. In antiquity, in order to protect temples that were repositories of great wealth from plunderers of various sorts, two strategems were used. On the one hand, temple police functioned as a small mercenary army to protect the temple precincts. On the other hand, a curse of the deity was leveled against anyone who violated the sanctuary (e.g., Polybius 31.9.3; Diodorus Siculus 14.63, 70; 22.5; 28.3; 31.189; Livy 29.18). It was not uncommon to hear stories of the tragic end of those upon whom such a curse came. Against this background, Paul could issue the warning associated with the Christian temple: "If anyone destroys God's temple, God will destroy him" (3:17a). Ministers are but equal servants of God, each with his own assigned task to build up the church whose unity and well-being are protected by the deity. Therefore, the implication is drawn: "So let no one boast of men" (3:21a).

The second part of the section, 3:5–4:7, comes in 4:1–7. Here again the Pauline contention is that missionaries are servants (*hypēretas*) of Christ and stewards (*oikonomous*) of the mysteries of God (4:1). In v.2 there is another Corinthian assertion: "Moreover it is required of stewards that they be found trustworthy" (perhaps echoing the Jesus-tradition now found in Luke 16:1–13). That this is the position of at least some of the Corinthians seems established by the fact that in 2:6–3:4 Paul is defending himself against the Corinthian charge that he did not teach the church the wisdom (about the gifts) that they had to receive later from other ministers. From the point of view of these Corinthians, Paul had not been a faithful steward of the mysteries of God. Furthermore, as spiritual men who now possessed a knowledge of these mysteries, they judged Paul unworthy. To the Corinthian assertion of v. 2, the apostle responds in vv. 3–5. It is not your place to judge me, a servant of Christ and a called apostle; that task belongs to the Lord (4:4; cf. 3:13) and will take place on the Day of Judgment (4:5; cf. 3:14–15). In 4:6–7 we have both the conclusion to this second part, 4:1–7, and the conclusion to 3:5–4:7 as a whole. When Paul says, "I have applied all this to myself and Apollos for your benefit" (4:6), he is referring back to 3:5: "What then is Apollos? What is Paul?" When he says that this use of himself and Apollos is aimed at their learning to live "not beyond what has been written" (4:6), the reference is probably to the instruction given young children about how to write. Teachers sometimes used outlines of letters for pupils to follow. The point of the model was that one should follow it, making the letter neither too small nor too large. One was neither to fall short of the model nor to exceed it (Plato *Protagoras* 326D; Seneca *Epistle* 94.51). The apostle is saying of himself and Apollos, Copy us, like a small child making his letters, and learn how not to write over the lines. Such a practice would result in their not being puffed up in favor of one minister against another (4:6b), so that divisions in the church would not occur.

Having answered the three rhetorical questions with which he began (1:13), Paul now comes to the conclusion of the entire section (4:8–21). The conclusion consists of three components: (1) a contrast (vv. 8–13), (2) an exhortation (vv. 14–17), and (3) a warning (vv. 18–21). In 4:8–13 we find a contrast being drawn between the Corinthian stance ("Already you are filled! Already you have become rich! Without us you have become kings!") and that of the apostles ("We are fools for Christ's sake, but you are wise in Christ. We are weak, but you are strong. You are held in honor, but we in disrepute. To the present hour we hunger and thirst, we are ill-clad and buffeted and homeless"; cf. 2 Cor 11:21–29; 4:7–12; 6:4–10; Rom 8:35–39). The Corinthian posture is what has been called an overrealized eschatology. These Christians live as though they were already in the New Age beyond the resurrection—beyond suffering, beyond tragedy, beyond poverty, beyond hard times (cf. 15:12, 19; 2 Tim 2:18). From this posture they, like kings, were judges of all things and judged by no one (2:15). It is this overrealized eschatology which forms the root problem that underlies many of the issues in the remainder of the letter. By contrast to the Corinthian triumphalism, the apostles clearly live within the limits of the Present Evil Age. Vv. 9–13 present the suffering apostle as a praiseworthy paradigm to be emulated by the Corinthians (cf. Epictetus 3.24.113–114).

There follows an exhortation to the Corinthians to be like the apostle, their spiritual father (4:14–17). In the rabbinic tradition, if someone teaches the son of another the Torah, it is as if he had begotten him (b Sanhedrin 19b). Since Paul is their spiritual father, he can urge them, "be imitators of me" (cf. 7:7a; 11:1). It was to this end that Paul sent Timothy to Corinth to remind these problem children of "my ways in Christ, as I teach them everywhere in every church" (4:17; cf. 1:2; 11:16; 14:33).

A warning about the consequences of failure to heed Paul's admonitions concludes the argument (4:18–21). Some are puffed up. But if the Lord wills, Paul will come to Corinth and confront these folks with the power of God. What shall it be? "Shall I come to you with a rod or with love in a spirit of gentleness?" (4:21b) These were strong words that would later be used against the apostle (e.g., 2 Cor 10:10).

Having traced the train of thought in 1 Cor 1:1–4:21, it is now necessary to attempt to summarize the positions of both the Corinthians and Paul insofar as the situation can be reconstructed (N. A. Dahl, "Paul and the Church at Corinth according to 1 Cor 1:10–4:21," in *Studies in Paul*

[Minneapolis: Augsburg, 1977], pp. 40–61). In 1 Corinthians Paul answers an official letter from the church at Corinth with its six questions (7:1, 25; 8:1; 12:1; 16:1, 12) brought to him by Stephanas, Fortunatus, and Achaicus (16:17). Before he could answer their questions, however, he had to come to terms with other information that had reached him unofficially through Chloe's people (1:11). They had told the apostle of divisions within the church caused by boastful attachments to various ministers (1:12; 3:21; 4:6). Some Christians at Corinth even resisted the idea of asking Paul for instructions, pointing both to his inadequacy (he did not teach us secret wisdom and is, therefore, an unfaithful steward of God's mysteries, 2:6; 3:1–4; 4:2) and their own independence (2:15–16a; 4:15, 19–20) based on their overrealized eschatology (4:8–13). Given this informal information, Paul begins his letter with an appeal for unity in the church which of necessity had to involve both a reassertion of his personal authority and the theological foundation for his argument to follow.

Paul's personal defense includes the following points. (1) I have been called by the will of God to be an apostle of Christ Jesus (1:1). (2) The confirmation of my preaching lies not in my rhetorical skill but in the power of God that was manifested among you (1:6; 2:1, 4–5). (3) My failure to teach you secret wisdom (i.e., about spiritual gifts, 2:12) was not due to my unfaithfulness as a steward of God's mysteries (4:1–3) but to your immaturity (3:1–4). (4) All ministers are to be regarded as equal (3:8), although each has a different task assigned by the Lord (3:5–15). So it is improper to be puffed up in favor of one over another (4:6b). Christ is our judge (4:4). (5) However, as the one who founded the church in Corinth, I am your spiritual parent (4:15) and you should pattern your life after me (4:16). (6) As an agent of the kingdom of God, I operate with God's power, not with empty words. Anyone who challenges my authority will have to stand up to this divine power when I come to Corinth.

Paul's theological foundation for much that will follow is his eschatological reservation. In 1:4–9, when he gives thanks for the gifts manifested in the Corinthian church, Paul will not allow the gifts to be the sign of the End. He speaks of waiting "for the revealing of our Lord" (1:7), who "will sustain you to the End, . . . the day of our Lord Jesus Christ" (1:8). In 4:8–13 when he speaks of the Corinthians' overrealized eschatology, Paul holds up apostolic example for a life-style that is far from triumphalist: "to the present hour we hunger and thirst, we are ill-clad and buffeted and homeless" (4:11). This eschatological reservation (cf. Rom 6:3–5) forms the theological underpinning of much that follows. There is a "not-yet" that must be taken into account along with the "now" of Corinthian enthusiasm.

1 Cor 1:1–4:21 has a preparatory function. It both establishes Paul's authority and calls on the Corinthians to emulate him and lays a foundation for the content of the answers to be given to many of the issues raised in the letter from the church. With this behind him, the apostle can move to the paraenetic section of the letter (chaps. 5–16).

SEPARATION FOR THE
SAKE OF SALVATION

1 Corinthians 5

With 1 Cor 5:1–13 there is a shift from the body of the letter (1:10–4:21) to the exhortations (5:1–16:12). Formally, chapter 5 is linked to what precedes it by several key terms: boasting (1:29, 31; 3:21; 4:7–5:6); power (4:19–20—5:4); being puffed up (4:6, 18, 19—5:2). Formally, it is related to what follows, 6:1–11 and 6:12–20, by means of an ABA' pattern:

> A. Sexual problem (incest) (5:1–13)
>   B. Problem of lawsuits (6:1–11)
> A'. Sexual problem (fornication) (6:12–20).

Logically, this entire complex (5:1–6:20) seem to be included here, not as answers to questions raised by the letter from the Corinthians (7:1, 25; 8:1; 12:1; 16:1, 12), but as proof that the Corinthians did need to hear from Paul because they were most definitely not self-sufficient.

1 Cor 5:1–13 is a major thought unit held together by an inclusion (v. 2c, "Let him who has done this be removed from among you"; v. 13b, "Drive out the wicked person from you"). A close reading of the chapter reveals four component parts: (1) a statement of the problem (v. 1); (2) two appeals for the excommunication of the guilty one, each with a similar pattern of arrangement (vv. 2–5; vv. 6–8); (3) a twofold clarification of a former letter (vv. 9–13a); and (4) a final exhortation (v. 13b). Each component needs individual attention.

(1) The problem specified in 5:1 is *porneia* (sexual immorality): one has his father's wife. The expression "father's wife" refers to one's stepmother in Lev 18:8 (cf. 18:7, where one's mother is a different entity). It is this incestuous relationship to which Paul refers in 1 Cor 5:1.

In the Old Testament, ancient custom was laxer about incest than later law. On the one hand, one hears that Abraham married his half sister (Gen 20:12), that Jacob married his wife's sister (Gen 29:21–30), that Reuben took his father's concubine while Jacob lived (Gen 35:22; condemned in Gen 49:4), that Moses was born of the union between a nephew and an aunt (Num 26:59), that Caleb married his father's widow (1 Chron 2:24), and of the assumption that a royal prince could marry his paternal half sister (2 Sam 13:13). On the other hand, Deut 27:20 condemns marriage with one's father's wife; Deut 27:22 condemns marriage with one's sister, whether the daughter of his father or the daughter of his mother; Deut 27:23 condemns marriage with one's mother-in-law. Lev 18:6–18 begins, "None of you shall approach any one near of kin to uncover nakedness." Fourteen areas are then specified: mother (v. 7), stepmother/father's wife (v. 8), sister (v. 9), son's or daughter's daughter (v. 10), father's wife's daughter begotten by your father (v. 11), father's sister (v. 12), mother's sister (v. 13), father's brother's wife, your aunt (v. 14), daughter-in-law (v. 15), brother's wife (v. 16), a wife's daughter (v. 17a), a wife's son's daughter (v. 17b), a wife's sister while the wife is alive (v. 18). Lev 20:11–21 reiterates eight of these areas: father's wife (v. 11), daughter-in-law (v. 12), wife's mother (v. 14), sister (v. 17), mother's sister (v. 19), father's sister (v. 19), uncle's wife (v. 20), brother's wife (v. 21). Ezek 22:10–11 indicates that these legal proscriptions were broken.

Postbiblical Judaism continued the prohibitions against incest, in some cases becoming even stricter than scripture. On the basis of the scriptural prohibitions, John the Baptist indicted Herod Antipas for having his brother Philip's wife (Mark 6:17–18). Antipas was not the only Herod who violated the incest taboo. Herod Agrippa II had an incestuous relation with his sister, Bernice, both being children of Herod Agrippa I (Acts 25:13, 23; 26:30; Juvenal *Satires* 6). Philo compares the strict Jewish laws of Moses against incest with the lax laws of the Athenians, Lacedaemonians, and Egyptians (*Special Laws* 3.22–28). The rabbis extended the limits of proscription beyond what scripture said (e.g., m Yebamoth 2:3). The sectarians who produced the Damascus Document also went beyond scripture's demands, branding as incest the marriage of a man with his niece (Damascus Document 5).

There were traditions about incest in the Greek world (e.g., Thyestes who had a son by his daughter, Oedipus who married his mother, and Macareus who committed incest with his sister). As portrayed in tragedy, their actions ended in disgrace and death, an indication of public disapproval of the matter (Plato *Laws* 838 ABC; Euripides *Hippolytus*; Tatian *Address to the Greeks* 28). That pagans used the charge of incest to discredit the Christians also indicates its disapproval by the general public (e.g., Justin Martyr *1 Apology* 26; Theophilus *To Autolycus* 3.4; Athenagoras *A Plea for the Christians* 3; Tertullian *Apology* 4, 7; Minucius Felix *Octavius* 9). At the same time, violations of the incest taboo were widespread enough in ancient Roman society that Juvenal could say of Roman females that there are "few whose fathers are not very much afraid of their kisses" (*Satires* 6).

In the New Testament three texts relate to the matter of incest. First, Acts 15:20, 29 and 21:25 proscribe four things, seemingly the same matters proscribed in Lev 17–18 for the alien residing in the land of Israel: (*a*) meat offered to idols (Lev 17:8–9); (*b*) the eating of blood (Lev 17:10 –12); (*c*) the eating of strangled animals (Lev 17:15; cf. Exod 22:31); and (*d*) sexual intercourse with close kin (Lev 18:6–18). In this context, *porneia* refers to sexual relationships within certain degrees of kinship. So understood, the decree calls for a sympathetic understanding of Jewish Christian sensitivities by Gentile Christians. Second, Matt 5:32 and 19:9 also speak of *porneia*. In Matt 15:19 *porneia* is distinguished from adultery. Since in the Matthean context any reference to premarital sex seems ruled out, the best interpretation seems to be marriage within the forbidden degrees, that is, incest. Third, 1 Cor 5:1–13, the passage under discussion, focuses on incest.

From the text it is not clear whether or not the father is still alive or is now dead. Either way, such an incestuous relationship was condemned by Jewish law (Lev 18:8; Deut 22:30; 27:20; Jubilees 33.10–13). It was also rejected by Greeks (e.g., Euripides *Hippolytus*; Andocides *On the Mysteries*; Tatian *Address to the Greeks* 28) and Romans (e.g., Institutes of Gaius; Cicero *Pro Cluentio* 14), so Paul could say the behavior was of a kind not found even among pagans. Christian morality had fallen below that of the outside world (cf. 10:32).

(2) There follow two appeals for excommunication of the guilty one, each with a similar pattern of arrangement (5:2–5, 6–8). The first appeal is found in vv. 2–5. It has five component parts: (*a*) the Corinthians' attitude: they are puffed up (v. 2a); (*b*) a Pauline question: Ought you not rather to mourn? (v. 2b); (*c*) a Pauline command: Let him who has done this be removed (v. 2c); (*d*) the basis for the command: For . . . I have already pronounced judgment (vv. 3–4a); (*e*) a concluding command: You are to deliver this man to Satan (vv. 4b–5). Each component deserves comment.

(*a*) The reference to the Corinthians' attitude shows that Paul is concerned not only about the individual's behavior but also about the community's part in the matter. The community was apparently pleased with the situation (cf. 4:6, where being puffed up in favor of one over another means being proud of or giving status to one and not another). How can this be understood? These Corinthians with their overrealized eschatology believed they were enriched with all knowledge (1:5; cf. 8:1) and as spiritual persons were as kings (4:8) who could judge all things but could be judged by no one else in the Christian community (2:15–16a). Part of their knowledge was the belief that they were, on the one hand, free from the moral law (6:12) and, on the other, free from any concern with the body (6:13a,b). This man, then, was acting out his newfound Christian freedom, judging that this sexual behavior was spiritually irrelevant. The others not only believed they could not judge him and his behavior but also were proud of his expression of Christian freedom.

(*b*) The apostle, however, regards pride as an inappropriate reaction to incest: "And should you not rather mourn?" (cf. 2 Cor 12:21) (*c*) The result of their mourning would be the removal of the one who had done this (v. 2c). Such was the community's responsibility (2 Cor 2:6). (*d*) The basis for this act of excommunication is a prophetic act on the part of Paul (vv. 3–4a). Just as Old Testament prophets pronounced judgment on kings in God's name (e.g., 2 Sam 12), so early Christian prophets voiced divine judgment on Rome (e.g., Rev 14:6–20) and on unbelievers who attended Christian services of worship (1 Cor 14:24–25). Now Paul, as one who has the mind of Christ (2:16b), speaks of his spiritual presence in the community and of the judgment he has already pronounced against this one who "already reigns" (4:6). The letter is Paul's proxy. This was the normal assumption in antiquity. For example, Seneca says:

> If the pictures of our absent friends are pleasing to us, though they only refresh the memory and lighten our longing by a solace that is unreal and unsubstantial, how much more pleasant is a letter which brings us real traces, real evidences of an absent friend. ("To Lucilium")

(*e*) The concluding command is addressed to the community. When assembled for worship, with Paul spiritually present, the church is "to deliver this man to Satan for the destruction of the flesh that his spirit may be saved in the day of the Lord Jesus" (v. 5). Some things about this command are fairly clear, others are difficult. "To deliver this man to

Satan" is a synonym for "Let him . . . be removed from among you" (v. 2c), for "Cleanse out the old leaven" (v. 7), and for "Drive out the wicked person from among you" (v. 13b). It refers to excommunication, a practice not uncommon in early Christianity (e.g., 2 Thess 3:14; 1 Tim 1:19–20; Titus 3:10–11; Matt 18:17; Lucian *Peregrinus*). Further, "that his spirit may be saved in the day of the Lord Jesus" (v. 5b) expresses the redemptive intent of the church's excommunication. The discipline of the early church was generally pastoral rather than penal, aimed at the reclamation of sinners rather than their lasting exclusion (e.g., 2 Cor 2:6 –7; Gal 6:1; Matt 18:21–35; 2 Tim 2:24–26; James 5:16, 20; Polycarp *To Philippians* 11.4). Difficulty arises when we try to be more precise about the meaning of "to deliver to Satan for the destruction of the flesh" (v. 5a). The key to understanding is the word "flesh." If "flesh" is taken to mean "the physical body," then "to deliver to Satan" involves some kind of cursing rite analogous to what we hear about in the Apocryphal Acts (e.g., Acts of Peter 2; Acts of Thomas 51–2) that resulted in physical suffering or death (cf. also 1 Cor 11:29–32; Acts 5:5, 10; 13:11). Then the excommunication would involve physical suffering or death that would allow the spirit to be saved at the Last Judgment (G. W. H. Lampe, "Church Discipline and the Interpretation of the Epistles to the Corinthians," in *Christian History and Interpretation*, ed. W. R. Farmer et al. [Cambridge: Cambridge University Press, 1967], pp. 337–61; Ivan Havener, "A Curse for Salvation—1 Cor 5:1–5," in *Sin, Salvation, and the Spirit*, ed. Daniel Durken [Collegeville, Minn.: Liturgical Press, 1979], pp. 334–44).

This line of argument seems problematic because Paul does not regard our physical body as an evil substance that must be destroyed in order to secure the salvation of the spirit. If "flesh" is taken to mean "an orientation to life characterized by self-sufficiency" (e.g., Gal 3:3; 5:24; 2 Cor 10:3; Rom 8:5–8; 1 Cor 3:3), then "spirit" would, of necessity, refer to that orientation characterized by absolute reliance on God (e.g., Gal 5: 16–17, 25; Rom 8:4, 9). The meaning of "to deliver to Satan" would be simply excommunication (cf. Ignatius *Ephesians* 13). Its purpose would be the repentance of the sinner (i.e., the destruction of the flesh) and God's approval of his life's orientation (spirit) at the Last Judgment (Rom 6:6–8). Then the excommunication, which might or might not involve physical suffering, would be seen as a shock to produce a change of orientation (e.g., J. Cambier, "La Chair et l'Esprit en 1 Cor 5:5," *NTS* 15[1968–69]:221–32). This reading seems more compatible with Paul's theology generally and is to be preferred. In this first appeal for excommunication, Paul's emphasis is on the benefits for the sinner to be had from the community's action.

The second appeal for excommunication (vv. 6–8) also have five component parts: (*a*) the Corinthians' attitude: boasting (v. 6a); (*b*) a Pauline question: Do you not know that a little leaven leavens the whole lump? (v. 6b); (*c*) a Pauline command: Cleanse out the old leaven (v. 7a); (*d*) the basis for the command: For Christ, our paschal lamb, has been sacrificed (v. 7b); and (*e*) the concluding command: Let us celebrate the festival (v. 8). Again, each component needs attention.

(*a*) The Corinthians were proud of the individual who lived in incest because he expressed his alleged Christian freedom in his style of life (v. 2a); they were also boasting about themselves as a community (v. 6a). Because of their spiritual status, they believed they were immune to danger from exposure to practices that might not be within God's will (e.g., 1 Cor 10 indicates some thought they could eat in an idol's temple and be spiritually safe). Hence, even if the community disagreed with the incestuous man's behavior, they did not have to worry. His sin could not touch them.

(*b*) The apostle disagreed. "Do you not know that a little leaven leavens the whole lump?" (v. 6b) One Christian's behavior affects the entire community (cf. 12:14–26). (*c*) His command follows: "Cleanse out the old leaven that you may be a new lump, as you really are unleavened" (v. 7a). (*d*) The basis for this action (excommunicating the incestuous man) involves Passover imagery. "For Christ, our paschal lamb, has been sacrificed" (v. 7b; Exod 12:21; John 1:29, 36; 12:1–8; 19:14). Whereas in Jewish practice the old leaven had to be disposed of before the sacrifice of the paschal lamb, in Christian practice God has taken care of the sacrifice first and now calls on the people to purge the old leaven (symbolic of evil) from their midst. (*e*) The concluding exhortation allegorizes the Passover symbols: "Let us . . . celebrate the festival, not with the old leaven, the leaven of malice and evil, but with the unleavened bread of sincerity and truth" (v. 8). Celebrating the festival means banishing the leaven (morally interpreted) from the community's midst (cf. Exod 12:15; m Pesahim 1 and 2; m Orla 11, 12; Gal 5:9). If the first call for excommunication had the sinner's repentance as its aim, the second is concerned about the spiritual safety of the community as a whole because of its exposure to unchecked evil.

(3) Following the two appeals for excommunication is a twofold clari-

fication of a former letter (5:9–13a). Apparently 1 Corinthians is not the first letter of Paul to the church in Corinth. No trace of the first letter remains, however. All that we can say is that in it the apostle had urged his converts "not to associate with immoral men" (v. 9). The Corinthians obviously did not understand this to refer to those of their own number; quite the contrary. So Paul had to clarify. On the one hand, he tells them what was not meant in the letter (vv. 9–10b). Three components comprise this statement. First, I wrote to you in my letter not to associate with immoral men (v. 9). Second, I did not mean the immoral of this world (v. 10a). Third, the reason for not meaning this is that it would have caused you to withdraw from the world (v. 10b). On the other hand, he tells them what was meant in his letter (vv. 11–13a). Again there are three components. First, I wrote. Second, what I meant was not to associate with one who bears the name brother (i.e., a Christian) who is guilty of immorality, not even to eat with such a one (v. 11; cf. Ahikar *Syr. A* 2.16: "My son, it is not becoming even to eat with a shameless man"). Third, the reason for this is that I have nothing to do with judging outsiders. God judges them. Christians are to judge those inside the church (vv. 12 –13a; cf. 1 QS 5.26–6:1. At Qumran the separation was the exact opposite of Paul's understanding). For Paul the rule is "strict discipline within the church; relative freedom of association outside it" (Barrett, *1 Corinthians*, p. 132).

(4) The final exhortation is given in the words of scripture (perhaps Deut 13:5b or 17:7b) with the implication "God says." V. 13b puts it with finality: "Drive out the wicked person from among you."

Having traced the train of thought in 1 Cor 5:1–13, we may now turn to the task of summarizing the positions of both Paul and the Corinthian problem children. The Corinthian position is a dual one. There is the matter of the incestuous individual's rationale for his behavior, and there is also the issue of the community's basis for its actions. The individual seems to have acted out his freedom from the law (cf. 6:12) and freedom from the body (cf. 6:13a,b), believing that one endowed with knowledge (1:5; 8:1) could judge all things and be judged by no one (2: 15–16a). The community seems to have agreed that it was the individual's place to judge what was proper for him and that the individual was immune to the church's judgment of him. The community seems also to have believed that exposure to behavior such as this would not harm them spiritually (cf. 9:24–10:22).

Paul's response involves a rejection of both individual and community rationales. Three things seem to concern the apostle. First, he is bothered by the fact that incest is behavior that even pagans reject (v. 1b). This would bother him because he advocated giving "no offense to Jews or to Greeks . . . just as I do to please all men in everything I do, not seeking my own advantage, but that of many, that they may be saved" (10:32; cf. 9:19–23). Such behavior would stand in the way of the evangelization of the pagans and Jews. Second, this behavior (living according to the flesh) would result in the destruction of the incestuous individual (cf. 1 Cor 6:9–10; Gal 5:19–21; Rom 8:6–8, 12–13). He must be shocked into repentance so that his new life-style (living according to the Spirit) would meet with God's acceptance on Judgment Day (2 Cor 5:10). Third, Paul believes that Christians who expose themselves to unnecessary evil run the risk of infection and the same end as the ancient Israelites, whose story serves as a warning to us (10:8, 11–12). The community is not immune to evil in its midst. "A little leaven leavens the whole lump" (5:6b; Gal 5:9). The answer to all three concerns Paul finds in excommunication of the incestuous man. This would shock him into repentance so that he would be saved. It would protect the church from becoming further infected. It would protect the good name of the Christian community in Corinth in the circles of outsiders. In pursuing his argument, Paul has contended that these Corinthians are not free from the moral law; they are not free from the body; they are not free from prophetic judgment in the name of the Lord Jesus; they are not free from community responsibility for one another; they are not free from responsibility for their influence on outsiders. Moreover, it takes their spiritual father (4:15) who has the mind of Christ (2:16b) to make all this plain for them.

THE COSTS OF
GOING TO COURT

1 Corinthians 6:1–11

1 Cor 6:1–11 is the B component of the larger ABA' pattern of 5:1–6:20. It is also linked formally to 5:1–13 by the key word "judge" (5:12, 13; 6:2, 3; cf. 6:5). A close reading of the text reveals that it falls into two parts, each with the same surface structure: (1) statement of the problem (vv. 1, 7a); (2) two arguments against the problem (vv. 2–6, 7b–11), one from tradition (vv. 2–4, 7b–10), the other from experience (vv. 5–6, 11). Our discussion will need to concentrate on each of the two parts in turn.

The first part of 6:1–11 comes in vv. 1–6, a unit held together by an inclusion (vv. 1 and 6). (1) The problem is stated in v. 1: "When one of you has a grievance against a brother, does he dare go to law before the unrighteous instead of the saints?" What the nature of the grievance was, we do not know. It could have been sexual, but it need not have been. Whatever the grievance, its redress was sought in the pagan courts before unbelievers instead of before a Christian court of arbitration analogous to the contemporary Jewish courts of arbitration. This airing of Christian dirty linen before unbelievers agitated the apostle, who wanted to give them no excuse for unbelief (10:32–33; 9:19–23; cf. 5:1). What Paul calls for, therefore, is the trying of Christian cases before Christian courts.

(2) Two arguments are marshaled against the practice of taking Christian cases before unbelievers and for taking them to Christian courts of arbitration, the one from tradition, the other from experience. The argument from tradition is twofold, each part beginning with "Do you not know" and continuing with "If," followed by a rhetorical question drawing out the implications of the information given in the tradition (vv. 2, 3–4). (a) "Do you not know that the saints will judge the world?" (v. 2) It was part of Jewish eschatological thought that God's people would participate in the Last Judgment (e.g., Dan 7:22–23; Wisd of Sol 3:7–8; Ecclus 4:11, 15; Jubilees 24.29; 1QpHab 5.4–5). This theological tradi-

tion was appropriated by Christians, as Rev 20:4 and Matt 19:28 show. The argument is from the greater to the lesser. "And if the world is to be judged by you, are you incompetent to try trivial cases?" If Christians will participate in eschatological judgment (so great a task), why is it impossible to try cases between Christians here and now (a trivial matter)? (*b*) "Do you not know that we are to judge angels?" (v. 3) Again, it was part of Jewish tradition that the saints of God were judges of angels (e.g., 1 Enoch 13.1-10). In Christian tradition, Jesus was believed to have pronounced judgment against the angels at his resurrection/ascension (1 Pet 3:18-20; 1 Tim 3:16?); from Paul's statement here, apparently the Corinthians knew of a Christian variation on the Jewish expectation. Again the argument is from the greater to the lesser. "How much more, matters pertaining to this life! If then you have such cases, why do you lay them before those who are least esteemed by the church?" (vv. 3-4) Based on the tradition of the saints' participation in the Judgment, Paul calls for the trying of the church's case before a Christian court of arbitration.

The argument from experience is framed in terms of a rhetorical question: "Can it be that there is no man among you wise enough to decide between members of the brotherhood?" (v. 5). The sarcasm is scathing. Given the Corinthians' experiential claim to possess the gifts of knowledge (1:5, 7; 8:1) and to be wise (3:18), surely someone would be capable of deciding these cases. Instead of using their wisdom to resolve the cases in the Christian community, Christians go to court and are judged by unbelievers.

The second part of 6:1-11 comes in vv. 7-11, a unit whose surface structure parallels that of vv. 1-6. (1) The problem is stated in v. 7a: "To have lawsuits at all with one another is defeat for you." From Paul's point of view, there should be no cases at all. His argument for Christian courts of arbitration was merely a concession to human sinfulness. This notion of a concession to human sinfulness was a Jewish concept (e.g., in the OT the monarchy was a concession to the people because of the hardness of their hearts; Jubilees says slavery is such; the rabbis generally regard marriage to a Gentile woman captured in war as such; at Qumran marriage was considered such; cf. David Daube, "Concessions to Human Sinfulness in Jewish Law," *JJS* 10[1959]:1-13) which was taken over into the Christian community (e.g., Mark 10:5) and employed by Paul (e.g., 1 Cor 7:6). The right thing to do would be for defending Christians to renounce their rights and for offending Christians to abstain from doing wrong. "To have lawsuits at all with one another is defeat for you" (v. 7a) because "while there is jealousy and strife among you, are you not of the flesh, and behaving like ordinary men?" (3:3)

(2) The twofold argument from tradition is found in vv. 7b–8, 9–10. (*a*) In vv. 7b–8 there are two rhetorical questions assuming tradition that address the offended party: "Why not rather suffer wrong? Why not rather be defrauded?" Behind these questions stands the paraenetic tradition found in various written forms in Matt 5:38–42 ("But I say to you, 'Do not resist one who is evil'"), Rom 12:17, 19 ("Repay no one evil for evil. . . . Beloved, never avenge yourselves, but leave it to the wrath of God"), 1 Pet 2:23 ("When he was reviled, he did not revile in return; when he suffered, he did not threaten; but he trusted to him who judges justly"), and in incarnate form in the lives of the apostles (1 Cor 4:12–13, "When reviled, we bless; when persecuted, we endure; when slandered, we try to conciliate"). If the offended party lives in accord with the standard of teaching to which he was committed (e.g., Rom 6:17; Eph 4:20–21), he will bear the wrong, allowing the evil to die in himself. (*b*) In vv. 9–10 the second argument from tradition reverts to the form used earlier in vv. 2–4. There is the question "Do you not know?" (v. 9a). What follows is a traditional list of vices characteristic of the ancient world (e.g., Cicero *De finibus* 3.35; Diogenes Laertius *Lives of Eminent Philosophers* 7.110; Wis of Sol 12:3; 14:22; Philo *Sacrifice of Cain and Abel* 32; *Posterity and Exile of Cain* 52, 4 Macc 1:20; 2:15; 1 QS 4.2–6, 9–11) and also employed by early Christians generally (e.g., Mark 7:21–22; 1 Pet 4:3; Rev 21:8; 22:15; Didache 5.1–2), including both the Deutero-Pauline letters (Col 3:5–8; Eph 4:31; 5:3–5; 1 Tim 1:9–10; 6:4–5; 2 Tim 3:2–5; Titus 3:3) and the genuine Paulines (Rom 1:24, 26–27, 29–31; 13:13; 2 Cor 12:20–21; Gal 5:19–21). This list is most like Gal 5:19–21, where the vices are accompanied by the assertion "those who do such things shall not inherit the kingdom of God." The form of 1 Cor 6:9–10 is ABA'B':

    A. The unrighteous
      B. will not inherit the kingdom of God;
    A'. the immoral, et al.,
      B'. will not inherit the kingdom of God.

The parallels elsewhere plus the traditional language "inherit the Kingdom of God" which is not distinctively Pauline, argue for traditional material being used here. We know from Gal 5:21 ("I warn you, as I warned you before") that this was part of Paul's usual instruction to new converts. The traditional list addresses those who wrong their Christian brethren ("But you yourselves wrong and defraud, and that even your own brethren," v. 8), that is, the offending parties. Although we cannot be sure which of the sins mentioned here lay behind the lawsuits, apparently some one or more did. Otherwise, why would the apostle have cited just this list? Also, he says, "And such were some of you" (v. 11a).

In this list of ten vices, two Greek terms in 6:9 (*malakoi* and *arseno-koitai*) are collapsed into one in the RSV ("homosexuals"), the TEV ("homosexual perverts"), and the NEB ("homosexual perversion"), although the NIV translates both ("male prostitutes nor homosexual offenders") as does the KJV ("effeminate nor abusers of themselves with mankind"). The two terms refer respectively to men and boys who allow themselves to be misused homosexually (i.e., the passive partners) and to males who practice homosexuality (i.e., the active partners). The challenge made to this reading has been unsuccessful (cf. J. Robert Wright, "Boswell on Homosexuality: A Case Undemonstrated," *ATR* 66[1984]: 79–94).

The Old Testament mentions both bisexual activity on the part of males (Gen 19:1–11; Judg 19:22–26) and male cult prostitutes (1 Kings 14:22–24; 15:12; 22:46; 2 Kings 23:7) but has nothing to report about female homosexuality. Old Testament legislation forbids any Israelite being a cult prostitute (Deut 23:17), male or female. It also forbids male homosexuality in general (Lev 18:22; 20:13) as a perverted sexual practice akin to adultery or bestiality. So Old Testament objections to homosexuality go beyond its associations with cult prostitution.

Ancient Judaism was likewise uniformly negative toward homosexuality. Wis of Sol 14:26 speaks about idolatry producing evil results, such as disorder in marriage, adultery, and confusion of sex. Philo condemns pederasty in particular (*On the Special Laws* 3.37–39; *Questions and Answers on Genesis* 4.37–38) and homosexuality in general as a perversion akin to adultery (*On Abraham* 26.134–36). "Do not be a sodomite or an extortioner or a murderer," exhorts the Sibylline Oracles (2.73). It later states that Jews do not hold unholy intercourse with boys as do Phoenicians, Egyptians, Latins, Greeks, and others (3.591–99), and it links idolatry with homosexual acts, prostitution, and incest (5.386–433). In his vision of the place of torment, Enoch is told it is for those "who dishonor God, who on earth practice sin against nature, which is child-corruption after the sodomitic fashion" (2 Enoch 10.4). Josephus refers to the unnatural vice rampant among the people of Elis and Thebes, incest and homosexuality, which were justified by the examples of the Greek gods (*Against Apion* 2.273–75). Pseudo-Phocylides says, "Do not give yourself over, against nature, to unpermitted love. Man's love to man is even detested by animals" (109–10) and "Do not have illicit intercourse or stir up a passion for another male, or lay plots, or stain your hand with blood" (3–5). Although the homosexuality condemned by ancient Judaism included pederasty, it was by no means limited to the corruption of boys. Sifra on·Lev 18:3, for example, condemns homosexual marriages, both male and female, among the Egyptians and Canaanites.

Greek literature provides evidence for homosexual activity among both males and females. Plato's *Symposium* regards homosexual love between males as alone capable of satisfying a man's highest and noblest aspirations. The love of a man and a woman is inferior, a purely physical impulse whose sole object is the procreation of children (cf. also, *Phaedrus*; the *Greek Anthology*, e.g., Strato, for homoerotic poetry; Aeschines' speech in *Against Timarchus* 40). Sappho's poetry is so widely thought to be homosexual in nature that the name of the island of her birth, Lesbos, has provided the popular designation for female homosexuality, lesbianism.

In Rome there were two streams of thought. On the one hand, traditional Roman values opposed homosexuality among citizens (Livy 38–39; Suetonius "Caligula"; Juvenal *Satires* 6).Homosexual activity had been illegal since the *Lex Scantinia* (either 223 or 149 B.C.), but the law was usually invoked only for political purposes. On the other hand, some Romans copied the Greek idealization of homosexuality (Plutarch *Eroticus*; Plautus *Pseudolus* and *The Braggert Warrior*; Suetonius "Nero," on Nero's homosexual marriage; Juvenal *Satires* 2, a reference to a homosexual marriage; cf. Hadrian's liaison with Antoninus). Others cynically recommended it as an alternative to marriage to a woman (Juvenal *Satires* 6) or just as a convenient liaison (Petronius *Satyricon*).

To summarize, in the Greco-Roman world homosexuality embraced both men and women. It involved prostitution, older-man–younger-man liaisons, woman-woman encounters, and also homosexual marriages. When negative opinions were expressed about the practice, they were not directed just against pederasty.

Early Christians continued the Old Testament and Jewish perspective on homosexuality. In the New Testament there are only four references to homosexuality. The first, Rom 1:26–27, speaks about both male and female homosexual activity resulting from idolatry, with either venereal disease or sterility as the result. This does not seem to refer to any particular type of homosexual practice (e.g., pederasty) but to speak of homosexuality in general. Homosexuality here is viewed as a condition of bondage ("God gave them up"). The second, 1 Cor 6:9–11, speaks about both the active and the passive participants in homosexual activity. Linguistic study shows that the term for the active partner speaks generally of male activity with males rather than specifically categorized male sexual engagement with boys (D. F. Wright, "Homosexuals or Prostitutes: The Meaning of *arsenokoitai* [1 Cor 6:9; 1 Tim 1:10]," *VigChr* 38[1984]:105–24). This passage assumes that homosexuals, like other types of sinners, can be changed by religious experience which breaks the bondage. The third, 1 Tim 1:10, mentions sodomites in a list of godless persons for whom the law functions as a fence. The fourth, Jude 7 (2 Pet 2:6) uses Sodom and Gomorrah as examples of those who engaged in unnatural lust and experienced God's judgment.

Among the early Christian fathers two things may be noted. First, the apologists criticize Greco-Roman homosexuality (Aristides *Apology* 17 refers to both male and female activity; Justin *1 Apology* 21, 25, 29; Athenagoras *A Plea for the Christians* 34; Clement of Alexandria *Exhortation to the Heathen* 2 claims that the pagan gods in their immorality did not abstain even from homosexuality). Second, there is a very similar note to that already sounded in the Old Testament, ancient Judaism, and the New Testament. The Didache says, "You shall not murder, you shall not commit adultery, you shall not corrupt boys" (2.1–2a). Polycarp asserts that those given to unnatural vice will not share in God's kingdom (*To the Philippians* 5.3). Justin opposes exposing infants because most are reared for immoral purposes, including sodomy (*1 Apology* 27, 36). The Apocalypse of Peter's vision of hell includes both male and female homosexuals. Clement of Alexandria says the sodomites burned with insane love for boys, so the city was destroyed (*Instructor* 3.8). Similar attitudes are found in Tertullian, the *Apostolic Constitutions*, Chrysostom, Basil, and Augustine (D. S. Bailey, *Homosexuality and the Western Christian Tradition* [London: Longmans, Green & Co., 1955]; Peter Coleman, *Christian Attitudes to Homosexuality* [London:SPCK, 1980]).

Such a survey allows two conclusions that are relevant. First, it is not possible to reduce Mediterranean homosexuality to pederasty. Second, it is not possible to reduce early Christianity's negative stance regarding homosexuality to its opposition to pederasty and prostitution. (Such conclusions run counter to the assertions of Robin Scroggs in *The New Testament and Homosexuality* [Philadelphia: Fortress, 1983].) Homosexuals, like idolaters, adulterers, thieves, the greedy, drunkards, revilers, and robbers, are mentioned in the list of vices characteristic of those who will not inherit the Kingdom of God.

In Paul's argument in 1 Cor 6:7b–10 tradition addresses both the offending party (if you act like this, you will not inherit the Kingdom of God) and the offended brother (why not rather suffer wrong?). There ought not to be lawsuits at all, whether in Christian courts of arbitration or outside.

The argument from experience comes in 6:11. It takes the form of a contrast between the lives of the Corinthians before Christ and after. Before Christ, he says, "and such were some of you" (v. 11a). But through Christ and by the Spirit, "you were washed, you were sanctified, you were justified" (v. 11b). Here Paul uses three different images for the same experiential reality, conversion to Christ. It is noteworthy that, of the three, the two signaling cleansing and holiness come first. The apostle wants to emphasize that the conversion of the Corinthians not only gave them forgiveness from the guilt of their sin but also involved a radical change of life (cf. Rom 6:6–11, death to sin, freedom from the power of sin, being set apart for God's will). As those who belonged experientially to God, the Corinthians were not to "yield your members to sin as instruments of wickedness, but [to] yield . . . your members to God as instruments of righteousness" (Rom 6:13). In other words, to be an offending party, and the cause of a lawsuit, is antithetical to one's religious experience. Experience supports tradition in the Pauline contention that there should be no lawsuits at all among Christians.

Now that we have traced the train of the argument in 1 Cor 6:1–11, we need to turn to the task of summarizing the positions of the Corinthians and Paul. There are two parts to the problematic of the behavior of the Corinthians. First, there is the issue of Christians going before the pagan courts against Christians. How could they justify this? Second, there is the matter of the community's detachment from the conflict between individual members. Why would they do this? Let us consider the second part of the problem first. At first glance, it seems strange that a church with at least some of its members coming out of the synagogue (cf. Acts 18:8 with 1 Cor 1:14; Acts 18:17 with 1 Cor 1:1) would not consider a Christian adaptation of the Jewish court of arbitration. On second thought, one sees that, just as in 5:1–13, the community would likely have stayed out of the matter because of the errorists' contention, "The spiritual man judges all things, but is himself to be judged by no one" (2:15). Behavior fitting for a spiritual person was to be discerned by the individual without interferences from the group (2 Cor 10:29b; Judg 21:25b). With this mentality there could be no thought of community arbitration. What justification could there be, then, for spirituals to take their brethren to court? The need for legal redress would lie in the belief by at least some of the Corinthians that by virtue of their relation to Christ through the Spirit they were free from moral law (6:12; 10:23): "All things are lawful for me." Given this justification for libertine behavior, someone was likely to be wronged or defrauded (6:8). Redress of the grievance would be needed. The basis for an offended one's going to pagan courts for assistance would lie in another of the Corinthians' beliefs, namely, belonging to Christ is a spiritual matter; the flesh is a spiritually/ morally neutral sphere (e.g., 6:13; 6:18b; 8:8–9). Just as in 5:1–8, some Corinthians believed that since the link with Christ was spirit to Spirit, what was done physically in the material sphere was outside the bounds of Christian concern. It would not matter, therefore, if one Christian acted against another in the arena of the empirical world. Moreover, since the civil courts belonged to this empirical world that is passing away, that would be where one would go. Go to the courts of the age that is passing away to deal with issues that belong to the world that is passing away. There was most definitely a logic to the Corinthians' positions.

The apostle Paul rejected the community's detachment here just as he did in 5:1–13 (and would later on, cf. 2 Cor 10:6). Christians who have the mind of Christ (2:16b), who are wise (v. 5), and who will act as judges of nations and angels at the Last Judgment (6:2a, 3a) can surely handle the trivial matters of this age. It is a scandal to think that you cannot (v. 5a). Clearly the apostle here too expects the community to deal with its members. Christian faith is communal, not totally individualistic.

Paul also rejected the rationale of both the offender and the offended. The common tradition of the churches (1:2; 4:17; cf. Gal 5:21–23) says to the offender that the realm of the flesh is most definitely religiously/ morally significant. It is the arena in which one acts out one's relation to Jesus through the Spirit. Not to grasp this is to miss the Kingdom (vv. 9–10), because it is to fail to live out of one's conversion experience (v. 11). The common tradition of the churches (v. 7b,c) also says to the offended the same thing. It is in the sphere of the flesh that one follows Jesus in not returning evil for evil. Further, to all parties in Corinth the apostle implies that the civil sphere, although passing away, is religiously important. One does not take a Christian brother before the civil courts because it interferes with Christian evangelism (cf. 9:19–23; 10:32–33). In 6:1–11 Paul, therefore, makes two points. First, there should not be abusive behavior between Christians. Second, if there is, however, it must be dealt with within the Christian community.

KEEPING THE BEDROOM ATTACHED TO THE REST OF THE HOUSE

1 Corinthians 6:12-20

1 Cor 6:12-20 is the third thought unit in the larger ABA' section, 5:1-6:20; like 5:1-13, it focuses on sexual sin, framing 6:1-11, which deals with lawsuits among Christians. There is a verbal link with 6:1-11, immoral (*pornoi*) in 6:9 linking with immorality (*porneia*) in 6:13. Tracing the train of thought in 6:12-20 is the task at hand.

The passage falls into two parts (6:12-18a and 6:18b-20), each of which is organized in the same way: (1) Corinthian assertions followed by their Pauline responses; (2) two Pauline arguments, usually beginning, "Do you not know?"; and (3) a concluding exhortation. The three components of 6:12-18a will be examined first.

(1) In vv. 12-14 there are three Corinthian assertions followed by Pauline qualifications. The first Corinthian assertion comes in v. 12a: "All things are lawful for me" (cf. 10:23), possibly a misunderstanding of Paul's preaching of Christian freedom (cf. Gal 5:1, 13) but certainly counter to Paul's thought (Rom 8:4; 13:8-10; Gal 5:23; 1 Cor 9). Paul responds, "but not all things are helpful" (v. 12b). The second Corinthian assertion repeats the first: "All things are lawful for me" (v. 12c). To which the apostle replies, "but I will not be enslaved by anything" (v. 12d), echoing the philosophical dictum that freedom cannot cancel itself by making one unfree (Seneca *Epistle* 14.1). The third Corinthian assertion is more complex. It comes in two parts: the moral principle (v. 13a, "Food is meant for the stomach and the stomach for food") and its basis (v. 13b, "God will destroy both the one and the other"). The moral principle reflects the Greek view that regarded sexual intercourse as just as natural as eating and drinking (e.g., Plutarch "Life of Solon" 31). In either case there is a physical hunger or thirst and physical objects to satisfy the need. In both cases, the act of satisfying a physical appetite

29

with a physical object is morally and religiously neutral (cf. 1 Cor 8:8). This is possibly another misunderstanding of a Pauline position (e.g., Rom 14:17). The basis for this contention is that both the appetite (be it hunger, thirst, or sexual desire) and its physical satisfaction (be it food, drink, or another human body) belong to this age that is passing away. Neither is anything more than a temporal, transient reality; neither is of the essence of the Kingdom of God. This is a dualism born not of a gnostic view of matter but of an eschatological error. This same rationale lies behind the Corinthian assertion of 1 Cor 15:12. It also seems to be a misunderstanding of a Pauline position (1 Cor 7:29–31). Just as the Corinthian assertion was given in two parts (moral principle, v. 13a; basis, v. 13b), so also the Pauline response is twofold: the moral principle ("The *body* is not meant for immorality, but for the Lord, and the Lord for the *body*," v. 13c), and its basis ("God raised the Lord and will also raise *us* up by his power," v. 14). In the statement of his counterprinciple, Paul personifies immorality (*porneia*) so that this life-style stands alongside the Lord as a rival. He then uses language characteristic of the marital union ("to be for," cf. Song of Sol 2:16; Rom 7:2–3) and says the Christian's body is meant not for union with Immorality but for union with the Lord. "Body" here is used in parallelism with the personal pronoun in v. 14 ("us") and so stands for the entire person or self (cf. Rom 6:12). Since humans act through their bodies (2 Cor 5:10; Rom 6:13), here body stands for the entire self but stresses the corporeal aspect of human life. This usage is in line with LXX practice (J. A. Ziesler, "*Sōma* in the Septuagint," *NovT* 25[1983]:133–45). The whole self, including its corporeal dimensions, is intended for intimate union with Christ, not Immorality. This is Paul's counterprinciple. The basis on which this moral principle rests comes in v. 14: "God raised the Lord and will also raise us up by his power." Just as Jesus was raised (cf. 1 Cor 15:4, 12), so God will raise Christians (cf. Rom 8:11). If the perishable nature of things physical was thought by the Corinthians to prove the moral and religious neutrality of the body, Paul's assertion of the bodily resurrection sets the seal to the moral and religious significance of the body. God's act to continue bodily life indicates that what is done in this sphere of human life has ultimate meaning.

(2) Two Pauline arguments follow the dialogue between Paul and his Corinthian opponents, each beginning with the question "Do you not know?" The first is found in v. 15: "Do you not know that your bodies are members of Christ? Shall I therefore take the members of Christ and

make them members of a prostitute? Never!" Whereas in a Palestinian or Jewish setting "Christ" (Messiah) was used as a title (the anointed king), in Paul's letters addressed to Hellenistic readers "Christ" functioned as a personal name (Jesus Christ, Christ Jesus, or simply Christ). Just as Israel could serve as the name of an individual (Jacob) or of a community (the people of Israel descended from the individual and identified with him), so could "Christ" (e.g., Phil 2:11, the individual; 1 Cor 12:12, the corporate personality). Here the name "Christ" is used as it is in 1 Cor 12:12 of the corporate personality, the Christian community. "Members" (*melē*) is Paul's term for the parts of the body through which the life of the body is expressed (cf. 1 Cor 12:12, 14–26; Rom 6:13). Paul is saying then that individual Christians in their corporeal existence are the various body parts of the corporate personality of Christ through which the life of Christ is expressed. Would it be proper to take Christ's body parts and make them the vehicle through which the life of a prostitute expresses itself? Of course not; such is unthinkable.

The Old Testament knows two kinds of prostitutes: (*a*) the secular harlot (e.g., Gen 38:14–15; Josh 2:4–16; Judg 16), who is judged negatively by the Law (Lev 21:7, 9; 19:29; 22:21) and the Wisdom tradition (Prov 5), and (*b*) the cult prostitute, male and female (1 Sam 2:22; 1 Kings 14:23–24; 15:12; 22:46; 2 Kings 23:7, 14; 2 Chron 15:16; Ezek 8:14; Hos 4:13–14; Jer 3:2), who is also treated negatively by the Law (Deut 23:17) and the prophets (Amos 2:7).

Ancient Judaism continued the Old Testament's negative judgment of prostitution. The LXX changed the references to sacred prostitution into prostitution generally. Farewell speeches in Tob 4:12 and Jubilees 20.3 warn the young against whoredom. Philo says that whereas men of other nations visit prostitutes from the age of fourteen, Jews do not do so at all (*On Joseph* 42–43). Josephus states that the Law said one was not to offer sacrifices out of the hire of a woman who is a harlot, for the Lord is not pleased with anything that arises from such abuses of the body (*Antiquities* 4.8.9 §206). He also indicates that no one ought to marry a harlot, whose matrimonial oblations, arising from the prostitution of her body, God will not receive (*Antiquities* 4.8.23 §245).

In Greece there were several types of prostitutes: (*a*) the *pornē* or the lowest class of prostitute (in the sixth century B.C., Solon had established houses of prostitution for such women in Athens [Plutarch "Life of Solon" 22–23]); (*b*) the higher class of courtesan, euphemistically called "companion" (*hetaira*); and (*c*) the true religious prostitute (*hierodulē*) such as the one thousand devotees of Aphrodite in Corinth before the destruction of the city in 146 B.C. The sexual lattitude allowed to men by Greek public opinion was virtually unrestricted. Sexual relations of males with both boys and harlots were generally tolerated. By the New Testament period, however, there were Stoics (e.g., Musonius Rufus) who had come to regard all sexual intercourse outside marriage as unlawful.

To the Romans prostitution was a trade. Prostitutes were required to register themselves in the office of the aedile (Tacitus *Annals* 2.85), with resulting supervision and protection by the state. Even moralists like Cicero and Cato condoned prostitution as necessary to protect and preserve marriage. Two anecdotes about Cato illustrate his stance. In the first, he is reported to have given his blessing to a young man coming out of a brothel, since by frequenting such a place he was not tempted to tamper with other men's wives. In the second, it is said that when he saw the young man repeatedly coming out of the same brothel, he remarked, "I praised you then, since I assumed you came here now and again, not that you lived here" (Horace *Satires* 1.2.32). In general, however, Romans felt more shame about visiting prostitutes than did the Greeks.

In the New Testament, the Gospels portray Jesus' forgiveness of a prostitute (Luke 7:37–50) and record him as saying that tax collectors and harlots (who have repented) go into the Kingdom of God before the religious leaders (who have not repented). Paul continues the Jewish hostility to involvement with prostitutes (1 Cor 6:15–16). The early fathers did not uniformly proscribe prostitution. Augustine, for example, continued the Roman position when he said, "Suppress prostitution and capricious lusts will overthrow society" (*De Ordine* 2.4.12). At the same time, the fathers believed a prostitute might repent, be saved (Jerome *Epistle to Furiam*), marry a Christian, and be received at the communion table (Council of Elvira, Canons 12 and 14).

A reading of Propertius reveals the contrary values of Christ and prostitution (exploitation, manipulation, greed, lying, unfaithfulness) (*Elegies* "In Lenam" 4.5; cf. Ovid *The Art of Love* 1.8 and Lucian *Dialogues of Courtesans* 6th dialogue, which reflect the values of courtesans in antiquity). A Christian would not want his selfhood linked to and used as a vehicle of such values, so Paul thought (Vern L. Bullough, *The History of Prostitution* [New Hyde Park, N.Y.: University Books, 1964]; William W. Sanger, *The History of Prostitution* [New York: Harper & Brothers, 1859]).

The second Pauline argument comes in vv. 16–17: "Do you not know that he who continually clings to a prostitute becomes one body with her? For it is written, 'The two shall become one.' But he who continually clings to the Lord becomes one spirit with him." The verbal form translated "continually clings to" is a present participle (*kollōmenos*) of the verb which is used in Gen 2:24 LXX and is translated "cleave to" in the RSV (cf. Matt 19:5, and Eph 5:31, which quote Gen 2:24). From this verbal form it may be inferred that, like the sexual behavior in 5:1 (*echein*, present infinitive) the problem is not a casual, one-time liaison with a prostitute but is an ongoing "cleaving to" one another. Such a relationship, as Gen 2:24 says, issues in a bonding in which "the two shall become one flesh." Likewise the same verbal form points to a continuous "cleaving to" the Lord by the Christian. Such a relation with Christ is not sexual, so it issues in a union described as "being one spirit." Although Paul describes the one relation as "being one body" and the other as "being one spirit," he does not intend to split the self in two. In his letters the apostle can use *sōma* (body) for the self, emphasizing the corporeal aspects and can likewise use *pneuma* (spirit) as a substitute for the personal pronoun (e.g., 2 Cor 7:13, where Titus and his spirit are used interchangeably), emphasizing the willing (e.g., Phil 1:27) and the self-awareness (e.g., 1 Cor 2:10–11) dimensions of the self. In a continuing relationship with an illicit sexual partner the whole self is involved, just as in the relation with the Lord the whole person is involved. For Paul, the two involvements are mutually exclusive; they are incompatible. In this context, the apostle does not make explicit why the two are incompatible, but the reason is implicit in the quotation from Gen 2:24 in v. 16. According to Genesis 2 (cf. Mark 10:2–9), the intention of God in creation is that sexual activity be within the marital relationship. Further, in Christ the redemptive activity of God aims not to cancel out creation but to free it from perversions and fulfill it. The bonding with a prostitute is incompatible with the bonding to Christ because the former violates the created order while the latter fulfills it. This is preferable as an explanation to the theory that the prostitute was a temple harlot and so the issue was idolatry (Manuel Miguens, "Christ's 'Members' and Sex," *Thomist* 39[1975]: 24–48, esp. p. 41).

(3) Given this fact, the concluding exhortation makes sense: "Shun immorality" (*porneian*, v. 18a).

The same three components in Paul's arguments found in 6:12–18a are also found in 6:18b–20. They must be investigated at this point. (1) In v. 18b we meet another Corinthian assertion: "Every other sin which a man commits is outside the body" (Jerome Murphy-O'Connor, "Corinthian Slogans in 1 Cor 6:12–20," *CBQ* 40[1978]:391–96). Taken at face value, the most natural meaning of this slogan is that the body has nothing to do with sin. The physical body is morally irrelevant, for sin takes place on an entirely different level of one's being. This is certainly not Paul's position. For the apostle, action is the only sphere in which commitment becomes real (Rom 6:19; 12:1–2; Gal 6:2). It does reflect the position of the Corinthian problem children, however. In 6:13 we have already seen that they denied the relevance of the body for the moral and religious life. Since no corporeal action has any moral importance, everything is permitted (6:12a,c; 10:23a). Sin belongs only to the level of motives, intentions, and human inwardness, according to the Corinthians. If this is so, then if a Christian's inner life is all right, an ongoing relation with a prostitute is of no consequence. This could have been a misunderstanding of a Pauline position (cf. Rom 14:14, 20b, as verbalized in the generation after Paul in Titus 1:15).

Paul's response is found at 6:18c: "but the immoral man sins against his own body." Again the presupposition for Paul's argument is the place of human sexuality in the created order. If God intended in creation that one's body be involved sexually within marriage, then if it is used otherwise, it is abused (cf. Musonius Rufus's assertion that the man who has intercourse with *hetairae* sins against himself).

(2) The dialogue between the Corinthians and Paul is followed by two Pauline arguments. The first begins with the phrase "Do you not know": "Do you not know that your body is a temple (*naos*) of the Holy Spirit within you, which you have from God?" (v. 19a). If this is so, then any abuse of one's body is ruled out (cf. Musonius Rufus's statement that by all unclean acts a man defiles the god in his own breast). In antiquity one violated a deity's temple at great risk (remember 1 Cor 3:16–17). The second argument does not have the standard introductory phrase "Do you not know." It simply states, "You are not your own; you were bought with a price" (vv. 19b–20a). The language here can be interpreted in two very different ways. On the one hand, this may be seen as an echo of the language of sacral manumission where a slave's purchase price was paid to his or her owner within a temple and was sealed by a standard inscription that included phrases like "for freedom _____ was set free" and "_____ was bought with a price." If this is the meaning of the statement, then Paul is saying a Christian does not have a right to enter again into a relationship of bondage (cf. Rom 6:17–23). On the

other hand, it could be taken as marital language. Paul says in 1 Cor 7:4 that Christians within marriage are not their own lords but rather belong to the other partner. Also, in the Old Testament (e.g., Neh 10:31; Ruth 4:5, 9, 10), "buying" is used of payment of a dowry, and "price" is also present in dowry contracts (e.g., Gen 20:16 LXX). If this is the frame of reference, again Paul is saying that a Christian does not have the freedom to enter another liaison but belongs to the present partner. Of the two, the latter seems out of place because the problem in Corinth is with men whereas the analogy applies only to women. Either way, the apostle says one's present status of belonging body and soul to another excludes a relationship that involves abuse of oneself.

(3) If Paul has argued the negative (do not act so as to abuse your body) in vv. 19–20a, he concludes with a positive exhortation: "So glorify God in your body" (v. 20b). In this context this can only mean living in line with the original intention of the Creator with reference to one's human sexuality.

Having traced the train of thought in 1 Cor 6:12–20, we now attempt to summarize the positions both of the Corinthians and of Paul insofar as the situation can be reconstructed. The Corinthians argued that Christian freedom permits sex outside of marriage. Their rationale was twofold. In the first place, sex, like all physical appetites, has its physical satisfaction and was meant to be satisfied. So satisfy it with no more qualms than you would your hunger by eating whatever food was at hand. After all, such physical acts are morally/religiously irrelevant, since both the appetite and its satisfaction belong to the physical world which will pass away. In the second place, sin does not involve the body; it is a matter of the spirit, of the inner motives, thoughts, and feelings. So sexual activity, which is a bodily function, has nothing to do with one's religious or moral life.

Paul argued first that unrestrained freedom is not always helpful to others and may be harmful to the individual if she or he becomes enslaved to something thereby. His response to the Corinthian rationale was two-fold. First, the whole self will be raised up to give an account to God of how it has responded to the Lord for whom it was meant. Since it is impossible to be in union with both Christ and an illegitimate sexual partner, illicit sex breaks the relations with Christ, something for which one will be judged. So, shun immorality. Second, since the physical dimension is part of the whole self, immorality affects the essential self or personality. This must be avoided because immorality defiles the temple of the Holy

Spirit and because a Christian's freedom was purchased in such a way that it makes him or her a slave of Christ. So, glorify God in your body.

A basic issue between Paul and the Corinthian problem children was over a proper understanding of the self. The Corinthians wanted to split the person into two parts, a physical part that was perishable and a spiritual part that was eternal. From their point of view, what happened to the physical part was irrelevant for the destiny of the spiritual part. Paul, however, stands firmly for the unity of the self. What happens to the physical involves the spiritual and vice versa.

A second issue between Paul and the Corinthians was over the relation of creation and redemption. The Corinthians believed that their redemption in Christ made them transcend creation. The result of their behavior was to contradict God's intention in creation in the name of their redemptive freedom. Paul stands squarely in the Jewish tradition when he sees redemption as fulfilling creation.

CHRISTIANS ARE NOT ANGELS

1 Corinthians 7:1-24

1 Cor 7:1-24 is a thought unit introduced by the statement "Now concerning the matters about which you wrote" (v. 1a). Paul apparently had two main sources of information about the Corinthian church out of which he wrote 1 Corinthians: (a) oral information from Chloe's people (1:11), and (b) an official letter from the church, asking the apostle a series of questions (7:1, 25; 8:1; 12:1; 16:1, 12). At 7:1 Paul begins to answer the questions raised in the letter. The passage falls into two parts, 7:1b–6 and 7:7–24, each of which is organized in basically the same way.

The first part, 7:1b–6, consists of a Corinthian assertion followed by a Pauline qualification given in chiastic form. 1 Cor 7:1b, "It is well for a man not to touch a woman," is a Corinthian assertion, probably conveyed to Paul in the letter. Formally, v. 1b belongs with v. 1a. It is one of the matters about which the church wrote. Its contents run counter to Paul's Jewish heritage, to Jesus, to Paul's theological assumptions (e.g., creation), to his explicit statements approving sexual relationships within marriage, and to the later Pauline school's understanding of his position (e.g., 1 Tim 4:3; Eph 5:21–33). The content is in line with the positions of spirituals in the Pauline churches elsewhere (e.g., Col 2:21–22a; 1 Tim 4:3). Since Origen, this has been recognized as a Corinthian assertion (W. E. Phipps, "Is Paul's Attitude Towards Sexual Relations Contained in 1 Cor 7:1?" *NTS* 28[1982]:125–31). The Corinthians who said this were advocating sexual celibacy.

The Jewish position regarding sex and marriage was positive (Gen 2:18; Tob 8:6; R. Johanan said, "He who is twenty years old and not married spends all of his days in sin" [b Kiddushin 29b]). The commandment to be fruitful and multiply was so important in the rabbinic tradition that only one rabbi, R. Simeon b. Azzai, was said not to have fulfilled it. Even he argued that his followers should (b Yebamoth 63a). Although some Essenes did not marry (Josephus *War* 2.8.2 §120), others did (Josephus *War* 2.8.13 §160–61; 1 QSa 1.4). Jesus, likewise, had sanctioned the marital union (Mark 10:2–12). At the same time, Jesus had apparently said that beyond the resurrection there would be no marrying or giving in marriage, but people would be like angels in heaven (Matt 22:30; Mark 12:25; Luke 20:34–35). This was a reflection of some Jewish thinking about the life after resurrection (e.g., 1 Enoch 51.4; 104.6; b Berakoth 17a; Genesis Rabbah "Bereshit" 8.11). In Pauline churches after the apostle's death, there were Christians whose overrealized eschatology led them to an ascetic stance with reference to sex and marriage (e.g., 1 Tim 4:3; cf. 2 Tim 2:18; Col 2:21). Since we know that some of the Corinthian Christians espoused an overrealized eschatology (1 Cor 4:8; 15:12, 19), it may very well be that this aversion to sex in Corinth derived from their application of Jesus' words about being like angels after the resurrection to themselves. Since they had already risen from the dead, they were now to live like angels, transcending their sexuality. Such an interpretation would have been supported by the asceticism of early Christianity's milieu (e.g., pre-Christian Jewish ascetics, the Rechabites, known from the narration of Zosimus; the Therapeutae, mentioned by Philo, who gave up normal conjugal relations in favor of spiritual intercourse with divine Wisdom [*Contemplative Life* 68]; a similar pattern is found in devotion to Isis, narrated by Apuleius [*Golden Ass* 11]).

The Pauline qualification comes in vv. 2–6. The pattern is ABCC'B'A' and looks something like this:

A. Possible acts of immorality (v. 2)
    B. Sexual union is all right (v. 3)
        C. Dependence of the woman on the man (v. 4a)
        C'. Dependence of the man on the woman (v. 4b)
    B'. Sexual union encouraged, except for special reason, and then
        only temporarily (v. 5a)
A'. Temptation to immorality (v. 5b).

Examination of the components in this concentric pattern is in order.

In (A) and (A') the apostle counters the demand for celibacy with the reality of sexual desire among Christians, which, if not satisfied within marriage, runs the risk of opening the door to Satan and of leading to immorality (cf. 1 Thess 4:3–8). In (B) and (B') Paul affirms the goodness of sexual relations within marriage ("The husband should give to his wife her conjugal rights, and likewise the wife to her husband," v. 3; cf. m Ketuboth 5:7) and does not approve abstinence within marriage except by mutual agreement, during a temporary period, for prayer (v. 5). Temporary abstinence from sexual relations within marriage is found in the Old Testament (Eccles 3:5; Joel 2:16; Zech 12:12–14), for example, before eating sacred food (1 Sam 21:4–6), when engaged in a military expedition (2 Sam 11:8–13), and before ratification of a covenant (Exod 19:14–15). In ancient Judaism it is found in the case of the high priest before the Day of Atonement (m Yoma 1:1). m Ketuboth 5:6 says a man may vow to have no intercourse with his wife for a very brief time (School of Shammai, two weeks if she consents; School of Hillel, one week only). Rabbis may abstain thirty days against the will of their wives for the study of the Law. T. Naphtali 8:8, says, "There is a season for a man to embrace his wife and a season to abstain therefrom for his prayer." Paul permits temporary abstinence also but only by mutual agreement. In (C) and (C') the apostle describes the mutual dependence of each partner on the other: "the wife does not rule over her own body, but the husband does; likewise the husband does not rule over his own body, but the wife does" (v. 4). In response to the Corinthian ascetics, Paul affirms the goodness of sexual activity within marriage and permits abstinence only for a limited time by mutual consent. In v. 6 when he says, "I say this by way of concession, not of command," he is referring to the "except perhaps by agreement for a season" (v. 5a). He is not commanding abstinence but, as a concession, allowing it under very special and limited circumstances. Taking vv. 1b–6 as a whole, one sees Paul not only sanctioning marriage but also disapproving of sexual abstinence within marriage. Since he did not have an overrealized eschatology, the apostle would not have considered Jesus' logion about being like angels beyond the resurrection applicable to Christian existence in the here and now.

The second part of 1 Cor 7:1–24 is vv. 7–24. In this section, once again the material consists of a Corinthian assertion followed by a Pauline qualification given in a chiastic pattern. V. 7a reads, "I wish all men to be as I am." The words are obviously Paul's (cf. 1 Cor 4:16; 11:1; Gal 4:12); however, in this context they do not reflect Paul's position. Paul does not wish *all* men to be unmarried. This is, however, part of the position of his opponents, as verbalized in v. 1b ("It is well for a man not to touch a woman"), and as proposed later in the chapter (i.e., if married, separate; if not married, stay that way). It seems best, therefore, to take v.7a as a Corinthian assertion using Paul's own celibacy as their authority (Barbara Hall, "Paul and Women," *TheolT* 31[1974]:53). Paul, they say, exhorts us to imitate him, and he lives in a single state.

The Pauline response comes in vv. 7b–24 and falls into a chiastic pattern, ABCB'A' that looks like this:

> A. Each has his or her own special gift from God and so lives (v. 7b)
>> B. *I say* to the unmarried and widows (vv. 8–9)
>>> C. *The Lord says* to the married (vv. 10–11)
>> B'. *I say* to those married to unbelievers (vv. 12–16)
> A'. Live in terms of the gifts assigned to you and in terms of your Christian calling (vv. 17–24).

Each component needs special attention.

Component (A) begins with a strong adversative, "But" (*alla*). Paul is correcting the Corinthian assertion that had the effect of making celibacy mandatory in the Pauline churches. "But each has his own gift [*charisma*] from God, the one this, the other that" (v. 7b). The apostle's point is that, rather than there being a general rule mandatory for all Christians in this regard, individual Christians are to live in accord with their particular gifts (cf. 1 Cor 12:4–30; Rom 12:3–8). This would seem to mean that if one had the gift of celibacy, it was an acceptable life-style; if one did not possess this gift, it was not all right.

Component (A'), vv. 17–24, is among the most difficult passages in the Pauline corpus to interpret. The place to begin is with the surface structure of the unit. It is composed of a general principle (v. 17) followed by two specific applications (vv. 18–24). The general principle in v. 17 reads, "To each as the Lord has apportioned; as the Lord has called each, so let him walk." Two things are being said here. In the first place, the term translated "apportioned" (*memeriken*) is the same word used in Rom 12:3 for God's assignment of spiritual gifts to various believers. It is so used in this context. Just as in (A), v. 7b, so here in (A') Paul is speaking about living in line with the gifts given by God. This is one half of the general principle. In the second place, Paul is saying that Christians should live in line with their calling.

In Paul's use of the "call" terminology (*kalein, klēsis, klētos*) one meaning is clear, two others are debated. First, it is agreed that in Pauline Christianity "to call" is a technical term for the choice of a person by God for salvation (Rom 8:28–30). The caller is God (Rom 9:11; Gal 5:8). The calling is to God's Kingdom and glory (1 Thess 2:2), to salvation (Rom 8:28–30; 2 Thess 2:13), to eternal life (1 Tim 6:12). The basis of the calling is the grace of God (Gal 1:6, 15; 2 Tim 1:9). The background for this meaning is the LXX's use of "to call" as an equivalent of "to choose" (e.g., Isa 41:9). Second, on the basis of Heb 5:4, where a priest is said to be called to his office, and Acts 13:2 and 16:10, where Paul and his helpers are said to be called to certain missionary work, the expression *klētos apostolos* in Rom 1:1 and 1 Cor 1:1 has often been taken to mean that Paul was called to be an apostle (e.g., "Paul, called to be an apostle of Christ Jesus," 1 Cor 1:1, RSV). If so, then "to call" may refer, in Paul as well as elsewhere, to the divine summons to an office or to a special work. It could just as easily be translated as the adjective it is, "Paul, a called apostle," with the meaning "a Christian missionary" (K. L. Schmidt, *TDNT*, 3:494). The latter understanding is preferred in this commentary. Paul understands apostleship as a gift (1 Cor 12:28; cf. Eph 4:8, 11). Third, since *hē klēsis* is sometimes used in nonbiblical literature to mean "station in life," "position," "vocation," certain exegetes wish to read 1 Cor 7:20 in this way (e.g., RSV, "every one should remain in the state in which he was called"). However, in Pauline literature *klēsis* refers everywhere else to the call to salvation (e.g., Rom 11:29; 1 Cor 1:26; Phil 3:14; 2 Thess 1:11; Eph 1:18; 4:1, 4; 2 Tim 1:9; cf. Heb 3:1; 2 Pet 1:10). There is no justification, then, for reading 1 Cor 7:20 in any other way.

Paul does not use "call" in relation to a specific occupation or station in life, although vv. 17 and 20 have been forced into that mold on more than one occasion. What is actually said here (v. 17) is that a person ought to live as she or he has been called by God. This is the same thing that is said in a slightly different way in Eph 4:1: "walk worthily of the calling of which you were called" ("as God has called you, live up to that calling," NEB). Paul's general principle, then, is twofold. Christians are to live (1) in line with their gifts and (2) faithful to their Christian calling.

In two specific situations Paul tries to work out the second part of this principle. Again, attention to the organization of the material is helpful. What follows are two paragraphs, each with three components: (*a*) an introductory, specific exhortation, (*b*) the basis for the exhortation, and (*c*) a concluding exhortation. Vv. 18a–20 constitute the first paragraph. (*a*) "Was anyone circumcised when called? Let him not seek to remove the marks. Was anyone in an uncircumcised state called? Let him not seek circumcision." (*b*) "Circumcision is nothing and uncircumcision is nothing, but keeping the commands of God [is what is important]." (*c*) "Each in the calling to which he was called, in this let him remain." The entire paragraph says what is important is being faithful to one's Christian calling (the second part of the general principle of v. 17); everything else is insignificant by comparison.

Vv. 21–24 constitute the second illustrative paragraph. (*a*) "Were you, a slave, called? Let it not worry you. But if you are even able to become

free, make the most of [your freedom]." (*b*) "For the slave called by the
Lord is a freedman of the Lord. Likewise, the called freedman is a servant of Christ." (*c*) "You were all bought with a price. Do not become
slaves of men. Each in the calling to which he was called, brethren, let
him remain with God." Again, the basic thrust of the paragraph says
what is important is being faithful to one's Christian calling (the second
part of Paul's general principle enunciated in v. 17). Three particular
problems call for comment, however.

In the first place, v. 21b is a notorious crux of interpretation. This is
due to the fact that in Greek the sentence is incomplete. It reads: "But if
you are even able to become free, make the most of _____." A dative
needs to be supplied after "make the most of" (*mallon chrēsai*). "Your
slavery," "your freedom," "the commands of God," and "your calling"
are all options (P. Trummer, "Die Chance der Freiheit: Zur Interpretation des *mallon chrēsai* in 1 Kor 7:21," *Bib*56[1975]:344–68; S. Scott
Bartchy, *First Century Slavery and 1 Corinthians 7:21* [Missoula, Mont.:
SBL, 1973]). The trend seems to favor "your freedom" (e.g., RSV; TEV;
NIV; NEB); it is the reading that is most natural in the context and is the
one favored here.

In the second place, if Christian slaves are able to gain their freedom,
they are to make the most of it. What this means is that they are to be
faithful to their Christian calling in their new freedom just as they were
in their former slavery. Whatever their status in society, they are to live
worthy of their Christian calling.

In the third place, the concluding exhortation is expanded to include
the specific injunction "You were bought with a price; do not become
slaves of men" (v. 23). Christians sometimes purchased the freedom of
slaves who were Christians (1 Clement 55.2; Ignatius *Polycarp* 4.3; Hermas "Mandate" 8.10; "Parable" 1.8). Sometimes this was done by Christians selling themselves into slavery. So 1 Clement 55.2 says, "We know
that many among ourselves have given themselves to bondage that they
might ransom others. Many have delivered themselves to slavery and
provided food for others with the price they received for themselves."
This is absolutely prohibited by Paul. If one reads, "that I may boast"
(*kauchēsōmai*) with P[46] in 1 Cor 13:3, the specific danger may have been
very real in Corinth. In any case, the dominant thrust of paragraph two
(vv. 21–24) is the same as that of paragraph one (vv. 18–20): Live according to your Christian calling; everything else is insignificant by comparison and makes no ultimate difference. Yet, if a relative difference for the

better is possible, avail yourself of it. Be sure, however, to adhere to your Christian calling whatever happens.

In the (B), (B'), and (C) components of the chiasm of vv. 7b–24, Paul utilizes the twofold principle he has enunciated in (A) and (A'). It remains for this to be demonstrated, first in (B) and (B'), finally in (C). In the (B) component of the section (vv. 8–9), Paul addresses the unmarried and the widows: "*I say* [italics added] that it is well for them to remain single as I do. But if they cannot exercise self-control, they should marry. For it better to marry than to burn." The very "to burn" could mean either "to be aflame with passion" (e.g., RSV; NIV; NEB) or "to be burned in the fires of judgment or Gehenna" (M. L. Barré, "To Marry or to Burn: *purousthai* in 1 Cor 7:9," *CBQ* 36[1974]:193–202; cf. 6:9–11; Gal 5:19–21). Either would fit the context. The point the apostle is making is that the never-married and the formerly married must decide their marital status on the basis of whether or not they have the gift of celibacy. The first part of the twofold principle (v. 17) is applicable here: "To each as the Lord has assigned."

In (B') (vv. 12–16) Paul addresses Christians married to unbelievers: "To the rest *I say*, not the Lord, that if any brother has a wife who is an unbeliever, and she consents to live with him, he should not divorce her. If any woman has a husband who is an unbeliever, and he consents to live with her, she should not divorce him" (vv. 12–13). The reason is given in v. 14: "For the unbelieving husband is consecrated through his wife, and the unbelieving wife is consecrated through her husband." An exception is offered: "But if the unbelieving partner desires to separate, let it be so" (v. 15a). The reason for the exception is given in v. 15b: "For God has called (*keklēken*) us to peace" (cf. Rom 12:18). V. 16 may be read optimistically (e.g., NEB—"Think of it: as a wife you may be your husband's salvation; as a husband you may be your wife's salvation") or pessimistically (e.g., RSV, NIV, TEV—"Wife, how do you know whether you will save your husband? Husband, how do you know whether you will save your wife?"). Either is possible. In any case, v. 15, "For God has called us to peace," shows that here (vv. 12–16) Paul is employing the second part of his twofold principle: Live in line with your Christian calling (v. 17; cf. Rom 12:18).

In (C) (vv. 10–11) the apostle addresses the married in the name of the Lord: "To the married I give charge, not I but the Lord, that the wife should not separate from her husband . . . and that the husband should not divorce his wife." Here Paul is using a logion attributed to Jesus in a form we know from Mark 10:11–12. He is using the saying to address an already existing situation ("but if she has separated" v. 11) rather than a hypothetical possibility (cf. Justin 2 *Apology* 2 and Acts of Paul for instances of women who divorce their husbands or renounce their engagements upon becoming Christians). In so doing he is once again applying the second part of his twofold principle: Live according to your Christian calling (cf. Eph 4:1, 20, where living a life worthy of one's Christian calling means living as one learned Christ).

Divorce was a fact in ancient Israel. No legislation institutes it. No legislation prohibits it, except in certain circumstances. It might be caused by a second wife's pressure (Gen 21:8–14), by the wife's father (Judg 14:19–20; 15:2, 6), by a wife's leaving on her own accord (Judg 19:1–3), by a man's putting his wife away (Mal 2:13–16), and by religious leaders forcing termination of marriages (Ezra 10:3, 9, 17, 44). Various laws were promulgated to regulate the practice. For example, when a divorced woman remarries and is divorced a second time, she is not to remarry her first husband (Deut 24:1–4, a rule that runs counter to the practice in 2 Sam 3:14–16 and Hos 3:1). When a man has slandered his wife (Deut 22:19) or when a man has seduced a virgin and is forced to marry her (Deut 22:28–29), divorce is forbidden. Further, priests are forbidden to marry divorced persons (Lev 21:14), but their daughters, if divorced, could return to them (Lev 22:13).

According to strict Jewish opinion, only the man could divorce the woman. Shammi said this could be done only if she was guilty of sexual immorality. Hillel said it was possible for anything offensive to the husband, for example, if she spoiled his food (m Gittim 9:10). Philo held that the husband could divorce his wife for any cause whatsoever (*Special Laws* 3.5.30). Josephus maintained the same position and was himself married three times and divorced twice (*Antiquities* 15.7.10 §259; *Life* 75, 76 §414, 416, 427). Although she could not divorce her husband, a Jewish woman could sue for divorce before the tribunal (m Ketuboth 13:10; 7:9–10; m Nedarim 11:12). At Qumran there was a prohibition of divorce (11 Q Temple 57.17–19; CD 4.12b–5.14a), showing that there were at least some Jews in the first century who proscribed it.

Where Jewish life was influenced strongly by non-Jewish mores, wives sometimes divorced their husbands; e.g., among the Jewish Aramaic writings found in Egypt and dating from as early as the fifth century B.C. are numerous marriage contracts which show that Jewish women in that community had the right of divorce (R. Yaron, *Introduction to the*

Law of Aramaic Papyri [Oxford: Clarendon, 1961], chap. 5); Josephus says of Salome, "she sent him (Costobar) a bill of divorce and dissolved her marriage with him, though this was against the Jewish laws" (*Antiquities* 15.7.10 §259); there is an example of divorce by mutual consent among Jews found in an extant deed of divorce dated A.D. 45 (George Milligan, *Selections from the Greek Papyri* [Cambridge: Cambridge University Press, 1927], pp. 41–42).

Divorce was commonplace among the Gentiles. Both husband and wife had equal rights to divorce in Roman society. Remarriage was the rule. Seneca said that some women count their age not by the consuls but by the number of their husbands: "Is there any woman that blushes at divorce now that certain illustrious and noble ladies reckon their years, not by the number of consuls, but by the number of their husbands and leave home in order to marry, and marry in order to be divorced" (*De Beneficiis* 3.16.2). Juvenal speaks of the woman who had eight husbands in five autumns, "a thing that merits a tribute on her tomb" (*Satires* 6).

There are two sayings about divorce and remarriage attributed to Jesus in the New Testament: (1) Mark 10:2–9//Matt 19:3–8; and (2) Mark 10:10–12//Matt 19:9; Matt 5:32; Luke 16:18; 1 Cor 7:10–11. Jesus stands absolutely against divorce in the form of the sayings in Mark 10:2–9 and in Mark 10:10–12; Luke 16:18; 1 Cor 7:10–11. The Matthean form of both sayings adds an except clause (*mē epi porneia*, 19:9; *parektos logou porneias*, 5:32). Since *porneia* is distinguished from adultery (*moicheia*) in Matt 15:19, the former may mean "marriage within forbidden degrees" as in Acts 15:20, 29 (Joseph A. Fitzmyer, "The Matthean Divorce Texts and Some New Palestinian Evidence," in *To Advance the Gospel* [New York: Crossroad, 1981], pp. 79–111).

Paul's position is nuanced. Marriage is a lifelong commitment (Rom 7:2–3; 1 Cor 7:10–11; 7:39), that is, no divorce and no remarriage if one separates. Divorce is permissible only if an unbelieving partner wants to separate (1 Cor 7:13–16). Remarriage is an option for one whose spouse is dead, but only in the Lord (1 Cor 7:39). The deutero-Pauline 1 Tim 3:2, 12, and Tit 1:6 specify as one qualification for bishops and deacons that such a person be the husband of one wife. Although clearly ruling out both celibacy and divorce, the text may be interpreted either as a prohibition of polygamy or as a rejection of remarriage. Which is correct is not at all clear.

Among the early fathers, divorce was forbidden except for adultery (Justin *1 Apology* 15; Athenagoras *Plea* 33; Irenaeus *Against Heresies*

4.15.2; Tertullian *Marcion* 4.34; *Apostolic Constitutions* 6.14; Lactantius *Institutes* 6.23.33). Remarriage in the earliest period (A.D. 110–80) was regarded as undesirable (Athenagoras *Plea* 33; Hermas "Command" 4.4.1). In the period A.D. 180–250, opinion was divided. The stricter Christians regarded second marriages as akin to fornication (Tertullian *Virgins* 10; Hippolytus *Refutation* 9.12; Clement of Alexandria *Miscellanies* 2.23). The laxer Christians (e.g., Callixtus) legalized them. In the period A.D. 250–313, second marriages were legal but frowned upon. A third marriage was considered the moral equivalent of prostitution (*Didascalia* 3.1).

Having traced the train of thought in 1 Cor 7:1–24, we now need to summarize the positions of Paul and his Corinthian opponents (D. R. Cartlidge, "1 Cor 7 as a Foundation for a Christian Sex Ethic," *JR* 55[1975]:220–34; P. H. Menoud, "Marriage and Celibacy according to Saint Paul," in *Jesus Christ and the Faith*, trans. E. M. Paul [Pittsburgh: Pickwick Press, 1978], pp. 1–18). It seems that some Corinthian spirituals were rejecting marriage, perhaps on the basis of their overrealized eschatology and their interpretation of Jesus' logion about life beyond the resurrection. Their rejection of marriage resulted in the contention that "it is good for a man not to touch a woman" (7:1). This was supported by their appeal to the words of Paul as used in other contexts: "I wish everyone was as I am" (7:7). Faced with this situation, the church sent a letter to the apostle asking in part about his opinions on this problem.

Paul's response can be summarized in three points. (1) Marriage, with full sexual involvement, is desirable *except* (a) when husband and wife abstain temporarily within marriage for prayer by mutual consent and (b) when one has the gift of celibacy. (2) Marriage is not to be dissolved *except* when a Christian's unbelieving partner desires to separate. (3) The general rule to follow about sex and marriage is the twofold rule followed in all Paul's churches (v. 17c): (a) Live according to the gifts God has given you (v. 17a); (b) Live according to your Christian calling (v. 17b) or God's commandments (v. 19b). By implication this means (a) if you have the gift of celibacy, live that way; if you do not have the gift, do not try to live that way; and (b) if you are married, stay that way (as the Lord has commanded).

WHEN A THEOLOGICAL GOOD BECOMES A PRACTICAL LIABILITY

1 Corinthians 7:25–40

In 1 Cor 7:25–40 Paul takes up the second question raised for him by the Corinthian letter: "Now concerning the virgins" (*parthenōn*, v. 25a). "Virgins" is a broad term that can include not only unmarried females but also males who have had no intercourse with women (cf. Rev 14:4). The context (e.g., vv. 27–28, 32–34, 36–38) seems to demand a meaning that will cover both sexes (cf. TEV, "unmarried people"). The section is held together by an inclusion; v. 25b ("I have no command of the Lord, but I give my opinion as one who by the Lord's mercy is trustworthy"); v. 40 ("I think that I have the Spirit of God"). The section begins with a statement of principles consisting of four components (vv. 26–28); what follows in the chapter is an exposition of each of the four components, but not in order (vv. 29–40). The statement of principles includes (1) a first reason to remain as is (v. 26), (2) an application of the injunction to remain as is (v. 27), (3) a statement of exceptions to the general rule (v. 28a), and (4) a second reason to remain as is (v. 28b). These four components are explained in what follows: (1) is explained in vv. 29–31, (2) in vv. 39–40, (3) in vv. 36–38, and (4) in vv. 32–35.

It will facilitate our understanding of the section, 7:25–40, if each of the four components is examined in connection with the explanation of it that follows. This, then, will be the procedure in what follows. (1) In v. 26 one meets a first reason to remain as is. Is it "considering *the present distress*, I think it is better for a man to stay as he is" (TEV) or "I think that in view of *the impending distress* it is well for a person to remain as he is" (RSV)? The Greek phrase, *tēn enestōsan anagkēn*, uses a perfect participle. In past tenses of the verb *enistēmi* the meaning is usually "to be present," "to have come" (e.g., 2 Thess 2:2, the day has come; Gal 1:4, the present age; Heb 9:9, the present time). Here, therefore, it seems preferable to translate "the present distress." At the very least, this would refer to the problems of a small band of Christians living in a large, corrupt city, subject to various types of abuse (e.g., Acts 18:1–17).

There is an exposition of this statement of principle in vv. 29–31 which adds to our understanding of the present distress:

> The time has been shortened.
> Let those having wives live as though they did not;
> those weeping as though they did not;
> those rejoicing as though they did not;
> those buying as though they had nothing;
> those dealing with the world as though they did not;
> for the form of this world is passing away.

There is comparative material in 2 Esd which speaks of the birth pangs of the New Age drawing near (16.37–39) and in which the readers are exhorted to "prepare for battle, and in the midst of the calamities be like strangers on the earth" (16.40). Here are selected portions:

> Let him that sells be like one who will flee;
> let him that buys be like one who will lose;
> let him that does business be like one who will not make a profit;
> . . . .
> them that marry, like those who will have no children;
> them that do not marry, like those who are widowed. (vv. 41–44)

Paul, then, is saying that the present distress experienced by Christians is the expected time of tribulation/messianic woes/birth pangs of the New Age. In this situation of battle, Christians are called upon to live "like strangers on the earth." He also says that this time of tribulation has been shortened (v. 29). This is similar to the statement in Mark 13:20. In the context of a section on the tribulation and its terrible sufferings that would be especially hard on those married (v. 17, "And alas for those who are with child and for those who give suck in those days!"), we are told, "And if the Lord had not shortened the days, no human being would be saved; but for the sake of the elect, whom he chose, he shortened the days." Christians, then, from Paul's point of view, are in the tribulation now, but this time has been shortened. Truly the form of this world is passing away. The End is at hand (cf. 1 Thess 4:15; 1 Cor 15:51). In such a time, Christians are to live "like strangers on the earth." This is a first reason to remain in the marital situation in which one finds himself or herself.

(2) In v. 27 we find Paul's application of the injunction to remain as is:

> Are you bound to a wife?
> Do not seek to be free.

> Are you free from a wife?
> Do not seek a wife.

The particular human circumstance on which attention is focused is marriage.

(3) In v. 28a the apostle gives exceptions to the general rule to remain as is:

> Even if you marry, you do not sin.
> If the virgin marries, she or he does not sin.

Components (2) and (3) of Paul's statement of principles are explained in vv. 36–38, 39–40. Vv. 36–38 give the apostle's exposition of (3), line two ("If the virgin marries she or he does not sin"). "If anyone thinks he is behaving dishonorably toward his virgin" (v. 36a) raises immediate problems. Who is the virgin? Who is the one who thinks he is behaving dishonorably toward her? Three possibilities have been offered. (*a*) The virgin is a daughter beyond marriageable age; the one who thinks he is behaving dishonorably is the father who thinks she should be married (e.g., Confraternity of Christian Doctrine, following Chrysostom; cf. NAB). (*b*) The virgin is a betrothed fiancée; the one who thinks he is behaving improperly is the man engaged to her (RSV; TEV; NIV). (*c*) The virgin is a young woman who has entered into a spiritual marriage with the man who now feels he is behaving dishonorably towards her because his feelings are no longer platonic (NEB—a practice perhaps reflected elsewhere as early as Hermas "Parable" 9.10–11 and later attacked by Cyprian, Chrysostom, and Athanasius and condemned by the Councils of Elvira in A.D. 306, Ancyra in 314, and Nicaea in 325). That vv. 36–38 explain component (3)'s exception (if the virgin marries, she does not sin) excludes the first possibility. That the practice of spiritual marriages cannot with any certainty be traced back into the first century eliminates the third possibility. The most probable reading is the second. Paul is saying to an engaged couple that neither the man nor the woman sins if they marry. However, it would be better if they did not. Why is this so? An answer to this question must be deferred until later.

Vv. 39–40 give Paul's exposition of component (2) and of component (3), line one ("Even if you marry, you do not sin"). In v. 27 the apostle says in effect that if you are married, do not separate; if you are not married, do not seek to get married. In v. 28a he says further that if one does marry, it is no sin. Vv. 39–40 concern wives, widows, and remarriage.

"A wife is bound to her husband as long as he lives" (v. 39a). This works out the principle that if you are married, you are not to separate (v. 27). "If the husband dies, she is free to be married to whom she wishes, only in the Lord" (i.e., to a Christian). This is an extension of the principle in v. 28a: "If you should marry, you do not sin." "But she is happier if she remains as is, according to my judgment," v. 40, derives from the principle in v. 27b which says if you are not married, do not contract a marriage. Once again the question arises, Why? Partial explanation was given in vv. 26, 29–31. Further explanation will follow in vv. 28b, 32–35.

(4) The fourth component in Paul's statement of principles (vv. 26–28) comes in v. 28b: "Tribulation in the flesh those who marry will have, and I want to spare you this." This is explained in vv. 32–35:

> I want you to be free from care.
> The unmarried man is anxious about the affairs of the Lord;
> the married man is anxious about worldly affairs.
> The unmarried woman is anxious about the affairs of the Lord;
> the married woman is anxious about worldly affairs.
> I say this for your own benefit,
>> not to lay any restraint on you
>> but to promote good order
>> and to secure your undistracted devotion to the Lord.

Here is Paul's second reason to remain as is.

This argument is best understood against the backdrop of attitudes in the Greco-Roman world. The question of whether or not marriage was desirable was a debated one in the Mediterranean area. For example, the first-century rhetorician Quintilian lists the topic "whether marriage is desirable" among those that provide the most attractive practice in the art of speaking (*Institutio Oratoria* 2.4.24–25). The ancient Greek tradition was divided, some being against marriage (e.g., the pre-Socratic Thales, so Plutarch *Table Talk* 3.63; Epicurus, so Diogenes Laertius *Lives of Eminent Philosophers* 10.118–19; Diogenes, so Diogenes Laertius 6.54), others being for it (e.g., Socrates, whose marriage to a shrewish wife left support for marriage to later philosophers; Xenophon *Concerning Household Management*). The Stoic tradition also reflected diverse perspectives. Some Stoics were against marriage because it hindered one's study of philosophy, no one being able to attend both to books and to a wife (Theophrastus *On Marriage*). Others were definitely for marriage because they believed a wife freed one for the pursuit of philosophy, one having in a wife someone to take care of the house and free him from everyday cares (Antipater *On Marriage*). Still others preferred marriage for humans generally but not for the Ideal Cynic, because present existence is like a battlefield where the Cynic ought to be free from distractions and wholly devoted to the service of God. Epictetus' own words make this third option clear:

> In such an order of things as the present, which is like that of a battlefield, . . . the Cynic ought . . . to be free from distraction, wholly devoted to the service of God. . . .

But if one is married, Epictetus says,

> he must show certain services to his father-in-law, to the rest of his wife's relatives, to his wife herself; finally, he is driven from his profession, to act as a nurse in his own family and to provide for them. To make a long story short, he must get a kettle to heat water for the baby, for washing it in a bathtub; wool for his wife when she has a child, oil, a cot, a cup (the vessels get more and more numerous); not to speak of the rest of his business, and his distraction. (3.22,69)

> (David L. Balch, "I Cor 7:32–35 and Stoic Debates About Marriage, Anxiety, and Distraction," *JBL* 102[1983]:429–39; O. Larry Yarbrough, *Not Like the Gentiles: Marriage Rules in the Letters of Paul* [Atlanta: Scholars Press, 1985])

Paul's position is closer to that of Epictetus than to the other Stoic options. Like Epictetus, the apostle thinks of the present as a battlefield (2 Cor 10:3–5), although he does not use this exact language in 1 Cor 7:26. Like Epictetus, Paul believes Christians should be wholly devoted to the service of God. Like Epictetus, Paul says marriage may not contribute to this end.

It is not at all uncharacteristic of Paul, when making a case, to use a Jewish and a philosophical argument side by side (e.g., 1 Cor 11:2–16). Significantly, when suggesting here that being free of marriage responsibilities is for one's benefit (given the distractions of family and the hardships of the present time), Paul does not aim to lay any restraint on his readers (v. 35; cf. 7:6). In this tightly organized section, 7:25–40, the apostle has taken up the question of the unmarried raised by the Corinthians in their letter and has said that *theologically* there is no problem with marriage, although *practically* there are arguments for remaining unmarried if one has "desire under control" (v. 37).

Having traced the train of thought in 7:25–40, we now have the task of summarizing, if possible, the positions of the Corinthians and Paul in relation to one another. In so doing, it will be necessary to draw on information about both already gleaned from 7:1-24. On the one hand, there are both a what and a why to the Corinthians' posture. First, what did they say? In 7:1-24 they argued that if one was married, he should separate. "It is well for a man not to touch a woman" (v. 1b). In 7:25-40 their emphasis seems to be that if one is not married, one should stay that way. Second, why did they say these two things? The explanation seems to have been their overrealized eschatology, which included their belief that they were now to live like the angels, transcending their sexuality. Their asceticism was rooted not in a belief in the inherent evil of matter (as with the Gnostics) but rather in their eschatological error.

On the other hand, there is a corresponding what and why to the apostle's positions. First, what did he believe? Throughout 1 Cor 7 Paul states that there is no theological problem with marriage. This is true for persons now married, for persons once married whose partner is now deceased and who want to remarry, and for persons who have not yet been married. There are, however, practical problems with being married (the distress in which Christians presently live and the need for an undistracted devotion to Christ) that say a lot for the option of being unmarried, assuming of course that one has the gift of celibacy (7:7b, 9a, 17a, 37). So from Paul's perspective both marriage and celibacy are legitimate Christian options. Second, why would the apostle come out at this point? Paul's eschatology had two poles to it. On the one side, Christians live where the ages overlap, so that the general resurrection of believers is still future (1 Cor 15). This being so, the institutions of creation, like marriage, continue. If so, the logion of the Lord prohibiting divorce still applies. From this eschatological perspective comes Paul's positive theological appraisal of marriage. On the other side, Paul believed in an imminent End, so that he, at this time at least, believed he would be alive when the Lord returned (1 Cor 15:51; 1 Thess 4:15). This belief would have arisen from his conviction that with the resurrection of Jesus the general resurrection had begun. Christ was "the first fruits of those who have fallen asleep" (1 Cor 15:20). If the first apple has turned red on the tree, can the harvest of the rest be far away? He also believed that Christians were even then living in the tribulation/messianic woes/birth pangs of the New Age and that people living in such circumstances needed a battle mentality in which there was an undistracted devotion to the Lord. Out of this aspect of his eschatology came the practical consideration favoring celibacy. At base, then, the arguments about marriage in 1 Cor 7:1–24 and 25–40 reflect the struggle to maintain a correct eschatological perspective and to work it out properly in one's sexuality.

The significance of the argument becomes clearer if looked at in the context of the larger issue, namely, the variety of attitudes towards sex, marriage, and celibacy in Mediterranean antiquity. The Jewish scriptures regarded human sexuality as part of the good creation (Gen 1:31). Within marriage, sexual relations functioned for procreation (Gen 1:28; cf. the view of childlessness as a curse, Gen 30:23; Judg 11:37–40; 1 Sam 1:3–9; Isa 4:1), for companionship (Gen 2:18, 24), and for pleasure (Deut 24:5; Prov 5:18–19; Song of Sol 1:2; 2:6–7; 7:1–12). Abstinence from marriage was unheard of in Old Testament history, apart from the isolated instance of Jeremiah (16:1–4). His sexual abstinence served as prophetic symbolism warning of national disaster. This Old Testament stance continued, for the most part, in postbiblical Judaism. Representative is m Yebamoth 6:6: "No man may abstain from keeping the law, 'Be fruitful and multiply,' ... for it is written, 'Male and female created he them.'" Only in certain restricted circles was celibacy advocated (e.g., the Therapeutae, about whom Philo speaks in *Contemplative Life*; the evidence about the Essenes is ambiguous, the Manual of Discipline and the Damascus Document disagreeing).

By the beginning of our era, the traditional Roman attitude toward sex (it was an activity as honorable as it was pleasurable; hence it was normal and proper to marry and have children; a woman should be a virgin when she married and should not participate in extramarital affairs, so the husband could be assured that the offspring were his) had split into two extremes: sexual indulgence and sexual asceticism. The critiques of Seneca (*Hostius*), Martial (e.g., *Perverted Phyllis* and *Roman Morals*), and Juvenal (*Satires* 2, 6, 9) may be extreme, but they are not inaccurate. Sexual indulgence of every kind is documented in the novels of Petronius (*Satyricon*) and Apuleius (*Metamorphoses*). Alongside indulgence, a tradition of sexual asceticism flourished. Its roots were ancient. Empedocles, a pupil of Phythagoras, denounced all forms of sexual intercourse (Diogenes Laertius 8.54). Diogenes the Cynic when asked when was the right time to marry, quipped, "For young men, not yet; for old men, never" (Diogenes Laertius 6.54). Epicurus maintained that sexual intercourse never benefited any man" (Diogenes Laertius 10.118, 132). The motives of this tradition were varied: for example, (*a*) passion is contrary to reason; it weighs the soul down and prevents mystical ecstasy (Platonists like Numenius); (*b*) sex is a distraction from duty (Stoics like Epictetus); (*c*) anything physical is inherently evil (Gnostics); (*d*) sex is so identified with excess and perversion that a person with moral sensitivity will shy away from it altogether (pagans like Juvenal).

In the New Testament both marriage and celibacy are regarded as legitimate life-styles for Christians. Marriage is the normal experience, being part of the created order and therefore good (Matt 19:4–6; 1 Tim 4:4), but celibacy is appropriate if one has the gift for it (Matt 19:10–12; 1 Cor 7:7b, 17). This acceptance of celibacy is for a different reason than that advocated by certain heretics (1 Cor 7:1b; 1 Tim 4:1–3). The problem children in Corinth take their position out of an overrealized eschatology; the heretics of the Pastorals appear to be dualists, perhaps Gnostics. The celibacy that is accepted in the New Testament is one that comes as the result of a spiritual gift. Unless one has received it, sexual activity within marriage is the norm.

The period after the New Testament finds an increasing tendency towards sexual asceticism in the church, with varied motives given for it. (*a*) Closest to the New Testament is the position that regards not sex itself but the immoral use of sex as obscene (Clement of Alexandria *Instructor* 2.6) and that sees celibacy as a gift and hence something about which one must not boast (1 Clement 38.2; Ignatius *To Polycarp* 5.2). (*b*) Continuing the overrealized eschatology of the heretics in Corinth, the Shepherd of Hermas tells how Hermas' spiritual progress brings him to the state of sexual transcendence where it is as though he were in a prepuberty existence again (*Parable* 9.11). (*c*) Continuing the Gnostic dualism of the heretics in the Pastorals are Saturninus (Irenaeus *Against Heresies* 1.24.1–2), Marcion (Tertullian *Marcion* 5.7; *Prescription against Heretics* 30), and Tatian (Irenaeus *Against Heresies* 1.28). (*d*) Some early Christians seem to reflect a platonic base for their asceticism (e.g., Athenagoras *A Plea for the Christians* 33, "You would find many among us, both men and women, growing old unmarried, in hope of living in closer communion with God"; perhaps the Acts of Paul, "Blessed are they who have kept the flesh pure, for they shall become a temple of God; Blessed are the continent, for to them God will speak"). (*e*) Other early Christians appear to echo the Stoic rationale for asceticism (e.g., Acts of Thomas 12–14, where the risen Christ appears to the bride and bridegroom on their wedding night, exhorting them to forgo sexual intercourse and be without care and grief that come from having children). Looked at in this way, it becomes clear that "Christianity did not make the world ascetic; rather the world in which Christianity found itself strove to make Christianity ascetic" (W. E. Phipps, *Was Jesus Married?* [New York: Harper & Row, 1970], p. 125). (*f*) The ascetic tendency in the ancient church found its strongest exponents in Tertullian *Exhortation to Chastity*; Jerome *Against Jovinian* and *Against Helvidian*; and Augustine *Incomplete Work against Julian* and *On Marriage and Concupiscence*. In all three of these fathers, to a greater or lesser degree, their bias against sexual activity was tied to their revulsion against the excesses and perversions either of their own past (so Augustine) or of their culture (Jerome; Tertullian) (Derrick S. Baily, *Sexual Relation in Christian Thought* [New York: Harper & Brothers, 1959]; Peter Harkx, *The Fathers on Celibacy* [DePere, Wis.: St. Norbert Abbey Press, 1968]).

THE LIMITS OF
CHRISTIAN FREEDOM

1 Corinthians 8:1–11:1

A t 8:1 ("Now concerning food offered to idols") one meets the third response of Paul to the questions raised in the Corinthian letter (cf. 7:1, 25). The large unit, 8:1–11:1, falls into a concentric pattern, as follows:

> A. Two issues, (1) and (2) (8:1–13)
> > B. The example of Paul (apostolic freedom and slavery) (9:1–23)
> > B'. The examples of Paul and Israel (necessity of self-control)
> > (9:24–10:13)
> A'. Two issues, (2) and (1) (10:14–11:1).

(John J. Collins, "Chiasmus, the ABA Pattern and the Text of Paul," *Studiorum Paulinorum Congressus Internationalis Catholicus* [Rome: Pontifical Biblical Institute, 1963], p. 582)

The component parts are likewise very carefully arranged.

In (A), 8:1–13, Paul deals with two issues: (1) the question of eating meat, originally killed or sacrificed in a pagan temple, now on sale in the marketplace (vv. 1, 4); and (2) the matter of eating at table in an idol's temple (v. 10). In pagan cults there were two kinds of sacrifices. First, there was a private sacrifice. The animal was divided into three parts: a token to be burned on the altar, a portion for the priests, and the remainder used by the worshiper for a banquet, usually at the temple of the god to whom the sacrifice had been made. Oxyrhynchus Papyrus 110 preserves an invitation to such a banquet. "Chaermon [the host] invites you to dine at a banquet of the lord Serapis in the Serapeum tomorrow, that is, the 15th, from the ninth hour" (Chan-Hie Kim, "The Papyrus Invitation," *JBL* 94[1975]:391–402). Could a Christian take part in such a feast? This was issue (2) in 1 Cor 8. Second, there was in pagan cults a public sacrifice. The animal was again divided into three parts: a token part to be burned, a share for the priests, and the substantial amount left to the magistrates. What they did not need, they sold to the shops and markets for resale to the public. Such meat was eagerly purchased by pagans. Aesop bought tongues of sacrificial pigs in the butcher shop (*Life of Aesop* 51). Pliny indicates the purchaser knew what she or he was buying (Letter to Trajan 10.96.10). Such food was prohibited to Jews because it was tainted with idolatry, it was not slaughtered in the proper way, and tithe had not been paid on it. So, instead of calling this meat "sacrificed for sacred purposes" (*hierothuton*), Jews termed it "sacrificed to idols" (*eidōlothuton*). Could a Christian buy or eat such meat? This was issue (1) in 1 Cor 8.

The chapter is organized in terms of three Corinthian assertions and their Pauline responses. The first two Corinthian assertions are explicitly related to issue (1), the eating of meat killed in a pagan temple (8:1, 4); the third is more general and allows a response that mentions issue (2), eating at table in an idol's temple (8:8, 10). The first Corinthian assertion comes in 8:1b: "all of us possess knowledge." Paul agrees ("we know," 8:1b) but qualifies the claim (vv. 1c–3). "'Knowledge' puffs up, but love builds up" (cf. 13:21, 14:1a). Further, our knowledge is limited (cf. 13:8–12); moreover, what is crucial in the relation with God is being elected by him ("known"—cf. 2 Tim 2:19; Num 16:5) and loving him in return (cf. 13:8, 13).

The second Corinthian assertion is found in vv. 4b–6, supported by appeal to a creedal statement. The Corinthians assert, (1) "an idol has no real existence" (v. 4b), and (2) "there is no God but one" (v. 4c). That is, one who is a monotheist does not accept the ontological reality of idols. The basis for this is given in vv. 5–6:

> For although there may be so-called gods in heaven or on earth—as indeed there are many 'gods' and many 'lords'—yet for us [at this point the creed begins]
>> There is one God, the Father
>>> from whom are all things
>>> and for whom we exist;
>> And one Lord, Jesus Christ,
>>> through whom are all things
>>> and through whom we exist.

In spite of the alleged existence of the many gods and lords (i.e., angels; cf. Clement of Alexandria, citing the apocryphal prophecy of Zephaniah, equates angels and lords [*Stromateis* 5.11.77]; Ps 82:1 and 138:1 equate angels and gods), Christians confess one God and one Lord

(1 Thess 1:9–10), as the creed states. Paul's response agrees with the contention ("we know," v. 4) but qualifies the implications of this knowledge for Christian behavior in v. 7: "But not all possess this knowledge. Now some, through being hitherto accustomed to idols, eat food as really offered to an idol; and their conscience, being weak, is defiled."

The third Corinthian assertion is found at v. 8a: "Food will not commend us to God" (J. Jeremias, "Zur Gedankenführung in den paulinischen Briefen: (3) Die Briefzitate in 1 Kor 8:1–13," in *Abba* [Göttingen: Vandenhoeck & Ruprecht, 1966], pp. 273–74; J. Murphy-O'Connor, "Food and Spiritual Gifts in 1 Cor 8:8," *CBQ* 41[1979]:292–98). This statement fits hand in glove with the Corinthian assertions in 6:12–13. As it is used here, it is a distortion of a Pauline position (Rom 14:17), a practice not uncommon at Corinth (cf. 1 Cor 5:9–12; 7:7). The Pauline response comes in vv. 8b–12. V. 8b belongs with Paul's qualification rather than the Corinthian assertion. If the Corinthians had said it, they would have put it, "we are no better off if we do not eat, and no worse off if we do." They would have meant that abstention from such food did not produce any increase in spiritual gifts, so the act was religiously irrelevant. The actual statement is exactly the opposite and forms Paul's qualification. He says to the knowledgeable who want to eat sacrificial meat, "We are no worse off if we do not eat, and no better off if we do." In other words, he agrees with their contention. However, he then goes on to qualify his agreement: "only take care lest this liberty of yours somehow become a stumbling block to the weak. For if any one see you, a man of knowledge, at table in an idol's temple (issue [2]), might he not be encouraged, if his conscience is weak, to eat food offered to idols? And so by your knowledge this weak man is destroyed, the brother for whom Christ died. Thus, sinning against your brethren and wounding their conscience when it is weak, you sin against Christ." In dealing with the Corinthian possessors of knowledge, the apostle makes the effect of one's behavior on others the criterion of Christian conduct (cf. Rom 14:13–15). While agreeing with the theological principles of the possessors of knowledge, Paul here sides with the weak, those Gentile Christians whose intellectual conviction that there was only one God had not yet been fully assimilated emotionally (Jerome Murphy-O'Connor, "Freedom in the Ghetto, 1 Cor 8:1–13; 10:23–11:1," *RB* 85[1978]:543–74).

The conclusion sums it up: "Therefore, if food is the cause of my brother falling, I will never eat meat, lest I cause my brother to fall (cf. Rom 14:20–21). This is a specific application of the principle enunciated at the first: "love builds up" (8:1b).

In (A'), 10:15–11:1, Paul deals with the same two issues mentioned in 8:1–13, although in reverse order. 1 Cor 10:16–22 treats the matter of eating at table in an idol's temple; 10:23–11:1 handles the problem of eating sacrificial meat from the market. Each section needs separate treatment.

After an introductory appeal in v. 15 ("I speak as to sensible men; judge for yourselves what I say"), the apostle turns to the matter of eating at table in an idol's temple (vv. 16–22). Two examples of sacred meals, one Christian and the other Jewish, serve as a backdrop for the discussion of pagan banquets. First, consider the Lord's Supper: "The cup of blessing which we bless, is it not a close fellowship produced by the blood of Christ? The bread which we break, is it not a close fellowship produced by the body of Christ? Because there is one bread, we who are many are one body, for we all partake of the one bread (vv. 16–17). In other words, the Christian meal produces an intimate relationship among those who partake. Second, "consider the practice of Israel; are not those who eat the sacrifices partners in the altar?" (v. 18) Paul's assumption is akin to that of Philo, who says that he to whom sacrifice has been offered makes the group of worshipers "partners in the altar, and of one table [with it]" (*Special Laws* 1.221). If this is what happens in the Christian and at Jewish meals, what inference can be drawn about pagan meals? "What do I imply then? That food offered to idols is anything, or that an idol is anything? No, I imply that what pagans sacrifice they offer to demons and not to God" (vv. 19–20a). In contrast to some Jewish polemical literature (e.g., Bel and the Dragon) that held the pagan gods to be nonexistent and with whom the knowledgeable Corinthians agreed (8:4–6), Paul regards them as ontological realities, namely, demons: "I do not want you to be partners with demons" (v. 20b). This posture is in line with certain other streams of both Jewish (Deut 32:17; Ps 106:37; Bar 4:7; 1 Enoch 19.1; 99.7) and early Christian thought (Rev 9:20) in which worship of pagan deities was regarded as offered to demons. It is difficult to avoid seeing here a Pauline belief that the pagan cult meals forged some type of relationship between the human participants and the spiritual powers (*koinōnous tōn daimoniōn*, partners of demons), just as Philo can say of Moses that he had *koinōnia* (fellowship, association, partnership) with God (*Life of Moses* 1.156) or 2 Kings 17:11 LXX can describe Israel's sin of idolatry as making *koinōnous*, that is, making allies with the gods of the pagans already in the land. If so, then from the three examples of cultic meals (Christian, vv. 16–17; Jewish, v. 18; and pagan, vv. 19–20), Paul infers two results: (1) such meals produce a relationship (*koinōnia*) among the individuals who participate, and (2) some meals effect a link between the human participants and demonic spiritual forces. In view of these convictions, the apostle's position is predictable. "You cannot drink the cup of the Lord and the cup of demons. You cannot partake of the table of the Lord and the table of demons" (vv. 20b–21). Eating at table in a pagan temple is absolutely ruled out. (For archaeological data about the Asclepion in Corinth, illustrating the Christians' dilemma, see J. Murphy-O'Connor, *St. Paul's Corinth: Texts and Archaeology* [Wilmington, Del.: Michael Glazier, 1983], pp. 161–65.) The apostle closes this section with two rhetorical questions designed to reinforce his point ("Shall we provoke the Lord to jealousy? Are we stronger than he?" v. 22), both implying a negative answer.

In 10:23–11:1 Paul turns again to the issue of eating meat purchased from the marketplace which may have been killed in a pagan temple. The section falls into two parts; 10:23–24 and 10:25–11:1. The first part consists of two Corinthian assertions followed by their Pauline qualifications (vv. 23–24). The first assertion repeats what was heard earlier in 6:12: "All things are lawful" (v. 23a). The Corinthians are doubtless echoing the cultural cliché: The Stoic wise man is he to whom all things are permissible (Dio Chrysostom 3.10). Paul responds: "but not all things are helpful" (v. 23b). The apostle's response continues with another cultural cliché: as Diogenes said, "It is not permissible to do that which is unprofitable" (Dio Chrysostom 14.16). The second assertion is but a repeat of the first: "All things are lawful" (v. 23c). Paul replies: "but not all things build up. Let no one seek his own good, but the good of his neighbor" (vv. 23d–24).

The second part of 10:23–11:1 consists of a continuing dialogue between the apostle and his problem children but in a different form. On the basis of the guideline enunciated in v. 24 (seek the good of your neighbor), Paul gives a specific directive: "Eat whatever is sold in the meatmarket without raising any question on the ground of conscience" (v. 25). He agrees with a Corinthian assertion, "For the earth is the Lord's, and everything in it" (v. 26; Ps 24:1; 50:12), and continues with a specific case: "If one of the unbelievers invites you to dinner [at his home, not at a pagan temple] and you are disposed to go, eat whatever is set before you without raising any question on the ground of conscience. But if someone says to you, 'This has been offered in sacrifice,' then out of consideration for the man who informed you, do not eat it" (vv. 27–29). The Corinthians' objection to vv. 28–29a follows: "Well then," someone asks, "why should my freedom to act be limited by another person's conscience? If I thank God for my food, why should anyone criticize me about food for which I give thanks?" (vv. 29b–30, TEV; cf. NEB). Paul's response is given in reverse order: 10:31 answers 10:30, agreeing as in 10:26, while 10:32 answers 10:29b, qualifying individual freedom with social responsibility. In 11:1 Paul gives his final exhortation: "Be imitators of me, as I am of Christ" (cf. 1 Cor 4:16; 1 Thess 1:6; Phil 3:17; 4:8–9).

Component (B), 9:1–23, in the large unit, 8:1–11:1, picks up just this emphasis of 11:1 and presents us with the example of Paul in the area of freedom and social responsibility. In line with the widespread use of rhetorical questions by philosophers of the time (e.g., Epictetus 3.22. 48), Paul opens in v. 1 with a series of four rhetorical questions, each with an implied affirmative answer: (1) Am I not free? (2) Am I not an apostle? (3) Have I not seen Jesus our Lord? (4) Are not you my workmanship in the Lord? V. 2 gives a response to questions (2) through (4): "If to others I am not an apostle, at least I am to you; for you are the seal of my apostleship in the Lord." Vv. 3–23 are Paul's response in light of question (1).

After an introductory statement in v. 3, in vv. 4–6 Paul states his thesis: I have a right to be paid by my churches and to be accompanied by a wife. This is put in terms of three rhetorical questions, the first two with an implied answer "Yes," the third with an implied "No."

The rest of this section falls into two structurally balanced arguments, vv. 7–12c and vv. 13–23, each of which says that although Paul has the right, he forgoes it. The first unit, vv. 7–12c, is composed of four components. (1) Argument one for Paul's right is found in v. 7. It consists of three rhetorical questions, each with the implied answer "No one," based on the analogies of soldier, farmer, and shepherd. (2) Argument two for Paul's right consists of an appeal to the law (vv. 8–12a). In his interpretation of Deut 25:4 Paul agrees with Philo when the latter says, "For the law does not prescribe for unreasoning creatures, but for those who have mind and reason" (*Special Laws* 1.260; cf. *Epistle of Aristeas* 144). (3) In v. 12b the apostle says that though both reason and the law establish his right to be paid by his churches, "Nevertheless, we have not made use of this right." (4) The reason for his not claiming his right is that "we endure anything rather than put an obstacle in the way of the gospel of Christ" (v. 12c).

The second unit of the section, vv. 7–23, is found in vv. 13–23. It contains the same four components as vv. 7–12 and argues the same thesis: although Paul has the right, he forgoes it. (1) Argument three for Paul's right is once again given in the form of a rhetorical question (v. 13), using the analogy of temple servants. (2) Argument four for Paul's right consists of an appeal to the Lord's command (v. 14; cf. Luke 10:7b; Matt 10:10b; 1 Tim 5:18; Didache 13.1). (3) In v. 15a Paul says that although reason and the Lord legitimate his right, "I have made no use of any of these rights, nor am I writing this to secure any such provision." (4) The reason for his not claiming his rights is twofold: (a) in vv. 15b–18 he says his reward is making "the gospel free of charge, not making full use of my right in the gospel"; (b) in vv. 19–23 he argues, "For though I am free from all men, I have made myself a slave to all, that I might win the more." Throughout 9:1–23 Paul has been at pains to show that he has certain rights and at the same time to demonstrate that he forgoes those rights for the sake of others. That is one reason why he could say to the knowledgeable Corinthians, "Imitate me."

Component (B′) in the concentric pattern of 8:1–11:1 consists of 9:24–10:14, the examples of Paul (9:24–27) and of Israel (10:1–13). If 9:1–23 used the example of Paul to deal with the problem of eating meat sacrificed to idols (you have the right, but do not use it if it harms others), 9:24–10:14 uses the examples of Paul and Israel to warn those who are tempted to eat at table in an idol's temple (10:15–22) of the dangers. In 9:24–27 Paul uses the images of a runner, a boxer, and a wrestler to remind the overly confident Corinthians that entry in a competition does not in itself guarantee a prize. Just as an athlete "in training submits to strict discipline" (TEV), so does Paul in order to gain the victor's prize. Here is an *exemplum* for the Corinthians to imitate.

1 Cor 10:1–13 uses the example of ancient Israel to issue a warning against overconfidence (v. 12). The section consists of two units followed by a conclusion (Wayne A. Meeks, "And Rose Up to Play: Midrash and Paraenesis in 1 Cor 10:1–22," *JSNT* 16[1982]:64–78). Vv. 1–6, the first unit, contain five clauses followed by a warning: (1) Our fathers were all under the cloud, and (2) all passed through the sea, and (3) all were baptized into Moses in the cloud and in the sea, and (4) all ate the same supernatural food, and (5) all drank the same supernatural drink (Pseudo-Philo speaks about the well of water following the Israelites in the wilderness [*Biblical Antiquities* 10.7; 11.15]; cf. t Sukka 3:11, 196; Targum Onkelos 16–19; Philo interprets the rock from which the water came as a reference to preexistent Wisdom [*Allegorical Interpretation* 2.86]. It was a

short step to christianize the Jewish tradition and say, "and the rock was Christ" [v. 4b]). "Nevertheless with most of them God was not pleased; for they were overthrown in the wilderness. Now these things are warnings for us, not to desire evil as they did." The second unit, vv. 7–11, contains four negative statements followed by a warning: (1) Do not be idolaters as some of them were (cf. 1 Cor 8:10; 10:14–22); (2) we must not indulge in immorality as some of them did (cf. 1 Cor 5:1–5; 6:12–20); (3) we must not put the Lord to the test as some of them did; (4) nor grumble as some of them did (cf. 1 Cor 9); "Now these things happened to them as a warning, but they were written down for our instruction."

The function of this section is to say that baptism and the Lord's Supper are no automatic guarantees of spiritual security. The case of ancient Israel who had been baptized into Moses and had eaten and drunk the supernatural food and drink declares that these events do not guarantee God's pleasure for those who engage in idolatry (cf. 10:20b–21) and immorality (cf. 5:1–13; 6:12–20). "Therefore, let anyone who thinks that he stands take heed lest he fall" (10:12). Specifically, this means "shun the worship of idols" (10:14). Be disciplined like Paul. Avoid the errors of ancient Israel, which had disastrous results. Do not eat at table in an idol's temple. "Shall we provoke the Lord to jealousy?" (10:22a) At this point Paul reflects the philosophical attack on nonethical sacramentalism in Mediterranean antiquity (e.g., Diogenes the Cynic complained that, from the point of view of the mystery religions, Pataecion the thief would after death have a better fate than the righteous Epaminindas, because the former had been initiated while the latter had not; cf. Plutarch *Quomodo Adulescens Poetas Audire Debeat* 4).

Having traced the train of thought in 1 Cor 8:1–11:1, we now summarize the positions of the two sides, Paul and the Corinthians. Since there were two issues discussed, it will be best to take them one at a time and see how the apostle and his problem children stood on each (Wendell Lee Willis, *Idol Meat in Corinth: The Pauline Argument in 1 Corinthians 8 and 10* [Chico, Cal.: Scholars Press, 1985]).

The first issue was that of eating food sacrificed to idols (8:4–7; 10:23–11:1). The Corinthians argued that it was all right for a Christian to eat such meat because (1) an idol has no real existence; there is no God but one, as the creed says (8:4–6); (2) all things are lawful, as scripture implies (10:23–26); and (3) a Christian's liberty should not be determined by another person's scruples. Paul's response was that it was all right to eat such meat, except in certain circumstances: (1) if another Christian is hurt by your eating, do not use your freedom (8:7), because a Christian is for others (10:24; 10:33) just as Christ was and Paul is (11:1; 9:1–23); (2) if an unbeliever raises a question about it, do not use your freedom (10:27–29a), because a Christian wants to give no offense to Jews or Greeks (10:32–33) so they may be saved.

The second issue was that of eating at table in an idol's temple (8:8–12; 10:16–22). The Corinthians argued that it was all right to do because (1) food does not commend us to God but is religiously neutral (8:8a), and (2) since we have been baptized into Christ and partake regularly of the Lord's Supper, we are protected from any harm spiritually (10:1–13). Paul's reply was negative because (1) it is not a religiously and ethically neutral act if another Christian is destroyed by it; it is then a sin against Christ (8:9–12); and (2) it is an act which makes one a participant in the pagan cult; it is then idolatry and subject to God's extreme displeasure (10:16–21, 1–14).

It is possible to sum up the Pauline arguments in terms of two directives. First, Christians have a responsibility not to use their freedom to injure another's spiritual life. Second, Christians have a responsibility not to use their freedom to endanger their own spiritual lives. Christian freedom is freedom for others and for Christ.

This position can be seen with greater clarity if viewed in the context of the larger Christian perspective on idol meat in the period of Christian origins. Acts 15:20, 29 and 21:25 seem to regard Gentile Christians as the Old Testament does the alien residing in Israel. Accordingly, the Jerusalem Decree forbids four of the things proscribed by Lev 17–18 for the alien: (1) meat offered to idols (Lev 17:8–9), (2) the eating of blood (Lev 17:10–12), (3) the eating of strangled animals (Lev 17:15), and (4) intercourse with close kin (Lev 18:6–18). If one accepts the essential historicity of the narrative, then prior to Paul's Corinthian ministry (Acts 18) there was a prohibition against eating meat sacrificed to idols (Acts 15). Its purpose was the facilitation of community between Gentile Christians and Jewish Christians. This was accomplished by Gentile Christians' concessions to Jewish Christian sensitivities.

In 1 Cor 8–10 the problem of Christians' eating meat offered to idols is one of two issues with which the apostle Paul has to deal (the other being eating at table in an idol's temple). Paul's position is nuanced. On the one hand, he stands for the principle of eating whatever is sold in the meat market without raising any question (10:25) on the grounds of the goodness of creation (10:26). On the other hand, he argues for abstaining from eating such meat if responsibility for a weaker brother, probably Gentile, demands it (8:7; 10:27–28; 10:32–33). Paul does not mention the Decree, perhaps because it was never intended to be applicable in a predominantly Gentile environment (cf. Acts 15:23; 16:1–4). At no point, however, does the apostle stand against the eating of meat sacrificed to idols because of the danger of an alliance with demons. That argument he saves for those who want to eat at table in an idol's temple (10:1–22).

In the period after Paul, two trajectories regarding idol meat are discernible. In the first place, there are heretics who espouse the eating of meat offered to idols (Rev 2:14, those who hold the teaching of Balaam; 2:20, false prophets; Justin *Trypho* 35, certain Gnostics; Irenaeus *Against Heresies* 1.6.3, Valentinians; 1.26.3, Nicolaitans; 1.24.5, Basilides; Eusebius *E.H.* 4.7.7, Basilides) because it poses no spiritual danger. In many respects these Christians are the heirs of the stance taken by Paul's opponents in Corinth (1 Cor 8:4b–6, 8) and Paul himself (1 Cor 10:25), though without the affirmation of creation's goodness assumed by both the apostle and his Corinthian converts (1 Cor 10:26, 30; cf. 1 Tim 4:3–5). In the second place, the main stream of Christian life stands solidly against the eating of meat sacrificed to idols (Rev 2:14, 20; Didache 6.3; Justin *Trypho* 34–35; Origen *Against Celsus* 8.29–31; Recognitions of Clement 2.71; *Apostolic Constitutions* 6.12; 7.21) because it is an idolatrous act that makes those who eat partners with demons, not because of one's responsibility for a weaker Christian. In this stream of Christian life, the prohibition of eating meat sacrificed in an idol's temple and sold in the meat market (so the Apostolic Decree) is connected with the danger said by Paul to be associated with eating at table in an idol's temple (1 Cor 10:14–22) (J. Brunt, "Rejected, Ignored, or Misunderstood? The Fate of Paul's Approach to the Problem of Food Offered to Idols in Early Christianity," *NTS* 31[1985]:113–24).

DIFFERENT THOUGH
EQUAL IN THE LORD

1 Corinthians 11:2–16

Whereas in 7:1–24, 25–40 and 8:1–11:1 Paul was answering questions raised by the Corinthians in their letter to him, in 11:2–34 he seems to be responding to a statement they made in it, perhaps something like, "we remember you in everything and maintain the traditions even as you delivered them to us." Paul's response is twofold, the first part coming in vv. 2–16, the second in vv. 17–34. This twofold response goes together with chapters 12–14 to constitute a three-part discussion of problems in the area of corporate worship:

A. Prayer and prophecy (11:2–16)
B. The Lord's Supper (11:17–34)
A'. Prayer and prophecy (chaps. 12–14).

Remember the earlier three-part discussion of 5:1–6:20 with a similar pattern.

1 Corinthians 11:2–16 is a thought unit held together by an inclusion, vv. 2 and 16. It falls into an ABA' pattern, something like this:

A. Sexual distinctions are rooted in creation and Christian worship must reflect them (11:3–10)
B. Sexual equality is rooted in redemption, and creation seen in its light, but sexual distinctions are not yet transcended (11:11–12)
A'. Sexual distinctions are rooted in the nature of things and Christian worship must reflect it (11:13–15).

Each of these components of the section needs attention.

Component (A), 11:3–10, consists of a midrash (commentary) on Gen 2:18–23 (vv. 3–9) followed by a concluding statement (v. 10). Its point is that sexual distinctions are rooted in creation and that Christian worship must reflect them. The midrash is arranged in a concentric pattern as follows:

(a) The origin of woman: an appeal to creation as a source of sexual
   distinctions (v. 3)
   (b) Man/ head not covered (v. 4)
      (c) Woman/ head covered (v. 5)
      (c') (For) woman/ head covered (v. 6)
   (b') (For) man/ head not covered (v. 7)
(a') (For) the origin of woman: an appeal to creation as a source of
sexual distinctions (vv. 8–9).

The pattern consists of three statements (a,b,c) and the bases for the
assertions (a',b',c'). (a) "The source [kephalē] of every man is Christ,
the source of woman is the man, and the source of the Christ is God" (v.
3). The basis of this statement is "For man was not made *from* woman,
but woman *from* man" (v. 8). The echo of the second creation story (Gen
2) is plain. This context demands that kephalē be translated "source," not
"head." The man was the source from which the woman came (i.e., the
rib—Gen 2:21–22). Since, in antiquity's way of thinking, origin determines purpose, Paul can say, "Neither was man created *for* woman, but
woman *for* man" (v. 9). The story of Gen 2 affirms creation as the source
of sexual distinctions between men and women. What do these distinctions mean in terms of social conventions?

(b) "Any man who prays or prophesies with his head covered dishonors his head" (v. 4). The basis is given: "For a man ought not to cover
his head, since he is the image and glory of God" (v. 7). (c) "But any
woman who prays or prophesies with her head unveiled dishonors her
head—it is the same as if her head were shaven" (v. 5). A shaven head
was a sign of a woman's humiliation and mourning (e.g., Deut
21:12–13). What did it mean for a woman to appear *akatakaluptō*?
There are two possibilities. On the one hand, the term may be translated
"unveiled" (RSV), "bare-headed" (NEB), "with nothing on her head"
(TEV), "uncovered" (NIV). In this case, the concern is for the wearing
of a head covering. Jewish women appeared in public only with their
heads covered (Sus 32; 3 Mac 4:6; Midrash Rabbah 1.139, so R. Joshua,
c. A.D. 90; b Nedarim 30b; Tertullian *De Corona* 4; *De Oratione* 22).
Evidence for non-Jewish practice is debated. The practice of veiling was
Oriental but reached as far west as Tarsus (Dio Chrysostom 33, 46). The
evidence for Greek women is not clear-cut. Some data suggests that
respectable Greek women also wore a head covering in public (Plutarch
Roman Questions 267a; Dio Chrysostom 16.48: Apuleius *Metamorphoses*
11.10), but it is far from compelling. Where the head covering was
worn, it appears to have been a social symbol attesting one's femaleness.

On the other hand, some have suggested that the term should be translated, "with unbound hair" (e.g., Abel Isaksson, *Marriage and Ministry in the New Temple* [Lund: C. W. K. Gleerup, 1965], p. 163; Elisabeth Sch8ussler Fiorenza, *In Memory of Her* [N.Y.: Crossroad, 1984], p. 227). In this case, the concern is that women keep their hair bound on top of their heads and not undo it, letting it hang loose. In a Jewish context, for a woman to go out with her hair unbound was regarded as the first step to adultery (m Ketuboth 7:6; cf. Num 5:18 LXX; Jth 10:3; 16:8). A man who once unloosed a woman's hair in the street was fined four hundred zuz (m Baba Kamma 8:6). In a pagan milieu, the sight of disheveled hair was connected with the worship of Oriental deities (Tibullus says a woman friend let her hair down twice daily in the worship of Isis [1.3.29–32]). Wearing the hair up on the head, then, symbolized responsible dignity. Which of these two readings is more probable? The linguistic evidence favors the former (*AGD*, 29). The major argument for the latter is v. 15 which refers to long hair. This need not be taken in a way that runs counter to the linguistic evidence, as later comments in this section will show. We, therefore, translate with the RSV: "For if a woman will not veil herself, then she should cut off her hair; but if it is disgraceful for a woman to be shorn or shaven, let her wear a veil" (v. 6).

From 11:16, it appears that the general practice in the Pauline churches was for women to keep their heads covered during worship. To cover the head was an act attesting a woman's sexuality. To remove the head covering, moreover, was a social symbol of one's transcendence of her sexuality. In *Joseph and Aseneth*, a pre-Christian Hellenistic Jewish propaganda tract, Aseneth is a virgin converted to Judaism through the agency of an archangel. Afterwards he orders her to remove her clothes of mourning and to put on radiant garments. This she does, including a head covering. When she returns, the angel orders her to take off the head covering, "because you are a holy virgin today and your head is as that of a young man." That is, in this Hellenistic Jewish document, Aseneth is believed to have transcended her sexuality as the result of her religious experience. With the transcendence of her femaleness goes the discarding of the social symbols of that sexuality (Robin Scroggs, "Paul and the Eschatological Woman: Revisited," *JAAR*, 42[1974]:532–37).

It seems likely that in Corinth also, because of their religious experience, certain women were discarding the social symbols of their sexuality. This may have been due to their misinterpretation of Paul (e.g., Gal 3:28) under the influence of an overrealized eschatology (cf. 1 Cor 4:8; 15:12).

In I Cor 7 a similar tendency of an overrealized eschatology expressed itself in certain men's belief that they had transcended their sexuality and were now to live as angels. Paul has no problem with women praying and prophesying in church; his difficulty is that they are doing these things in a way that denies their created sexuality. For the apostle, scripture says that men and women are different by the Creator's design. "That is why a woman ought to have a sign of authority on her head, because of the angels" (v. 10). The sign of authority refers to the head covering which serves as a social symbol of the women's femaleness. Of the many interpretations of the angels, the context demands that they be taken to mean the angelic beings entrusted by God to watch over the orders of creation (1 Enoch 60.12, 16–21; 61.10; 72.1; 82.3; Jub 2:2–3; 1 QH 1.10–11). Paul's point is that wearing a veil means acceptance of one's created sexuality.

Component (A'), 11:13–15, roots sexual distinctions in nature. The problem is the same as in 11:3–10: "Judge for yourselves; is it proper for a woman to pray to God with her head uncovered?" (v. 13). Paul's argument here is based upon the assumptions of his cultural context, assumptions illustrated by a passage like this:

> Let us leave the chief works of nature..., and consider merely what she does in passing. Can anything be more useless than hairs on a chin? Well, what then? Has not nature used even these in the most suitable way possible? Has she not by these means distinguished between the male and the female? Does not the nature of each one among us cry aloud forthwith from afar, "I am a man; on this understanding approach me, on this understanding talk with me, ask nothing further; behold the signs"? Again, in the case of women, just as nature has mingled in their voice a certain softer note, so likewise she has taken away the hair from their chins.... Wherefore, we ought to preserve the signs which God has given; we ought not to throw them away; we ought not, so far as in us lies, to confuse the sexes which have been distinguished in this fashion. (Epictetus 1.16. 9–14)

In Paul's world certain things were social symbols of femaleness and maleness. They distinguished the sexes. Among the signs of femaleness was long hair. (On the eve of her marriage in the Acts of Paul, Thecla is converted to celibate Christianity. After baptism, she cuts her hair short and dresses like a man. This act said she had transcended her sexuality.) For a woman to be shaven was degrading to her (Deut 21:12–13 says women taken captive in war shaved their heads; Lucian says it is unnatural for women to shave off their hair [*Dialogi Meretricii* 5.3]). Therefore, Paul could say, "Does not nature itself teach you ... if a woman has long hair, it is her pride? For her hair was given to her for a covering" (vv. 14–15). If nature has shown the way in giving women long hair as a covering, then Christian worship ought to follow this guidance and expect women to wear a head covering. As Cicero says, "If we follow nature as our guide, we shall never go astray" (*De Officiis* 1.28.100).

Whether it is the philosophical argument from nature or the Jewish argument from scripture (remember a similar combination in 7:25–40), Paul's point is the same. The sexual distinctions between men and women are real and have not been transcended by Christian religious experience. Any behavior (in this case, the discarding of head coverings) that claims otherwise is to be rejected.

In (B), I Cor 11:11–12, Paul says sexual equality is rooted in redemption but even there sexual distinctions are not transcended. In vv. 8–9, the assumption that origin determines purpose seemed to say that, by virtue of creation (Gen 2), since the man existed originally without the woman and was woman's origin, the man was woman's purpose. In v. 11 the apostle says that in the Lord (i.e., as Christians in the church) "woman is not without (*chōris*) man, nor man without (*chōris*) woman." Neither exists before the other or without the other. This is explained in v. 12: "as woman was made from man, so man is now born of woman." If origin defines purpose, then in the Lord (in the Christian community) one sees that even creation testifies that each is for the other (cf. 7:4). While sexual distinctions remain (i.e., we are still male and female), even in our sexuality we are equals, though not identicals. So Paul says men and women are both different and equal. In this passage his concern is to protect the created and natural distinctions of the sexes from a distorted view of equality. "And all things are from God" (v. 12b); that is, both our created differences and our redemptive equality are divine gifts. Creation is not cancelled out by redemption. If you want to argue about this, "we recognize no other practice, nor do the churches of God" (v. 16; cf. 1:2; 4:17; 7:17; 14:33).

Now that the train of thought has been traced in 1 Cor 11:2–16, it remains to summarize the positions of the two sides in the debate. Among the Corinthians were some women who, when praying and prophesying in public worship, removed their head coverings. The reason they did this was complex, involving several ingredients. (1) If Greek women sometimes went to public ceremonies with uncovered heads, there may have been a question about why in church this practice was discontinued. (2) Paul elsewhere (Gal 3:28) argued that in Christ there is neither male nor female. This could easily be taken to mean that sexuality had been transcended in the Christian community. (3) The Corinthian overrealized eschatology elsewhere (1 Cor 7) had led to the belief that Christians were now living like the angels, with sexuality a thing of the past. As a result of some combination of such factors, certain Corinthian women discarded their head coverings and led in public worship (cf. 14:26–33) in a way that said to their culture, "We have transcended our femaleness."

Paul rejected any female participation in public worship which did not involve the wearing of a head covering. His arguments were three. (1) Scripture grounds our sexuality in the creation, over which God has set guardian angels to preserve his original intent. Christian worship must reflect creation. (2) Nature shows that women are intended to be covered (e.g., women's long hair), so social custom and Christian worship must be in line with nature's leading. (3) If scripture and reason do not suffice, there is the authority of universal practice in the Pauline churches. If you are following the Pauline traditions as you claim (v. 2), women must wear head coverings in worship.

The issue as Paul defines it seems to be whether redemption (religious experience resulting from Christ) cancels out creation (human sexuality) or whether creation and nature are from God just as are redemption and being in the Lord. The Corinthian women acted as though their redemption had caused them to transcend their created sexuality. Paul's posture grows out of his conviction that creation (sexual differences) is not cancelled by redemption (Christian equality) but rather is enhanced. Hence 1 Cor 11:2–16 does not aim to silence Christian women but rather to guarantee that in their self-expression they were not denying an integral part of themselves (Derwood C. Smith, "Paul and the Non-Eschatological Woman," *OJRS*, 4[1976]:11–18).

How well was Paul's point understood by the early church? It is interesting to note that in North Africa near A.D. 200, Tertullian wrote *On the Veiling of Virgins*. In this piece, he attempted to enforce the wearing of a veil that covered the space that would be covered by the hair when unbound by both married and unmarried women. His appeal was both to custom (throughout Greece the majority of churches keep their virgins covered) and to 1 Cor 11:2–16. Whereas Paul seems to restrict the wearing of a veil to women involved as leaders in Christian worship, as a way of clarifying the relation between creation and redemption in the face of an overrealized eschatology, some later Christians seem to extend the wearing of a head covering to all Christian women past puberty both in public and in church for reasons of sexual modesty.

THE SOCIAL SIGNIFICANCE OF THE SUPPER

1 Corinthians 11:17–34

1 Cor 11:17–34 is the second of three sections dealing with matters of public worship at Corinth (11:2–16; 11:17–34; chaps. 12–14). It is linked to the previous section by v. 17a, "But in the following instructions I do not commend you," which echoes v. 2, "I commend you because you remember me in everything and maintain the traditions even as I have delivered them to you." In vv. 17–34 Paul makes very clear that the Corinthians are not maintaining the tradition associated with the Lord's Supper. The section falls into three main parts (vv. 17–22, the problems in the Corinthian eucharistic observance; vv. 23–26, the tradition which serves both as a critique and as a basis for a solution; and vv. 27–34, the solutions offered), followed by a concluding comment (v. 34b). Each of these main parts deserves examination.

Vv. 17–22, the first main section, are held together by an inclusion, v. 17a ("But in the following instructions I do not commend you") and v. 22b ("Shall I commend you in this? No, I will not commend you"). The subsection is divided into two balanced halves (vv. 17b–19 and vv. 20–22a), each with an indictment followed by the reason for the charge. The first half's indictment reads, "When you come together it is not for the better but for the worse" (v. 17b). The reason is given: "For [*gar*] when you assemble as a church, I hear that there are divisions among you; and I partly believe it, for there must be factions among you" (vv. 18–19). Did Paul's knowledge of these divisions come from oral reports, perhaps given by the same people whose information about divisions is mentioned in 1:11? Perhaps. Paul's belief of the report is supported by the divine necessity (*dei*) of factions (v. 19). Other writers independently echo such a saying (Justin Martyr *Dialogue with Trypho* 35 [Christ said, "There will be divisions and heresies"]; the Syrian *Didascalia* 6.5 [Our Lord said, "There will be heresies and divisions"]; and the Pseudo-Clementine *Homilies* 2.17 and 16.21. That they attribute it to Jesus may mean

73

that the apostle is here quoting an agraphon not found in the canonical gospel tradition (cf. Acts 20:35 for an analogous situation). Such divisions associated with the common meal would be viewed as tragic by Paul, who saw the meal as the catalyst for Christian fellowship (10:16–17, "The cup of blessing which we bless, is it not a fellowship created by the blood of Christ?. . . Because there is one loaf, we who are many are one body, for we all partake of one loaf").

The second half's indictment reads, "When you meet together, it is not to eat the *Lord's* supper" (v. 20). The reason is given: "For [*gar*] each one proceeds to eat *his own* supper, and one is hungry and another is drunk" (vv. 21–22). To understand this matter better, the social context must be described, namely, what was eaten, where it was eaten, and when.

(1) What was eaten? Two items of background information assist us at this point. First, Plutarch describes a banquet at which guests brought their individual meals and complains that this resulted in many banquets and the destruction of fellowship. He says, "Where each guest has his own private portion, fellowship perishes" (*Table Talk* 644C). 1 Cor 11:21 indicates that this was part of the problem in Corinth: "Each goes ahead with his own meal." Various members brought their own food and consumed it on their own schedule (cf. Jude 12). Second, there was a Roman custom to serve different types of food to different categories of guests (Pliny the Younger *Letters* 2.6; Juvenal *Epigrams* 3.60; 4.85). Juvenal tells of a dinner with a patron that reflects this practice:

> You're given a wine that even a poultice would not take . . . but your host drinks vintage wine, bottled when consuls wore long hair and beards.
> You're served bread you can scarcely break, a hard lump of dough already spread with mold, impervious to teeth and sure to crack your jaws. But a loaf made out of fine flour, snow-white and soft as gauze, is served your host.
> Look at that mammoth lobster, with garnish of asparagus, being served your host . . . For you a shrimp is served in state—one shrimp afloat on one half of one egg on a tiny plate.
> Look, that half-eaten hare he'll give us now, or from the haunch of boar some bits; we'll get what's left of the capon soon. So all of you sit in silence, ready, with bread held tight, untasted, and wait. (*The Satires of Juvenal*, trans. H. Creekmore [New York: Mentor Books, New American Library, 1963], 5)

Given such a custom, it would have been normal behavior for the wealthier members not to have any qualms about eating their bountiful provisions and letting the poorer do the best they could.

(2) Where was the meal eaten? In the average well-to-do house of the Roman era, a dining room accommodated about nine people, the atrium thirty to forty. In any large Christian gatherings at Gaius's house (Rom 16:23), some would have been in the dining room, others in the atrium outside. It would have been the natural procedure for the host's social equals to gather early in the dining room and for the lesser lights to find their places in the atrium.

(3) When was the meal eaten? Since the Corinthian church was composed of well-to-do (e.g., Gaius, Rom 16:23; 1 Cor 1:14; Titius Justus, Acts 18:7; Crispus, Acts 18:8), as well as slaves (e.g., 1 Cor 1:26; 7:21–23), the time of arrival would differ. The well-to-do could come early, while the slaves would arrive late. The latecomers would doubtless find no place to be besides the atrium of the house and would be entering hungrily a scene where others had already reached the point of satiety.

These three factors enable one to conceptualize the situation like this. The wealthy came early, joined the host in the dining room for the best food and drink. By the time the slaves gathered in the atrium to partake of the meager amount that they brought or that was left, the early arrivals would be in their cups ("and another is drunk," v. 21) (Jerome Murphy-O'Connor, *St. Paul's Corinth* [Wilmington, Del.:Michael Glazier, 1983], pp. 156–61). What Paul refers to is a real meal, but one with a religious purpose. The purpose of the supper forgotten by the Corinthians, customary social convention prevailed and divisions resulted. Paul was incensed: "Do you not have houses to eat and drink in? Or do you despise the church of God and humiliate those who have nothing?" (v. 22).

It is interesting to note that the meals of other religious communities of the times suffered from similar strains. From a Bacchic society of the second century B.C., one finds regulations like, disruptive behavior at the meetings is not to be tolerated. If anyone starts a quarrel, he is to be excluded until a fine is paid (F. W. Danker, *Benefactor* [St. Louis:Clayton Publishing House, 1982], pp. 158–59). From the regulations of the guild of Zeus Hypistos of the first century B.C., one hears: "It shall not be permissible . . . to make factions" (C. Roberts, T. C. Skeat, A.D. Nock, "The Guild of Zeus Hypsistos," *HTR* 29[1936]:39–87). One does not make rules that are not needed. The problem in Corinth, then, was that cultural norms took precedence over Christian distinctives at the meal.

Having spoken about the problems in the Corinthian eucharistic observance in vv. 17–22, Paul turns in vv. 23–26 to the tradition of the Last Supper, which will be both the basis of his critique and of his correction of the Corinthian excesses. In v. 22b he declared: "I will not commend you"; in v. 23 he says why: "For [*gar*] I received from the Lord what I also delivered to you." In both Jewish and Greek worlds, "to receive" and "to deliver" were technical terms (e.g., Pirke Aboth 1; Wisd of Sol 14:15; Diodorus Siculus 5.49.5; 12.13.2). Paul used them for learning and teaching oral tradition (cf. 1 Cor 15:3). He does not claim that the tradition to follow was given him personally by the earthly Jesus or the risen Christ, but that the Lord was the origin of the tradition he passed on. The tradition is found in vv. 23b–25:

> The Lord Jesus, on the night on which he was betrayed,
> took bread and, having given thanks, he broke it,
> and said: This is my body which is for you. Go on doing
> this for my remembrance.
> Likewise also the cup, after supper, saying:
> This cup is the new covenant in my blood. Go on doing
> this, as often as you drink, for my remembrance.

It is necessary to speak both about the meaning of the tradition and about its use by the apostle.

Several details are a necessary preliminary to understanding the meaning of the tradition. (1) In both Jewish and early Christian writings, "to remember" is something that both God (Gen 9:16; 19:29; 30:22; Deut 9:27; Judg 16:28; 1 Sam 1:11; 2 Kings 20:3; Isa 38:3; Jer 2:2; 1 Macc 1:2–6; 4:9–10; Tob 3:3; Bar 3:4–7; 2 Esd 8:27–30; Psalm of Solomon 10.1–5; Acts 10:31; Rev 18:5; Didache 10.5) and humans do (Deut 5:15; 7:18; 8:18; 15:15; Judg 8:33–34; Jonah 2:8, 10; 1 Macc 12:11; Tob 1:11; Wisd of Sol 19:9–10; 2 Bar 84.7–11; 2 Tim 2:8; Eph 2:11). When sin is acknowledged, God remembers and forgiveness comes (Lev 5:11–13). When sin is not acknowledged, God remembers and punishment results (Num 5:15). God is said to remember the covenant (Lev 26:42; Luke 1:68–73); he asks to be made to remember (Isa 43:25–26); he says he will remember his people (Jer 31:20); he will make a new covenant with them, forgiving their iniquity and remembering their sin no more (Jer 31:31–34); he says he remembers his covenant and will establish an everlasting covenant with his people with the result that the people will remember (Ezek 16:60–63). Moreover, God is reminded or caused to remember by an archangel (Tob 12:12), by the people's sacrifices (Ecclus

50:16), by Moses (Testament of Moses 11.16–18), by angels (1 Enoch 99.3; 104.1), by the apostle Paul (1 Thess 1:2–3, "We give thanks to God always for you all, constantly mentioning you in our prayers, remembering before our God and Father your work of faith and labor of love and steadfastness of hope"; Rom 1:8–10, "I thank my God through Jesus Christ for all of you ... without ceasing I make remembrance of you"), by the church at worship (Didache 10.5, "Remember, Lord, your church"). In such references the terminology may be either *hē anamnēsis* and cognates or *to mnemosunon* and cognates.

(2) The phrase that is usually translated "in remembrance of me" (vv. 24, 25) does not contain an objective genitive (of me) but rather an adjective that is normally translated "my." Here it should be rendered "for my remembrance" or "as my memorial."

(3) In vv. 24, 25, the command is "Go on doing this." It is not "eat this" (v. 24) or "drink this" (v. 25), but "do this." Do what? To what does "this" refer? It must be more inclusive than just the eating and the drinking. It includes disciples sharing a meal, the focus of which is the death of Jesus as the seal of the new covenant. It is this meal focused on the death of Jesus that facilitates the fellowship (*koinōnia*) in the one body, the church (1 Cor 10:16–17).

Taking these details together, it would be possible to read the tradition in any one of several ways. In the first place, one could understand the supper as an occasion for human beings' remembrance of Jesus' death, analogous to the Israelites' remembrance of the Exodus at Passover time (Deut 16:2–3; m Pesahim 10:4), the Epicurean school's remembrance of Epicurus and Metrodorus at their annual celebration (Diogenes Laertius *Lives of Eminent Philosophers* 10.16–22), or the feasts in memory of the passion of the Syrian goddess (Lucian *Syrian Goddess* 6). In the second place, one could understand the supper as a time when the disciples called to God's remembrance the death of Christ as the seal of the new covenant, analogous to the priestly acts of Simon the high priest, followed by the response of the sons of Aaron "for a remembrance before the Most High" (Ecclus 50:1, 14–16), or Didache 10.5, where in the context of the Lord's Supper the disciples pray, "Remember, Lord, your church, to save it from all evil and to make it perfect in your love." In the third place, one could interpret the meal as a time when the community called the Lord Jesus to remember his death for the sake of the new covenant so that he would intercede for his saints before the Father (cf. Rom 8:34; Heb 7:25; 9:24), analogous to 1 Enoch 99.3, where the righteous raise their prayers as a memorial before the angels who will then bring the sins of sinners for a memorial before God, and passages like 1 Enoch 104.1 and Tob 12:12, where angels bring a remembrance/reminder before God on behalf of humans. In the fourth place, it would be possible to see some combination of the first and the second or third readings. For example, in the meal the disciples remember the death of Jesus and call on God or Christ to remember the new covenant as well (so Fritz Chenderlin, *Do This as My Memorial* [Rome:Biblical Institute Press, 1982], on whom the preceding paragraphs are heavily dependent). Whatever interpretation one gives of the tradition, 1 Cor 10:16–17 makes clear that Paul saw the meal as facilitating a fellowship among those who shared it, just as 10:18 says Israelite sacrifices made the participants partners. This, of course, is precisely the point in 11:17–34.

Paul adds his explanation to the tradition in v. 26: "For as often as you eat this bread and drink the cup, you proclaim the Lord's death until he comes." Does this addition demand a reading of vv. 23–25 only in terms of the first understanding mentioned above? Not necessarily. The proclamation is indeed addressed to humans. That does not mean, however, that the eating and the drinking of this specific bread and the particular cup is only for human reminder. To give thanks to God for the new covenant sealed by Christ's sacrifice involves not only disciples' remembering but also a reminder to God/Christ of the new covenant with the implied request for him/them to protect and deliver. In what sense, then, can the meal be a proclamation of Christ's death? One possibility is that the repetition of the words of institution within the meal is a proclamation of the death of the Lord. Another possibility is that the unity of the disciples created by a meal that focuses on Jesus' death is itself a proclamation (cf. Phil 2:15 in the context of 2:1–16; John 17:23). Perhaps it lies rather in the very stated purpose of the meal.

In the invitations to the sacred meals from pagan antiquity, there would often be a statement of the occasion of the feast, for example, the coming of age of a man's brothers, the birthday of a daughter, sacred rites in honor of a deity (Wendell Lee Willis, *Idol Meat in Corinth* [Chico, Cal.: Scholars Press, 1985], pp. 40–42, gives examples). The stated purpose of the meal made it a public announcement of a certain cause. So a Christian meal held for the purpose of focusing on the sacrifice of Christ as the seal of the new covenant became a public proclamation of his death. Throughout vv. 23–26 the apostle's point has been the purpose of the common meal for Christians: "for my remembrance." Only thereby is it the Lord's Supper and not one's own supper. This is the basis of Paul's critique of Corinthian practice.

In vv. 27–34a the apostle offers his twofold solution to the problem of eucharistic divisions in the church. The two parts correspond to the two indictments and their reasons in vv. 17b–22. (1) In vv. 27–32 the apostle says: Discern the body, that is, the church as the body of Christ. This section falls into an *aba'* pattern, like this:

(*a*) Danger in wrong behavior (v. 27)
   (*b*) Exhortation to proper behavior (v. 28)
(*a'*) Danger in wrong behavior (vv. 29–32).

In (*a*), v. 27, Paul says: "Whoever eats the bread or drinks the cup of the Lord unworthily will be guilty of the body and blood of the Lord." To be guilty of the blood of someone is to be responsible for someone's death (Deut 19:10). To eat and drink unworthily is clarified in v. 29. Basically it means to treat the supper of the Lord as one's own supper (11:21). In (*a'*), vv. 29–32, Paul says, "For anyone who eats and drinks without discerning the body eats and drinks judgment upon himself." Given the context, failure to discern the body can mean only inability to perceive the Christian unity rooted in the sacrifice of Christ and actualized in the sacred meal (1 Cor 10:16–17; cf. Didache 14.2, "let none who has a quarrel with his fellow join in your meeting until they are reconciled, lest your sacrifice be defiled"). The judgment is specified in v. 30: "That is why many of you are weak and ill, and some have died." Already in 10:7–10 Paul has used the example of ancient Israel in the wilderness to show how sin was followed by punishment that sometimes issued in death. A third-generation Tanna, R. Jose the Galilean, has a similar saying: "Come and see the awful effect of sin. Before the crime of the golden calf, there were no issues of blood, no cases of leprosy, in Israel. But as soon as they sinned, these diseases sprang up among them" (Sifre on Num 5:1). The judgment about which the apostle speaks, then, is not the Last Judgment but the present suffering of the afflictions mentioned. This suffering is remedial: "But when we are judged by the Lord, we are chastened so that we may not be condemned along with the world" (v. 32; cf. 5:5). The suffering is also unnecessary. "But if we judged ourselves truly, we should not be judged" (v. 31). Given the dangers of partaking unworthily (i.e., without discerning the body), in (*b*), v. 28, Paul offers an exhortation to proper behavior: "Let a man examine himself and so let him eat of the bread and drink of the cup."

(2) The second part of Paul's twofold solution to the eucharistic problems of the Corinthians comes in vv. 33–34a: "So then, my brethren, when you come together to eat, wait for one another—if anyone is hungry, let him eat at home—lest you come together to be condemned." Remember that at this time the special eucharistic celebration of Christians took place during the course of a meal of fellowship. To correct the abuses evident here in Corinth, Paul said, (*a*) wait for one another, and (*b*) if you are too hungry to wait, eat at home before you come. In saying this, the apostle took the first step toward the transformation of a real meal which included the eucharistic celebration into a purely liturgical celebration distinct from a common meal.

In v. 34b the apostle gives his concluding comment: "About the other things I will give directions when I come." The other things must be matters connected with the sacred meal.

Having traced the train of thought in 1 Cor 11:17–34, we will describe the positions of the Corinthians and Paul as they are reflected in this text. It is important, in depicting the Corinthians' posture, to distinguish between any problem reflected in 11:17–34 and that inferred from 10:1–22. Whereas in 10:1–14 the problem seems to be a mechanical understanding of the Supper and baptism—if we partake, we are safe—in 11:17–34 the issue appears to be due to the social conventions of the community which interfered with the religious significance of the meal. The former might conceivably be connected with an overrealized eschatology that plagued some in Corinth; the latter arises from an underrealized eschatology, that is, the failure to allow the spiritual power available through Christ to transform the social mores of the culture within the congregation. Against the former, Paul warned, "Therefore let anyone who thinks that he stands take heed lest he fall" (10:12). Against the latter, he said, Eat worthily (11:27), discern the body (11:28), wait for one another (11:33). The other Pauline statements about the Lord's Supper likewise are conditioned by the contexts in which they are uttered. (1) 1 Cor 5:11 says the meal is not to be shared with overtly immoral Christians. (2) 1 Cor 10:1–14 says the Supper, like baptism, does not operate mechanically or magically. (3) 1 Cor 10:16–17 says the Supper is a catalyst for fellowship among those who look to the death of Christ as a saving event. (4) 1 Cor 11:17–34 says the Supper's purpose is "for my remembrance" and must be partaken of with full sensitivity to its social ramifications. (5) 1 Cor 16:20b–24 may be a liturgical transition from the homily as represented by 1 Corinthians into the meal which would conceivably follow.

REGULATION, NOT SUPPRESSION, OF SPIRITUAL GIFTS

1 Corinthians 12–14

A t 12:1 Paul returns to the questions raised in the Corinthian letter (7:1, 25; 8:1): "Now concerning the spiritual gifts" (14:1 predisposes one to translate "spiritual gifts" instead of "spiritual persons"). This is a topic discussed by the apostle elsewhere in Rom 12:6–8 (cf. 1 Thess 5:19–22), by the Pauline school in Eph 4:11, and by 1 Pet 4:10–11. In chapters 12–14 the apostle treats the third in a series of matters relating to corporate worship (a. 11:2–16; b. 11:17–34; a'. chaps. 12–14). These three chapters consist of an initial statement of the criterion by which truly Christian religious experience can be discerned (12:2–3), followed by an ABA' pattern:

> A. Spiritual gifts (12:4–30)
>   B. Proper motivation in manifesting the gifts (12:31–14:1a)
> A'. Spiritual gifts (14:1b–40).

Each of these components must be examined in turn.

In 1 Cor 12:2–3, Paul gives the Christological criterion for evaluating any alleged gift. He is concerned at the very first to distinguish what is and what is not Christian religious experience. Two examples, one pagan and the other Jewish, show that not all religious experience is Christian. On the pagan side: "You know that when pagans you were regularly led astray to dumb idols as you were moved" (cf. Lucian *Dialogi Mortuorum* 19.1). On the Jewish side: "No one speaking by the Spirit of God says, 'Jesus is anathema'" (as certain Jews did in the synagogues—cf. Justin *Dialogue* 16.4; 47.4; 96.2; 137.2). As in Deut 13:1–5, Paul's criterion is the content of one's confession: "No one is able to say, 'Jesus is Lord,' except by the Holy Spirit" (v. 3b). In the early church a variety of criteria was employed to distinguish truly Christian religious experience: (a) Matt 7:6 and Didache 11.8–12 specify ethical conduct as the test; (b)

81

Hermas "Command" 11.7–16 and 3 Corinthians 3 (part of the apocryphal Acts of Paul) make their judgment on ecclesiastical grounds; while (c) 1 John 4:1–3 and 1 Cor 12:2–3 employ a Christological criterion. Both pagans and Jews have religious experience, Paul acknowledges, but only that which points to Jesus as Lord is deemed by the apostle to be due to the Holy Spirit (cf. John 15:26). Within these boundaries, Paul accepts the gifts as manifestations of the Spirit. His concern, then, is not the suppression but the regulation of the gifts.

(A), 12:4–30, deals with the variety of gifts in the one body. Once again the pattern is *aba'*:

> (a) the variety of gifts (vv. 4–11)
> (b) the one body (vv. 12–27)
> (a') the variety of gifts (vv. 28–30).

Vv. 4–11, (a) is a thought unit held together by an inclusion (vv. 4 and 11, "the same Spirit"). Not only is the term "Spirit" the dominant word in the paragraph, it is also the link word that ties vv. 4–11 to the previous unit, vv. 2–3. The theme of vv. 4–11 is the variety of gifts. Included here as samples are the utterance of wisdom (v. 8; cf. 1 Kings 3:16–28; Isa 11:2; Luke 21:15; Acts 6:10), the utterance of knowledge (v. 8; John 14:26), faith (v. 9; not saving faith nor faith as a fruit of the Spirit, Gal 5:22, but "faith that moves mountains," 1 Cor 13:2; Matt 17:20), gifts of healing (v. 9; Luke 9:2; 10:9), the working of miracles (v. 10; cf. John 14:12; Acts 4:29–30), prophecy (v. 10; cf. Jer 1:9; 2 Chron 20:14–15; Joel 2:28– 29; Acts 2:16–18), the ability to distinguish between spirits (v. 10; cf. 1 Kings 22; 1 John 4:1), various kinds of tongues (v. 10; Acts 10:44–45; 19:6), the interpretation of tongues (v. 10; 1 Cor 14:27–28). "All these are inspired by one and the same Spirit, who apportions to each one individually as he wills" (v. 11; Rom 12:3).

First, note that this is not the same list that appears in Rom 12:6–8 (prophecy, service, teaching, exhortation, contributing, giving aid, acts of mercy). It is clear from such a comparison that for Paul both unusual and more usual types of action fall within the sphere of the gifts of the Spirit (also 1 Pet 4:10–11).

Second, note that such phenomena continued in the patristic period, at least in some circles. Hermas sets the tone: "If you bear his name but possess not his power, it will be in vain that you bear his name" ("Parable" 9.13). Representative sources include the following. (a) Eusebius tells how in the time of Trajan prophecy and miracles continued (*Ecclesiastical History* 3.37, 39). (*b*) Justin says, "For one receives the spirit of understanding, another of counsel, another of strength, another of healing, another of foreknowledge, another of teaching, and another of the fear of God" (*Dialogue* 39); he also says, "the prophetical gifts remain with us, even to the present time" (*Dialogue* 82, cf. 87–88; *2 Apology* 6). (*c*) Eusebius tells how in the time of Marcus Aurelius many wonderful works of the grace of God were still being wrought up to that time in the churches (*E. H.* 5.3.4). (*d*) Also in the time of Marcus Aurelius, Irenaeus relates,

> "some . . . drive out devils . . . others have foreknowledge of things to come: they see visions and utter prophetic expressions. Others still heal the sick by laying their hands upon them, and they are made whole. Yea, moreover, as I have said, the dead even have been raised up, and remained among us for many years. And what shall I say more? It is not possible to name the number of gifts which the church, scattered throughout the whole world, has received from God." (*Against Heresies* 2.32.4)

Irenaeus tells about "many brethren in the church who possess prophetic gifts, and who through the Spirit speak all kinds of languages" (cf. 5.6.1; 5.16, 17 on prophecy). (*e*) Tertullian *A Treatise on the Soul* 9; *Against Marcion* 5.8. (*f*) Eusebius *E.H.* 6.9, for the time of Caracalla; cf. also 6.43.11, 14 (fifty-two exorcists in the Roman church of that time). (*g*) Origen says, "And there are still preserved among Christians traces of that Holy Spirit which appeared in the form of a dove. They expel evil spirits, and perform many cures, and foresee certain events" (*De Principiis* Preface 3; *Against Celsus* 1.46). (*h*) Novatian *De Trinitate* 29. (*i*) Eusebius *E.H.* 10.4.66 (about events in his own time). (*j*) *Apostolic Constitutions* 8.1. (*k*) Cyril of Alexandria *Catechesis* 16.15–16; (*l*) Gregory the Great asks, "Which one of us does not think himself close to God when he sees himself overwhelmed with favors from on high, when he receives the gift of prophecy, . . . the grace of curing the sick?" (*Moralia* 9.13, 20). Given this evidence, it is clear that Paul is not speaking about something that was restricted to Corinth or to the first century.

Third, note that most of the gifts mentioned here are christologically grounded, for example, the utterance of wisdom (Luke 20:20–26); utterance of knowledge (Luke 7:39–50); faith (John 11:41–42); gifts of healing (Luke 7:22); working of miracles (Luke 9:10–17); prophecy (Luke 18:31–33 with Luke 22–23; Luke 11:13 with Acts 1:14 and Acts 2); ability to distinguish between spirits (Luke 4:1–13; 9:49–50).

Fourth, note that this diversity of gifts is not only from the one Spirit but is also for the common good (v. 7). This is a thread that will run throughout chapter 14.

In vv. 12–27, (*b*), a unit held together by an inclusion (vv. 12 and 27, body/members/Christ), Paul focuses on the organic unity of the Christian community. To do this, he employs a fable of the body and its limbs that was widely used in antiquity (e.g., Livy tells how Menenius Agrippa used it with the plebians in Rome [2.32]; Epictetus shows how the Stoics used it for political life [2.10.3]; Midrash Tehillim on Ps 39:2 employs it in a Jewish context): "For just as the body is one and has many members, and all the members of the body, though many, are one body, so it is with Christ" (v. 12). Christ here is not the name of an individual, Jesus, but of the community which derives its existence and identity from the individual. Just as in the Old Testament Israel could serve as the name of an individual (Gen 32:28) and of a people, so in Paul the name Christ is used both for the individual (1 Cor 2:2; Rom 5:17) and for the Christian community (1 Cor 15:22). The Christian community, Paul is saying, is like the human body. It is an organic unity with a multiplicity of parts.

This organic unity is created by the Spirit: "For in one Spirit we were all baptized into one body . . . and all were made to drink of one Spirit" (v. 13). Two images are used here. The first is "baptism in the Spirit." The expression is that used in the Gospels (Luke 3:16; John 1:33) and Acts (1:5; 11:16) and with the same meaning. Here the Spirit is not the baptizer but the one in whom all are baptized. One is immersed in the Spirit. The other image is that of drinking the Spirit. Although the verb is different, the thought is the same as that in John 7:37–39 (cf. John 4:14). Taken together, the two pictures say that the Spirit is both within and all around believers. In the Pauline churches, this experience normally occurred in the context of proclamation (Gal 3:1–5; 1 Cor 2:1–5; 1 Thess 1:5), as in the narrative of Acts 10:44–48 about Peter and Cornelius. It is this experience of the Spirit that incorporates people into the Christian community.

This organic unity demands a view of Christian diversity of gifts that fits with the oneness of the body of Christ rather than detracting from it: "The eye cannot say to the hand, 'I have no need of you,' nor again the head to the feet, 'I have no need of you'" (v. 21); "If one member suffers, all suffer together; if one member is honored, all rejoice together" (v. 26).

In (*a'*), vv. 28–30, Paul returns to his emphasis on the varieties of gifts. In v. 28 his list is different in part from that in vv. 4–11. Here he speaks of apostles, prophets (1 Cor 12:10; Rom 12:6), teachers (Rom 12:7), workers of miracles (1 Cor 12:10), healers (1 Cor 12:9), helpers (Rom 12:8 ?), administrators, speakers in various kinds of tongues (1 Cor 12:10). There is no intention in this list to rank the gifts. The terms "first" (*prōton*), "second" (*deuteron*), "third" (*triton*), "then" (*epeita*), are merely used to enumerate a sequence (*AGD*, 726). If Paul were ranking gifts here, he would be involved in the very problem he is seeking to combat in the Corinthians' behavior. He would be saying that he, because of his apostleship, outranked them because they were not apostles. This kind of one-upmanship is the very thing that Paul wants to avoid.

In vv. 29–30 there are seven rhetorical questions, each one demanding a negative answer. "Are all apostles?" No. "Are all prophets?" No. "Are all teachers?" No. "Do all work miracles?" No. "Do all possess gifts of healing?" No. "Do all speak with tongues?" No. "Do all interpret?" No. The gifts are diverse and not every Christian is a recipient of all (cf. Rom 12:6, "Having gifts that differ according to the grace given to us, let us use them"). Not only are there diverse gifts, but also different people are used by the Spirit to deliver the different gifts for the common good.

1 Cor 12:31–14:1a, (B) in the larger pattern, focuses on the proper motivation in manifesting the gifts. The unit is introduced in v. 31a with a sentence that can be translated either as an imperative ("But earnestly desire the higher gifts," as the RSV) or as an indicative ("But you are eagerly desiring," so the NIV margin). Two arguments support the indicative reading. First, Paul distinguishes between the gifts of the Spirit and the fruit of the Spirit (Gal 5:22–23, "But the fruit of the Spirit is love, joy, peace, patience, kindness, goodness, faithfulness, gentleness, self-control"). Gifts reflect the activity of Jesus; fruit reflect the character of Jesus. If one reads an imperative, "Earnestly desire the higher gifts," then Paul seems to be saying his readers should strive for love as the higher gift. For the apostle, however, love is a fruit of the Spirit, not a gift of the Spirit. Second, in chapter 12 it seems that the Corinthians were in fact distinguishing between the greater and the lesser gifts and were coveting the greater. It seems also that Paul had urged them to be content with the gift(s) apportioned them. If one reads an imperative in v. 31a, Paul would then be reinforcing such distinctions and their quest. If one reads an indicative, "But you are eagerly desiring the higher gifts," then the apostle would merely be reporting the sad state of affairs in Corinth. The Corinthian spirituals were interested in gifts not for the common good (12:7) but for their own personal status. Their motivation

in manifesting the spiritual gifts was wrong. Paul, therefore, responds, "And I will show you a still more excellent way" (12:31b). Chapter 13, then, focuses on love as the motivation for applying the gifts.

1 Cor 13:1–13 is an aretalogy of love (cf. a similar aretalogy of truth in 1 Esd 4:34–40) that falls into an *aba'* pattern: (*a*) the superiority of love (vv. 1–3); (*b*) the characterization of love (vv. 4–7); and (*a'*) the superiority of love (vv. 8–13). Vv. 1–3, (*a*), are organized around a three fold repetition of the refrain, "If I . . . but have not love, I am/gain." This section speaks of the incompleteness of tongues, prophecy, faith, and sacrifice without love as motivation. Vv. 4–7, (*b*), characterize love in three ways: first, what love does in two positive descriptions ("Love is patient and kind"); second, what love does not do in eight negatives ("love is not jealous or boastful; it is not arrogant or rude. Love does not insist on its own way; it is not irritable or resentful; it does not rejoice at wrong"); and third, what love does in five positives ("rejoices in the right. Love bears all things, believes all things, hopes all things, endures all things"). Vv. 8–13, (*a'*), resume the theme of the superiority of love, emphasizing its permanence ("Love never ends," v. 8a; "so faith, hope, love abide," v. 13a) over against the transience of prophecy ("as for prophecies, they will pass away," v. 8b), of tongues ("as for tongues, they will cease," v. 8c), and of knowledge ("as for knowledge, it will pass away," v. 8d). The time for the passing of the gifts is "when the perfect comes" (v. 10), that is, at the parousia. Love, then, stands supreme as the more excellent motivation for the manifestation of spiritual gifts. The unit concludes with the Pauline exhortation "Make love your aim" (14:1a). In saying this, the apostle does not aim to replace the spiritual gifts with love (cf. 14:1—"make love your aim" followed by "zealously see the spiritual gifts") but to undergird them with the fruit of the Spirit.

1 Cor 14:1b–40, (A'), returns to the focus on spiritual gifts. This unit is held together by an inclusion (vv. 1 and 39, "seek to prophesy"). It falls into two sections, (1) vv. 1b–19, a Pauline thesis in two parts with supporting arguments, and (2) vv. 20–36, two Corinthian assertions followed by their Pauline responses, after which comes a concluding summary (vv. 37–40). (1) In the first section, vv. 1b–19, the thesis is formulated in vv. 1b–5: (*a*) in public worship, prophecy is preferable to tongues (vv. 1b, 5a,b) (*b*) unless the tongues are interpreted (v. 5b). The ultimate test of comparison is benefit for the church (v. 5b, "so that the church may be edified"; cf. 12:7, "for the common good"). What follows are two clusters of arguments (vv. 6–12 and vv. 13–19).

In the first cluster there are three arguments in favor of prophecy in public worship (vv. 6–12). First, if Paul came speaking only tongues, the Corinthians would not benefit (v. 6; cf. 15:1–11). Second, if musical instruments do not communicate unless their sounds are arranged in an intelligible pattern, then the Corinthians should not expect to communicate in church unless their speech is intelligible to others (vv. 7–9). Third, if language is not understood, then people are foreigners to each other (vv. 10–12). Throughout these three arguments the social concern of the apostle has been uppermost. Hence the cluster is concluded, "strive to excel in building up the church" (v. 12b).

In the second cluster there are three arguments in favor of the interpretation of tongues in public worship (vv. 13–19). V. 13 sets forth the theme: "he who speaks in a tongue should pray for the power to interpret." First, Paul argues, since what is said in tongues is not framed by the mind, nothing is communicated to others present at worship (vv. 14–15). Second, language that is not intelligible to all in public worship prevents the other Christians from responding with their "Amen" (vv. 16–17). Third, Paul's apostolic example is to be considered. "I thank God that I speak in tongues more than you all; nevertheless, *in church* I would rather speak five words with my mind, in order to instruct others, than ten thousand words in a tongue" (vv. 18–19). Throughout these three arguments is the same social concern noted in the previous cluster. What is said in church is to be intelligible to all present. If tongues are used, therefore, they must be interpreted (v. 13). In corporate worship uninterpreted tongues are inferior to prophecy as a vehicle for church edification.

(2) In the second section, vv. 20–36, there are two Corinthian assertions, followed in each case by their Pauline response. Prior to the two dialogue parts is the apostolic admonition: "Brethren, do not be children in your thinking . . . in thinking be mature." The first Corinthian assertion and Pauline reply come in vv. 21–25. Reading it this way avoids the contradiction between vv. 21–22 and vv. 23–25. It also avoids attributing to Paul a position that is clearly not his (vv. 21–22) (B. C. Johanson, "Tongues, A Sign for Unbelievers?: A Structural and Exegetical Study of 1 Corinthians 14:20–25," *NTS* 25[1979]:180–203). The Corinthian assertion is found in vv. 21–22. It consists of a quotation from scripture (Isa 28:11–12, "By men of strange tongues and by the lips of foreigners will I speak to this people, and even then they will not listen to me, says the Lord") followed by its interpretation in two stages. (*a*) Tongues are a

sign not for believers but for unbelievers. The reason why the Corinthians held to such a position may have been that in antiquity there is evidence that the sure sign of an inspired speaker was that the deity authenticated the message previously delivered in an understandable language by means of the tongues that followed (T. W. Gillespie, "A Pattern of Prophetic Speech in First Corinthians," *JBL* 97[1978]:74–95). (*b*) Prophecy is not for unbelievers but for believers.

Paul responds in vv. 23–25, dealing with the two stages of the Corinthian interpretation of Isa 28 with two illustrative situations, perhaps out of their experience. (*a*) "If, therefore, the whole church assembles and all speak in tongues, and outsiders or unbelievers enter, will they not say that you are mad?" (v. 23) That is, the non-Christian world will identify the Christian community with the ecstatic pagan cults in which ritual madness was highly desirable. Paul is asking, "Is this what you really want?" (*b*) "But if all prophesy, and an unbeliever or outsider enters, he is convicted by all, he is called to account by all, the secrets of his heart are disclosed; and so, falling on his face, he will worship God and declare that God is really among you." Such a reading both makes sense of what otherwise seems to be contradictory and fits the sense of the chapter as a whole. In this context, prophecy functions to disclose the secrets of the human heart, to produce conviction of sin, and to lead to a vindication both of God and of the Christian community (cf. John 16:7–11; Acts of John 56–57).

Prophecy was a phenomenon found in both the Greco-Roman and Jewish traditions in antiquity (J. Panagopoulos, ed., *Prophetic Vocation in the New Testament* [Leiden: Brill, 1977]; David Hill, *New Testament Prophecy* [Atlanta: John Knox, 1979]; M. Eugene Boring, *Sayings of the Risen Jesus: Christian Prophecy in the Synoptic Tradition* [Cambridge: Cambridge University Press, 1982]; David E. Aune, *Prophecy in Early Christianity and the Ancient Mediterranean World* [Grand Rapids: Eerdmans, 1983]). The pagan world had its oracular places and persons just as the Jewish heritage did.

Early Christians understood prophecy within the church as a continuation or renewal of the prophecy of ancient Israel (e.g., Luke 1–2; 7:26, 39; Acts 2:16–21). When Justin Martyr said, "the prophetical gifts remain with us even to the present time" (*Dialogue* 82), he was expressing a widespread Christian belief. References to early Christian prophets and prophecies are extensive: 1 Thess 5:20; 1 Cor 12–14; Rom 12:4–6; Eusebius's reference to a prophecy telling Christians in Jerusalem to move to Pella (*E.H.* 3.5.3); Eph 3:5; 4:11; 1 Tim 1:18; 4:14; Acts 11:27–28; 13:1–3; 15:22, 32; 19:6; 21:4, 9, 10–11; Rev 11:10, 18; 16:6; 18:20, 24; 22:6, 9; Didache 10.7; 11.3, 7–11; 13.1–6; 15.1–2; Ignatius *Phil* 7.1–2; Hermas "Command" 11.7, 12, 15, 16; Martyrdom of Polycarp 5.2; 12.3; Odes of Solomon 42.6; Quadratus (so Eusebius *E.H.* 3.37.1); Melito of Sardis (so Eusebius *E.H.* 4.26.20); Ammia of Philadelphia (so Eusebius *E.H.* 5.17.3–4), etc. This early Christian prophecy was not just preaching and teaching but was regarded as a supernatural gift. According to Paul, it was a gift given to an individual (1 Cor 14:30); it had a spontaneous quality (14:30); it did not force one to speak against one's will (14:30, 32a); it enabled the prophet to know something from a divine perspective (14:24–25); it functioned for evangelism (14:24–25), for upbuilding, encouragement, and consolation of the church (14:3), as well as for learning (14:31); it was to cease at the parousia (13:8, 10). Just as in ancient Israel, so in the early church false prophets and prophecy became a problem: 2 Thess 2:2; Matt 24:11, 23–24; 7:15–23; Mark 13:22; 1 John 4:1–3; Rev 2:20; 16:13; 19:20; Didache 11.8–12; 13.1–7; Hermas "Command" 11.7; the Gnostic Marcus (so Irenaeus *Against Heresies* 1.13.3–4); Montanism (so Eusebius *E.H.* 5.16.6–9); Lucian *Peregrinus* 11–13; Acts of Thomas 79; *Apostolic Constitutions* 8.2.1, etc. Because of the problems with false prophecy, the gift of prophecy itself eventually fell into disuse and sometimes disrepute.

The New Testament speaks about two different phenomena with the label "tongues": (1) xenolalia (Acts 2) and (2) glossolalia (1 Cor 12, 14). In the former case, to speak in other tongues (Acts 2:4) is a gift of the Spirit (2:4, 17–18) that enables people listening to hear in their own language (2:11). In the latter case, to "speak in a tongue" (1 Cor 14:4, equals to "pray in a tongue," 14:14, or to "speak in the tongues . . . of angels," 13:1) is a gift of the Spirit (12:10) that is intelligible only to God unless interpreted (14:15–19) and that is controllable, so that no state of trance, frenzy, or loss of control is involved (14:27–28).

The question of parallels to these phenomena is exceedingly difficult. Most alleged parallels do not carry conviction (E. R. Dodds, "Supernormal Phenomena in Classical Antiquity," in *The Ancient Concept of Progress* [Oxford: Clarendon, 1973], pp. 156–210; S. D. Currie, "Speaking in Tongues: Early Evidence Outside the New Testament Bearing on Glossais Lalein," *Int* 19[1965]:274–94; R. A. Harrisville, "Speaking in Tongues: A Lexicographical Study," *CBQ* 38[1976]:35–48; David Christie-Murray, *Voices from the Gods: Speaking in Tongues* [London: Routledge & Kegan Paul, 1978]; Morton T. Kelsey, *Tongue Speaking: The History and Meaning of Charismatic Experience* [New York: Crossroad, 1981]). From the pagan world, the only possible analogy to xenolalia, to my knowledge, is a passage of Herodotus where the diviner in the temple of Ptoan Apollo speaks Carian to Mys of Europa who had come to consult him (*Histories* 8.135). Possible analogies to glossolalia are found in Quintilian, who mentions the "more unusual voices of the more secret language which the Greeks call 'glossai' (*Instituto Oratorio* 1.35), in Dio Chrysostom who speaks of the language of the gods and hints at sham glossolalia in referring to "persons who know two or three Persian, Median, or Assyrian words and thus fool the ignorant" (10th *Discourse* on Servants), and in Lucian's *Alexander*, where he says the false prophet uttered "unintelligible vocables which sound like Hebrew or Phoenician" (cf. Celsus, in Origen *Against Celsus* 7.9).

From the Jewish world instances of xenolalia are unknown to me. The most persuasive instance of glossolalia is found in the Testament of Job, where Job's three daughters speak in the angelic language, praising God separately and together in the exalted dialect (48–52). In two places the Babylonian Talmud says Rabbi Johanan ben Zakkai understood not only Torah but also the language of the ministering angels and the matters of the throne chariot of Ezek 1 (b Baba Bathra 134a; b Sukkah 28a).

In the patristic period xenolalia is difficult to discover but is not unknown (e.g., Irenaeus *Against Heresies* 5.6.1; Chrysostom *Homily* 29 on 1 Cor 12:1–11). References to glossolalia are to be found easily. We hear that as Isaiah was taken up into heaven, when he reached the sixth heaven he "praised along with them (the angels) . . . and our praise was like theirs" (Ascension of Isaiah 8). Irenaeus tells of Christians who "have received the Spirit of God, and who through the Spirit of God do speak in all languages, as he [Paul] used himself also to speak. In like manner we do also hear many brethren in the church . . . who through the Spirit speak all kinds of languages" (*Against Heresies* 5.6.1). Tertullian deals with the gifts of the Spirit and assumes that tongues and interpretation of tongues occur in the mainstream church (*Against Marcion* 5.8). Viewed in the context of the four types of prayer in ascetical theology (meditation, contemplation, mystical union, ecstasy), glossolalia is one kind of contemplative prayer. Like the other kinds of contemplative prayer and prophecy, glossolalia has analogues in other traditions. What makes it Christian, from Paul's perspective, is its source (the Holy Spirit), its locale (it occurs in a community making the confession, Jesus is Lord, 12:3), and its results (it edifies the individual Christian who prays this way, 14:4; when interpreted, it may benefit the church, 14:5, 13).

Following the first Corinthian assertion and Pauline response (14:21–25) is a concluding summary (vv. 26–34a) whose thesis is, "Let all things be done for edification" (v. 26b) in public worship. Two things are necessary if this is to be the case. First, what is said must be capable of being understood by all. "If anyone speak in a tongue . . . , let one interpret. But if there is no one to interpret, let each of them keep silence *in church* and speak to himself and to God" (vv. 27–28). Second, everything should be done in order. "Let two or three prophets speak, and let the others weigh what is said. If a revelation is made to another sitting by, let the first be silent. For you can all prophesy one by one, so that all may learn and be encouraged" (vv. 29–31). Just as with tongues (v. 28), Paul believes prophecy, although a gift/happening, is controllable: "and the spirits of prophets are subject to prophets" (v. 32). Although this could conceivably mean that one prophet is subject to the discernment of another prophet (a point already made in v. 29), the context favors interpreting Paul's language to mean that prophecy is not accompanied by a trance (T. Callan, "Prophecy and Ecstasy in Greco-Roman Religion and in 1 Corinthians," *NovT* 27[1985]:125–40). V. 33 continues the argument for order in corporate worship: "For God is not a God of confusion but of peace, as in all the churches of the saints" (cf. 4:17 and 11:16, where the appeal to general practice concludes Paul's argument; so here also, contra RSV, TEV, NIV, NEB, etc.).

The chapter concludes (14:34–40) with a second Corinthian assertion (vv. 34–35) and the apostolic response (v. 36), followed by a summary (vv. 37–40). Justification of this position begins with an analysis of the individual components of the paragraph in the RSV (14:33b–36). V. 33b, "as in all the churches of the saints," goes with the previous thought unit as its conclusion. Vv. 34–35 consist of two admonitions and their bases. Admonition one: "the women should keep silence in the churches." Basis one: "for they are not permitted to speak, but should be subordinate, as even the law says." Admonition two: "if there is anything they desire to know, let them ask their husbands at home." Basis two: "for it is shameful for a woman to speak in church." Two things stand out about these words. First, they reflect the general cultural values: (*a*) Livy's account of a speech by the consul Cato against Roman women has Cato ask: "Could you not have asked your husband the same thing at home?" (34:1–8); (*b*) Juvenal speaks disparagingly of a woman who boldly rushes around the whole city intruding on the councils of men, and talks down leaders in military clothes, in front of her husband (*Satires* 6); (*c*) Philo says, "The husband seems competent to transmit knowledge of the laws to his wife" (*Hypothetica* 8.7.14); (*d*) Josephus says, "The woman, says the Law, is in all things inferior to the man. Let her accordingly be submissive ... that she may be directed, for the authority has been given by God to the man" (*Against Apion* 2.201). Second, the position taken in vv. 34–35 runs counter to that taken by Paul elsewhere: (*a*) Gal 3:27–28, "For as many of you as were baptized into Christ have put on Christ. There is neither Jew nor Greek, there is neither slave nor free, there is neither male nor female; for you are all one in Christ Jesus," affirms Christian equality between the sexes in Christ; (*b*) 1 Cor 11:5, "any woman who prays or prophesies," and 11:12, "a woman to pray to God," imply that Corinthian women prayed and prophesied in church and that Paul had no problems with the practice so long as their heads were covered. Since there is no evidence in the text that different women are involved in 1 Cor 11:2–16 and 14:34–35 (e.g., celibate in chap. 11, wives in chap. 14) or that different parts of the service are referred to (e.g., time of prayer and prophecy in chap. 11, discussion after the sermon in chap. 14), one is forced to conclude that if 14:34–35 is from Paul, it contradicts his stance elsewhere.

When a text in Paul is clearly contradictory to the apostle's thought expressed everywhere else, there are two different expedients often used to resolve the difficulty. On the one hand, the contradictory text may be declared to be a later interpolation. This has frequently been suggested for 1 Cor 14:34–35. On the other hand, the discordant note may be regarded as the position of Paul's opponents, cited by the apostle before his refutation. This has, of late, also been suggested for vv. 34–35.

Can v. 36 ("What! Did the word of God originate with you, or are you the only ones it has reached?") assist in deciding between these two options? V. 36 begins with a particle (*ē*, translated "What!" by the RSV) whose force indicates that what has come before is refuted by the twofold rhetorical query that follows (as at 1 Cor 11:22; David W. Odell-Scott, "Let the Women Speak in Church: An Egalitarian Interpretation of 1 Cor 14:33b–36," *BTB* 13[1983]:90–93). Further, v. 36 is not directed to the women exclusively. The second question of v. 36 ("or are you the only ones it has reached?") uses a masculine plural (*monous*) for the term translated "only ones." This masculine plural can be understood to refer

either to multiple male persons or to people in general in a gender-inclu-
sive sense, but it cannot address only female persons. Taken together,
these two observations lead to the conclusion that v. 36 is not the natural
conclusion of the argument in vv. 34–35. Rather, if vv. 34–36 are read
together, then v. 36 is a refutation of vv. 34–35. This leads very naturally to the reading that takes vv. 34–35 as a Corinthian assertion, analogous to other such assertions in 1 Corinthians and like some of them appealing to the Law (2:15, citing Isa 40:13; 10:23, 26, citing Ps 24:1 or
50:12; 14:21–22, citing Isa 28:11–12). If so, then v. 36 is the Pauline response rejecting the Corinthian stance about women. This interpretation would yield a coherent, uniformly positive stance of Paul regarding
women in the church.

If one takes vv. 34–35 as a post-Pauline interpolation with a viewpoint
similar to that of the deutero-Pauline 1 Tim 2:11–12 (most recently,
Jerome Murphy-O'Connor, "Interpolations in 1 Corinthians," *CBQ*
48[1986]:81–94), then v. 36 was originally a response to vv. 26–33, the
concluding summary asking that everything in worship be done for edification and in order. The difficulty with this reading is that v. 36 is addressed to "you all" (plural), whereas, if a response to vv. 26–33, it ought
to be "you" (singular). Paul has been saying in vv. 26–33, "If any *one*
speak in a tongue, let . . . But if there is no *one* to interpret, let *each* of
them keep silence . . . If a revelation is made to *another* sitting by, let the
first be silent." That is, he is addressing unbridled individualism and is
asking individuals to subordinate their personal expression of spiritual
gifts to the corporate good. If he then says indignantly that the word of
God has not gone forth from and come to them only, it ought to be addressed to the individuals addressed in vv. 26–33, not the church as a
whole or the group of prophets within it. This difficulty is sufficient to
tip the scales in favor of taking vv. 34–35 as a Corinthian assertion and
v. 36 as an indignant Pauline reply. This yields a coherent position with
reference to the place of women in the church in Paul's genuine letters.
He is seen as taking a stand, in the name of Christian equality, against
the values of the culture.

If one grants the unity of the historical Paul's attitude towards women
in the church, there still remains the problem of the stance of his school,
as reflected in 1 Tim 2:11–12: "Let a woman learn in silence with all
submissiveness. I permit no woman to teach or to have authority over
men; she is to keep silent." The general rule to follow in such ethical
matters is twofold: (*a*) look at the entire range of New Testament evi-

dence, not just one text, and (*b*) examine the historical context out of which the various texts come (Brevard Childs, "Biblical Theology's Role in Decision-Making," in *Biblical Theology in Crisis* [Philadelphia: Westminister, 1970], pp. 123–38; a position approved by Bruce C. Birch and Larry L. Rasmussen, *Bible and Ethics in the Christian Life* [Minneapolis: Augsburg, 1976]).

(*a*) 1 Tim 2:11–12 needs to be set alongside Acts 18:24–28, a text from a document that also has connections with the Pauline school near the end of the first century. If the Pastorals prohibit a woman's teaching or having authority over men, Acts 18:26 says Priscilla and Aquila expounded to Apollos the way of God more accurately. The latter passage not only has a woman teaching a male preacher but also listed in the dominant role (cf. Acts 13:2, Barnabas and Saul; 13:13, Paul and his company; where the shift in whose name goes first is a sign of who is the dominant figure in the relationship). Why would two deutero-Pauline documents differ so radically on the function of women in the church?

(*b*) The Pastorals reflect a situation in which Gnosticism is infecting the church and is making inroads especially among the women (2 Tim 3:6–7, "For among them are those who make their way into households and capture weak women, burdened with sins and swayed by various impulses, who will listen to anybody and can never arrive at a knowledge of the truth"). As a defense against error, the author of the Pastorals appeals to a principle of succession. The true tradition was passed from God to Paul and from the apostle to Timothy and Titus and from them to the faithful men who will teach others also (2 Tim 1:11–12, 13–14; 2:2). It is the author's belief that if the faithful men (obviously the church officials for whom the qualifications are given in 1 Tim 3:1–7—e.g., v. 2, "an apt teacher") properly teach the true tradition, then heresy will be defeated. In such a context, the defense of the tradition would not be committed to those most swayed by heresy (the women). Such people would rather be prohibited from exercising authority and from teaching. On the other hand, in Acts Priscilla and Aquila represent the true Pauline tradition which completes a deficient faith or theology. In this context where the woman is a representative of the true tradition there is no reluctance to depict her as the teacher of a male preacher. The constant in the two cases is the faithfulness to the true tradition of Paul. What is variable is how that faithfulness is insured. In one case it is by the exclusion of women from teaching; in the other it is by the inclusion of women in the act of teaching. Such an observation precludes taking 1 Tim 2:11–12 as timeless truth.

Following the second Corinthian assertion (14:34–35) and Paul's reply (v. 36), there comes the final summary (vv. 37–40) which stands at the end of the entire argument. It has two components. There is first of all an assertion of apostolic authority: "If any one thinks that he is a prophet, or spiritual, he should acknowledge that what I am writing to you is a command of the Lord. If any one does not recognize this, he is not recognized" (vv. 37–38). Presumably this covers Paul's directives in the entire thought unit (1 Cor 12–14). There is then a reiteration of his positions: (*a*) earnestly desire to prophesy, (*b*) do not forbid speaking in tongues, (*c*) do all things decently and in order (v. 39).

Having traced the train of thought in 1 Cor 12–14, we will now attempt to formulate briefly the positions of the two sides, the Corinthians and Paul. On the one hand, the Corinthian spirituals (1) contended that some gifts were better than others; (2) indicated that they wanted the higher gifts; (3) took the position that tongues were a sign for unbelievers, prophecy for believers; and (4) held that women should not occupy a leadership role in Christian worship. On the other hand, the apostle (1) argued that there are a variety of gifts and that each one makes its own contribution to the common good; (2) showed love to be the indispensible motivation for the manifesting of any gift; (3) insisted that understandable speech is mandatory in corporate worship for both believer and unbeliever; and (4) stood firm for the principle that Christian corporate worship is not a male-dominated enterprise.

THE HUMAN TRANSFORMATION
YET TO COME

1 Corinthians 15

1 Cor 15:1–58 is a thought unit held together by an inclusion (vv. 1–2, brethren/in vain; v. 58, brethren/in vain). There is no indication that it is a response to the Corinthian letter addressed to Paul (note the absence of "now concerning," as in 7:1, 25; 8:1; 12:1). It is most likely the apostle's response to information received orally either from Chloe's people (1:11) or from the bearers of the letter from Corinth (16:17, assuming that Stephanas, Fortunatus, and Achaicus are different from Chloe's people). The chapter which deals with the resurrection consists of three major parts: (1) a reminder of the gospel of Christ's resurrection (vv. 1–11); (2) two Corinthian assertions together with their Pauline responses (vv. 12–34); and (3) two Corinthian questions followed by their Pauline answers in reverse order (vv. 35–58). Each of these three major components must be examined in turn.

(1) Vv. 1–11 constitute a unit held together by an inclusion (vv. 1–2, preached/believed; v. 11, preached/believed) that falls into three sections: (a) vv. 1–2, (b) vv. 3–8, (c) vv. 9–11. (a) Vv. 1–2 are organized into two parts around the repetition "the gospel I preached (*euēggelisamēn*) to you" (v. 1) and "by which word you were evangelized" (*euēgglisamēn*, v. 2). Thereby Paul reminds the Corinthians that the gospel he preached to them when the church was founded is the one by which they are saved, but only if they hold it fast. What is that gospel? (b) In vv. 3–8 the apostle reiterates the gospel preached on that first occasion: "I delivered to you as of first importance what I also received" (v. 3a). Just as in 1 Cor 11:23, Paul uses the technical terms for passing on (delivered) and learning (received) of oral tradition. What follows in vv. 3b–8, except for Paul's comments in v. 6b ("most of whom are still alive, though some have fallen asleep") and v. 8 ("last of all, he appeared to me"), is traditional material used both in Paul's preaching and in that of the other apostles (v. 11). As a whole, the unit is built around four verbs

relating to Christ: Christ *died*, he was *buried*, he was *raised*, and he *appeared*. The last verb occurs, either actually or by implication, six times and in a concentric pattern:

> He appeared (*ōphthē*) to Cephas;
>   Then (*eita*) to the Twelve;
>   Then he appeared (*epeita ōphthē*) to more than five hundred;
>   Then he appeared (*epeita ōphthē*) to James;
>   Then (*eita*) to all the apostles;
> He appeared (*ōphthē*) also to me.

The points of the apostle are two. First, the common tradition of the church which was preached when the Corinthian congregation was founded asserts the fact of the resurrection. Keep in mind that for the Jewish mind there was only one resurrection, the general resurrection. So if the tradition said one man (Christ) had been raised, and that event was legitimated by the appearances, then the general resurrection had begun. To say that Christ has been raised, therefore, is to establish the fact of the resurrection from the dead. Second, by his insertion into the tradition of his comment in v. 6b ("most of whom are still alive, though some have fallen asleep"), Paul establishes that death has not yet been destroyed, not even for those who have experienced the risen Lord. This means that the resurrection of all besides Christ is still future. These two concerns of the apostle are taken up explicitly in vv. 12–20 and vv. 21–28. At this point, Paul is interested in grounding them in the tradition of the gospel through which the Corinthian church was founded. (*c*) Vv. 9–10 focus on the one who preached to the Corinthians. He shares with the other apostles both a common experience (v. 8, "last of all . . . he appeared also to me"; cf. 9:1) and a common gospel (v. 11, "Whether then it was I or they, so we preach"). His apostleship is as much a miracle of God's grace ("by the grace of God I am what I am, and his grace toward me was not in vain," v. 10a) as the Corinthians' conversion (cf. 1:26–31). On the foundation of vv. 1–11, Paul's argument in the rest of the chapter will be constructed.

(2) In vv. 12–34 there are two Corinthian assertions followed in each case by a Pauline response. The first Corinthian assertion is echoed in v. 12: "Now if Christ is preached as raised from the dead" (vv. 3–8), Paul asks, "how can some of you say, 'There is no resurrection of the dead'?". When the Corinthians made their statement, they were not saying with Aeschylus, "When the earth has drunk up a man's blood, once he is dead,

there is no resurrection" (*Eumenides* 647–48). They obviously accepted Christ's resurrection (15:1, "the gospel which you received") and apparently believed they were risen with him (4:8, "already you are filled! Already you have become rich! Without us you have become kings! And would that you did reign, so that we might share the rule with you"). What they seemed to deny was a future resurrection for Christians (cf. 15:19). The Corinthians, then, would be like the heretics named in 2 Tim 2:17–18: "Among them are Hymenaeus and Philetus, who have swerved from the truth by holding that the resurrection is past already." Their denial of a future resurrection would be yet another expression of the pervasive overrealized eschatology in some segments of the Corinthian church. Their resurrection they believed to have already taken place in the sense that they already experienced the resurrection mode of existence. Paul's response is given in two stages, vv. 13–15 and vv. 16–18. In both, the apostle's argument rests on the assumption that there is only one resurrection of the dead, the general resurrection. In vv. 13–15 Paul says the consequences of the Corinthian assertion (there is no resurrection of the dead) are (*a*) Christ has not been raised, (*b*) our preaching is in vain, and (*c*) your faith is in vain. In vv. 16–18 the apostle continued to enumerate the consequences of the Corinthian denial of a future resurrection: (*a*) Christ has not be raised, (*b*) your faith is futile, and (*c*) those who have fallen asleep in Christ (v. 6b) have perished.

The second Corinthian assertion comes at v. 19: "If in this life in Christ, we are *hoping only*, we are of all men most pitiful." This is the epitome of the Corinthian overrealized eschatology. It is the same sentiment that is expressed in the later Gospel of Philip: "Those who say 'They will die first and rise again' are in error. If they do not first receive the resurrection while they live, when they did they will receive nothing" (121.1–5). Tertullian, in his *On the Resurrection of the Flesh*, tells of a similar problem. Some claimed that what is usually thought of as death is not really so. Death is instead the ignorance of God. Resurrection, therefore, means that moment when one bursts forth from the sepulchre of the old man. It follows, then, that those who have attained this resurrection are with the Lord after they have once put him on in baptism. Woe, then, to anyone who has not risen in the present body. As the Corinthians put it earlier, "If we are *hoping only* [italics added], we are most pitiful" (15:19) (J. H. Schütz, "Apostolic Authority and the Control of Tradition: 1 Corinthians 15," *NTS* 15[1969]:439–56).

Paul's response is threefold (vv. 20–28; v. 29; vv. 30–32) and affirms the future character of the resurrection for Christians. (*a*) In vv. 20–28 his reply is framed in terms of an apocalyptic scheme of stages in salvation history. Christ's resurrection belongs to one stage ("Christ has been raised from the dead, the first fruits of those who have fallen asleep," v. 20), the Christians' resurrection belongs to another ("in Christ *shall* all be made alive. But each in his own order: Christ the first fruits, then at his coming those who belong to Christ," vv. 22b–23). Between Christ's resurrection and parousia is his heavenly rule ("For he must reign until he has put all enemies under his feet. The last enemy to be destroyed is death," vv. 25–26). Since death has not yet been destroyed (cf. 15:6, "some have fallen asleep"), there remains the resurrection of those in Christ, which belongs to the time of his ultimate victory and parousia. The resurrection is not past already; it is future.

(*b*) The second part of Paul's threefold response comes in v. 29: a future resurrection is implied in the meaning of Christian baptism. Although often translated and interpreted in terms of vicarious baptism as known among heretical groups in early Christianity (e.g., Marcionites, so Tertullian *Against Marcion* 5.10; Chrysostom *Homilies on 1 Cor* 40.1; Cerinthians, so Epiphanius *Heresies* 28; Montanists, so Philaster *Heresies* 49), there is no assurance that the practice was as early as the first century. V. 29 is better understood in terms of Rom 6:5: "For if we have been united with him in a death like his, we shall certainly be united with him in a resurrection like his." In early Christian baptism, the bodies of believers were immersed in a sure hope of resurrection (cf. 1 Pet 1:3). Not only the kerygma (15:3–7) but also the liturgy implied a future resurrection for believers. So understood, a translation might read, "Otherwise [i.e., if there is not a future resurrection] what will those being baptized accomplish for the corpses? If corpses are not raised at all, why are they being baptized for them?" Here, in agreement with the Greek fathers, corpses refer to the bodies of the people being baptized. If in baptism one's body is immersed in water (dying and being buried with Christ) in hope of being united with Christ in a resurrection like his, if there is no future resurrection, then what is the point of the baptismal liturgy? The common Christian experience of baptism demands belief in a future resurrection. (See B. M. Foschini, "Those Who Are Baptized for the Dead. 1 Cor 15:29," *CBQ* 12 [1950]:260–70; 379–88; 13[1951]:46–78, 172–98, 276–83, for a survey of the options; see K. C. Thompson, "I Cor 15:29 and Baptism for the Dead," *Studia Evangelica*, II, ed. F. L. Cross [Berlin: Akademie Verlag, 1964], pp. 647–59, for a position similar to that espoused here.)

(*c*) In vv. 30–32 the third part of the apostle's threefold response to the Corinthian denial of a future resurrection is found. Here he argues that sufferings are meaningful only in light of the future resurrection: "What do I gain if, humanly speaking, I fought with beasts at Ephesus? If the dead are not raised, 'Let us eat and drink, for tomorrow we die'" (cf. Heb 11:35; 2 Macc 7:9–20). The entire section concludes with the general exhortation in vv. 33–34: "Do not be deceived. . . . Come to your right mind." So ends the first half of the chapter in which Paul has argued for the resurrection of Christians and, more especially, its futurity.

(3) Vv. 35–58 consist of two Corinthian questions followed by their Pauline answers in reverse order. The first question, "How are the dead raised?" (v. 35a), is answered in vv. 50–57. The second question, "With what kind of body do they come?" (v. 35b), is answered in vv. 36–49 (Joachim Jeremias, "'Flesh and Blood Cannot Inherit the Kingdom of God,' 1 Cor 15:50," *NTS* 2[1951]:151–59).

"With what kind of body do they come?" (v. 35b; cf. 2 Baruch 49.2, "In what shape will those live in Thy day?"). This was a stock question of those skeptical about a future resurrection in Mediterranean antiquity. For example, the second-century rabbi Meir was asked the question, "When the dead rise, will they rise naked or in their clothes?" Rabbi Meir's answer is instructive. He replied that there was an analogy in a grain of wheat. If the grain of wheat is put into the earth naked and grows up in who knows how many garments, how much more should one expect appropriate attire for the raised righteous ones who are buried in their clothes (b Sanhedrin 90b).

In vv. 36–49 Paul's reply is given in two parts: (*a*) vv. 36–45 and (*b*) vv. 46–49. (*a*) Vv. 36–45 argue that the resurrection body is a different type from the body that is buried. The argument here, like Rabbi Meir's, is based initially on the analogy of a grain of wheat (vv. 36–38): "What you sow does not come to life unless it dies. And what you sow is not the body which is to be, but a bare kernel. . . . But God gives it a body as he has chosen, and to each kind of seed its own body." The apostle's point is that the plant that emerges is the same being but has a different body. There is continuity in the life-principle, but the form of its expression changes. Paul's argument then shifts to another analogy (vv. 39–45). In antiquity it was believed the different classes of animals were composed of different kinds of matter. Galen, for example, thought the flesh of lions differed from that of lambs. So Paul says, "Not all flesh is alike, but there is one kind for men, another for animals, another for birds, and another for fish" (v. 39). Likewise, it was believed that the character of the heavenly bodies (sun, stars, moon) differed from that of earthly forms and it was recognized that each of the heavenly bodies had its own distinctive radiance (sun, stars, moon). "So is it with the resurrection of the dead. What is sown is perishable, what is raised is imperishable" (v. 42). The point is the same as with the first analogy: the resurrection body is different from that which is buried. (*b*) Vv. 46–49, the second part of the apostle's reply to the question, "With what kind of body do they come?" (v. 35b), argue that the resurrection body comes after the fleshly body: "It is not the spiritual which is first but the physical, and then the spiritual" (v. 46).

"How are the dead raised?" (v. 35a). This may be taken in either of two ways. On the one hand, it may be read as a rhetorical question meaning, "Is it possible for the dead to be raised?" (R. J. Sider, "The Pauline Conception of the Resurrection Body in 1 Cor 15:35–54," *NTS* 21[1975]:428–39). Paul's answer is that it is no more incredible for the dead to be raised than for the living to be changed. Both are necessary because "flesh and blood [i.e., those alive at the parousia] cannot inherit the kingdom of God, nor does the perishable [corpses in decomposition] inherit the imperishable" (v. 50). Or on the other hand, the question may be taken to mean, "How will it happen?" Paul's answer comes as the revelation of a mystery (v. 51; cf. Rom 16:25–26; Eph 3:4–5, 9–10; Col 1:26–27; Rev 10:7; 1 Enoch 103.2; 104.10, 12) whose content is similar to that of 1 Thess 4:15–17: "We shall not all sleep, but we shall all be changed" (v. 51), that is, some will live until the parousia, but even they will be transformed. "For the trumpet will sound, and the dead will be raised imperishable, and we shall be changed. For this perishable nature must put on the imperishable, and this mortal nature must put on immortality" (vv. 52–53). Immediately at the parousia, the dead are raised and those alive (among whom Paul reckoned himself, "we") are transformed. At this point (the parousia), "Death is swallowed up in victory" (v. 54b). How is this process possible? "Thanks be to God, who gives us the victory through our Lord Jesus Christ" (v. 57; cf. 15:26). "How are the dead raised" (v. 35a)? Paul's answer is that God does it; he does it through Christ's defeat of God's enemies, including death; and he does it at the parousia when the dead are raised and the living are changed.

The positions taken in 1 Cor 15 are sharpened when they are seen against the backdrop of Jewish expectations of the period. Belief in resurrection from the dead has its roots in the Jewish soil out of which Christianity came. At the same time, it is also necessary to say that there is no single Jewish doctrine of life after death as late as the first century A.D. A spectrum of opinion is helpful in sensitizing one to Jewish diversity. (*a*) A number of Jewish sources are silent about life after death (e.g., Ecclus, Jth, Tob, Aristeas, 1 Bar, 1 Macc, 3 Macc, Letter of Jeremiah, Assumption of Moses, Martyrdom of Isaiah). Whether this is due merely to the fact that such a reference was inappropriate, given the subject matter, or to the possible continuation of the old Israelite conception of immortality as limited to the perpetuation of one's name through offspring would need to be argued in each case. (*b*) Some Jews explicitly denied life after death (e.g., the Sadducees, so Josephus *War* 2.8.14 §165; *Antiquities* 18.1.4 §16; Mark 12:18; Acts 23:8; m Sanhedrin 10:1; certain unnamed heretics who may or may not be Sadducees, so m Berakoth 9:5c). (*c*) Certain Jews thought of life after death in terms of the immortality of the soul, exclusive of the body (e.g., the Essenes, so Josephus *War* 2.8.11 §154–57; *Antiquities* 18.1.5 §18; Testament of Abraham; 4 Macc; Wisd of Sol). (*d*) Others looked for the resurrection of a physical body, either this one or a new one, for life on this earth (Sibylline Oracles 4.171–90; Genesis Rabbah 14.5; Leviticus Rabbah 14.9; the morning benediction). (*e*) Still others who thought in terms of a resurrection conceived of it as a transformation or glorification of the body for life in a new heavens and earth (1 Enoch 51.1, 4; Pseudo-Philo *Biblical Antiquities* 3.10; 4 Ezra 8:52–54; Apocalypse of Moses 13.3–6). (*f*) On occasion, combinations of the immortality of the soul and either of the two resurrection positions are found, with the former sometimes relegated to an intermediate state (Josephus's own position; Pseudo-Phocylides 99–115; Testament of Job; Testament of Twelve Patriarchs). (*g*) On occasion, a combination of the two views of resurrection are found, the restoration of life to dead corpses followed by their transformation or glorification (2 Baruch 49–52). (*h*) In at least one case, there is a type of realized eschatology. The reception of a proselyte signifies her resurrection to new life, including a transformation and glorification which resembles the one expected for the righteous in the new world in the more futuristic eschatological texts (*Joseph and Aseneth*) (Hans C. C. Cavallin, *Life After Death: Paul's Argument for the Resurrection of the Dead in 1 Cor 15, Part I—An Enquiry into the Jewish Background* [Lund: Gleerup, 1974]).

Against this background, one can see the Corinthians positioned near (*h*), a realized eschatology. Paul in 1 Cor 15 fits into a stance like (*e*), resurrection conceived of as a transformation or glorification of the body for life in a new environment. If one takes into account the apostle's statements elsewhere (e.g., 2 Cor 5:6–9; Phil 1:21–24), then he would seem to fit into category (*f*), with the immortality of the soul viewed as an intermediate state prior to a transforming bodily resurrection. If this is so, then Paul's is not an anthropological monism but an anthropological dualism of sorts. He believes that it is possible for the soul or spirit alone to survive death. This does not commit him, however, to the belief that matter or the body is evil as such. Nor does it commit him to the preexistence of the soul. He looks forward to the resurrection of the dead. And since he does have this hope, he can conclude the chapter with an exhortation: "Therefore, my beloved brethren, be steadfast, immovable, always abounding in the work of the Lord, knowing that in the Lord your labor is not in vain" (v. 58).

Now that the train of thought in 1 Cor 15 has been traced, it may be helpful to summarize the positions of Paul and his opponents. Let us look first of all at the Corinthian stance. Their position is captured in their four contentions/questions. (1) "There is no resurrection of the dead." In light of 1 Cor 4:8 and other signs of an overrealized eschatology among certain of the Corinthians, it seems best to take this in terms of 2 Tim 2:18 to mean a denial of a future resurrection on the basis of their present religious experience. (2) "If Christians look only to the future, they are to be pitied." This is to be taken as a condescending comment by Christians who believed they already participated in a resurrection mode of life. (3) "How are the dead raised?" This was a stock skeptical inquiry. It questioned both whether resurrection was at all possible and the method of its happening. (4) "With what kind of body do they come?" This was another stock mocking question which implied the ridiculous nature of belief in a future resurrection (cf. Mark 12:18–27 for a similar mocking question).

The Pauline response is twofold. On the one hand, he says that the consequences of denying a future resurrection are impossible to contemplate. If one denies the future resurrection, it means (*a*) a denial of the common kerygmatic tradition of the apostles; (*b*) the futility of the religious experience of the Corinthian Christians; (*c*) a denial of the facts of everyday experience (i.e., that death still exists); (*d*) an emptying of the act of baptism of its meaning; (*e*) a removal of a major incentive for enduring suffering in the present. On the other hand, the apostle reiterates the Christian stance about the resurrection: (*a*) it lies in the future; it will occur at the parousia of Christ; and (*b*) it will involve transformation of both the living and the dead.

PLANS, PRESCRIPTIONS, AND PLEASANTRIES

1 Corinthians 16

1 Cor 16:1-24 consists of three components. The first is Paul's answers to the two final questions raised in the Corinthians' letter (vv. 1-11, "now concerning the collection"; v. 12, "now concerning Apollos"). The second is the concluding paraenesis (vv. 13-18). The third is the closing of the letter form (vv. 19-24). Each merits separate attention.

The first component of 1 Cor 16 is vv. 1-12, which falls into two parts (vv. 1-11 and v. 12), each introduced with the standard signal for a Pauline answer to a question raised in the letter sent by Corinth to the apostle (7:1, 25; 8:1; 12:1; 16:1, 12, "now concerning"). Vv. 1-11 begin, "Now concerning the contribution for the saints." The reference is to the collection Paul was undertaking in his Gentile Christian churches for the Jewish Christian poor in Jerusalem (cf. Gal 2:10; 2 Cor 8-9; Rom 15:24-33; Acts 24:17). V. 12 begins, "Now concerning our brother Apollos." The reference is to the eloquent preacher who worked alongside Paul in the Aegean area (1:12; 3:5-6; 4:6; Acts 18:24-19:1). The entire section is tied together by the link word "come" (*elthō*, v. 2; *eleusomai*, v. 5; *elthē*, v. 10; *elthō, elthē,* and *eleusetai*, v. 12). This indicates that vv. 1-12 function, in part at least, as communication of travel plans, Paul's and others'.

Paul's travel plans are initially tied to the collection (vv. 1-4). The procedure the apostle recommends for gathering the collection in Corinth is the same he suggested for Galatia. On the first day of the week (i.e., Sunday was already the Christians' day of worship), "each of you is to put something aside and store it up [i.e., systematically], as he may prosper [i.e., proportionately], so that contributions need not be made when I come [i.e., not under duress]." The procedure he proposes for getting the collection to Jerusalem involves two parts, one clear-cut, the other a possibility. For sure, the gift will be taken by those whom the Corinthians approve (v. 3a). It is not clear whether the letter that will accompany

105

the delegates is sent by the Corinthians as part of their accreditation (so RSV) or by Paul as their introduction (so NEB). Either is possible. Further, if it seems advisable, Paul will go along (v. 3b).

The apostle envisions staying in Ephesus (where 1 Cor was written) until Pentecost (late spring) because of the effectiveness of his work there at the moment (vv. 8–9). Then he plans to go through Macedonia (v. 5) and on to Corinth where he hopes to stay for a while, even the winter (winter was no time for journeys, especially on the sea, Acts 27:9–12), before going on elsewhere (vv. 6–7). At this point, Paul did not foresee the necessity of the painful, intermediate visit that would have to be made (2 Cor 2:1) nor the difficult time he would have getting the Corinthians to complete their part of the collection (2 Cor 8–9).

1 Cor was delivered by Timothy (16:10; 4:17). Paul asks both for a good reception for him ("put him at ease," v. 10; "let no one despise him," v. 11) and for assistance in his return journey to Ephesus ("speed him on his way," v. 11).

The Corinthians had obviously asked about Apollos. Paul's explanation that he had tried to persuade Apollos to go to Corinth and that it was Apollos's decision not to come at this time (v. 12) may indicate a Corinthian suspicion that the apostle had hindered Apollos's arrival. At this point, travel plans give way to paraenesis.

The concluding paraenesis in vv. 13–18 falls into two groupings. The first, in vv. 13–14, calls for the hearers to be watchful, to stand firm, to be courageous, to be strong, to act in love. The second, in vv. 15–18, urges the Corinthians to give recognition and to be subject to the household of Stephanas, the first converts in Achaia. Three key terms used here (be subject, watch, stand) are found in the deutero-Paulines and elsewhere in household codes (be subject, Eph 5:21, 24; Col 3:18; 1 Tim 2:11; Tit 2:9; 3:1; 1 Pet 3:1; 5:5; James 4:7; watch, Col 4:2; 1 Pet 5:8; stand, Eph 6:11, 13–14; Col 4:12; 1 Pet 4:12). Whether or not such Christian household codes existed as early as the time of 1 Corinthians, we do not know. We, therefore, do not know if the language here reflects Paul's knowledge and use of such material.

The closing of the letter form comes in vv. 19–24. There are first of all the greetings (vv. 19–20a). Note that Aquila and Priscilla are now in Ephesus. Paul, though dictating the letter, adds his greeting in his own hand. Then comes what may be a liturgical sequence. There are several parts to it: (1) the holy kiss (v. 20b, cf. 1 Thess 5:26; Rom 16:16; 2 Cor 13:12); (2) the pronounciation of the anathema (v. 22a, cf. Didache

10.5, 6–7; Lucian *Alexander* 38); (3) the prayer *maranatha* (v. 22b, cf. Rev 22:20; Didache 10.6); (4) the grace (v. 23); (5) the Amen (v. 24b) (John A. T. Robinson, "The Earliest Christian Liturgical Sequence?" *Twelve New Testament Studies* [London:SCM, 1962], pp. 154–57; G. Bornkamm, "On the Understanding of Worship," in *Early Christian Experience* [New York: Harper & Row, 1969], pp. 161–79). On the basis of later Christian practice (e.g., Didache 9.5, "But let no one eat or drink of your Eucharist but those who have been baptized in the name of the Lord"; 10.6, "If anyone is holy, let him come; if any one is not, let him repent" 10.7, "Lord, come quickly. Amen"; Justin *1 Apology* 65, "When we have ceased from prayer, we salute one another with a kiss. There is then brought to the president bread and wine"; Acts of John 84–85, exclusion from the Eucharist before celebration) and pagan analogies ("If any atheist or Christian or Epicurean has come to spy on the rites, let him be off, and let those who believe in the god perform the mysteries, under the blessing of heaven" [Lucian *Alexander* 38]), it has been suggested that 1 Corinthians functioned as the sermon in a Corinthian worship service and that 16:20b–24 served as a transition to the celebration of the Eucharist which would follow. Whether what was clearly a part of later Christian worship existed this early remains uncertain.

THE SORRY NECESSITY OF SELF-PRAISE

2 Cor 10–13 is a large thought unit which falls into an ABA' pattern:

    A. Looking forward to his presence with them (10:1–11)
     B. Proper and foolish boasting (10:12–12:13)
    A'. Looking forward to his presence with them (12:14–13:10).

Except for 13:11–14, it has the character of a body of a letter (note the request formula, 10:1–2). If this is part of a separate letter, as this commentary contends, then it has lost its beginning.

The first subsection, (A), is 10:1–11. This material is held together by an inclusion (v. 2, "when present"; v. 11, "when present"). The unit consists of either echoes or quotations of five assertions made by Paul's Corinthian challenger and his sympathizers together with the apostle's response to each. That this was a standard literary technique may be seen from Apuleius of Madaura's *Apology*, a long defense against the charge of magic in which Apuleius quotes the accusations raised against him before answering them.

The initial charge against Paul is echoed in v. 1b: "I who am humble when face to face with you, but bold to you when I am away." The charge is basically that of the fifth assertion in v. 10: "His letters are weighty and strong, but his bodily presence is weak, and his speech of no account." In a sense, v. 10 is the clue to the interpretation of the entire subsection, 10:1–11.

In v. 10 the term *phēsin* may be translated in a number of ways (he, she says; one says; it is said). As it is used here, it is typical of the diatribe form of antiquity (e.g., Epictetus 4.9.5–6; Chrysostom *Epistle to Colossians* chap. 3, homily 8.5) and should be read either as "one says" or as "it is said," following the best Greek text (contra RSV, "they say") George L. Kustas, *Diatribe in Ancient Rhetorical Theory* [Berkeley, Cal.: Center for Hermeneutical Studies, 1976], p. 11). Granting that "one says" allows the objection to be presented in typical diatribe style, why would this contention and that of 10:1b have been made? By whom? The explanation that seems to fit the facts best is the following. In 1 Cor 4:18–21 Paul had said he would discipline those who were out of line when he came again and in 1 Cor 5 had written a bold excommunication order for one violator. When he returned on his intermediate visit, however, he did not follow through and act either as he had promised or as he had done in his letter (1 Cor 5). This led to a charge by one individual in the Corinthian church that Paul was not really a spiritually authoritative apostle but only a man of the flesh. When Paul withdrew without responding to this attack as well, the charge found sympathy among at least some of the church's membership. Near the time that Paul's behavior was being judged inadequate by some Corinthians, certain visiting apostles came through Corinth. Their behavior embodied both the ideals of the individual who attacked Paul and those of the attacker's sympathizers. Consequently the attack on the apostle became like a two-sided coin. On the one side, Paul's behavior in Corinth on the intermediate visit was weak. On the other side, the visiting apostles demonstrated what Paul had not—spiritual authority. Vv. 1b and 10 echo the first side of the coin and reflect both the individual's attack on Paul (v. 10, "one says") and some community support for the attacker's position (v. 2, "some"). The "anyone" of v. 7 probably reflects the claims of the visiting apostles (11:23) as verbalized by Paul's Corinthian attacker and his sympathizers as a disparagement of Paul. In 2 Cor 10:1–11, therefore, one is not hearing charges made against Paul by the interlopers so much as attacks made upon Paul by a Corinthian individual and his cohorts in light of Paul's behavior on his intermediate visit (Francis Watson, "2 Cor 10–13 and Paul's Painful Letter to the Corinthians," *JTS* 35[1984]: 324–46; Derk William Oostendorp, *Another Jesus: A Gospel of Jewish-Christian Superiority in 2 Corinthians* [Kampen: J. H. Kok, 1967], pp. 17–27). The one side of the coin is dealt with in 10:1–11; the other side will be handled in 10:12–12:13.

In response to charges one and five (vv. 1b, 10), Paul counters with a plea ("Please do not make it necessary for me to be bold when present," v. 2a) and a promise ("Let such people understand that what we say by letter when absent , we do when present," v. 11). Doubtless the type of behavior that was expected and which he would reluctantly employ is that exemplified in Acts 5:1–11 and 13:8–11.

The second accusation made against Paul is that he is walking according to the flesh (v. 2b). This could be understood in either of two ways: either Paul is accused of acting out of worldly motives with egocentric conduct, or he is charged with being without spiritual power (1 Cor 3:1). The latter reading fits this context better. Since Paul did not act in a spiritually authoritative manner on his painful visit, he must be merely a man of flesh, not a spiritual man of power. To this he responds, "While walking in the flesh, we do not carry on a war according to the flesh. For the weapons of our warfare are not fleshly but are powerful in God" (vv. 3–4a). Paul, like his later followers (Eph 6:11–17; 1 Tim 1:18; 2 Tim 2:3–4; 4:7), understood the Christian life not only as a walk but also as a warfare. As such, it was conducted with spiritual weapons associated with divine power (1 Thess 5:8; 2 Cor 6:7). The divine power manifested in Paul's ministry accomplishes three things: (1) it demolishes fortifications (v. 4b), that is, every obstacle to the knowledge of God; (2) it takes captives (v. 5b), that is, every thought captive to Christ; and (3) it punishes resistance (v. 6), that is, those who need discipline because of improper conduct. But note that Paul has delayed (3) until the Corinthians as a community have completed their obedience, that is, sided with Paul against his opposition. The apostle acts in continuity here with his expectations elsewhere (1 Cor 5:1–13; 6:1–11) that the Corinthians as a community are to deal with deviant behavior (A. J. Malherbe shows how Paul uses the common language of warfare from his milieu ["Antisthenes and Odysseus, and Paul at War," *HTR* 76 (1983):143–73]).

Charges three (v. 7b, "I am of Christ," says someone, with the obvious inference "but Paul is not") and four (v. 8a, "Paul boasts too much of his authority," with the obvious inference "but does not actualize it when it is needed") are two sides of the same coin. The issue is still that Paul has not acted with a demonstration of power as one who belongs to Christ would. Paul can only say that he does belong to Christ but that his authority is for building up the Corinthians, not destroying them (vv. 7b, 8b; contrast Acts 5:1–11; 13:6–12; Jer 1:9b–10). 2 Cor 10:1–11, then, has focused on the Corinthian individual's charges against Paul, together with the apostle's responses. The conclusion looks forward to his presence with them and the possibility that he may indeed have to use the power he has to date withheld (v. 11).

The second and major subsection of 2 Cor 10–13 is (B), 10:12–12:13, Proper and Foolish Boasting. In this unit Paul focuses firstly on proper boasting, vv. 12–18. An inclusion ("commend," v. 12; "commends,"

v. 18) holds the section together. It is composed of an introduction (v. 12) followed by two corresponding parts, vv. 13–14 and vv. 15–18. In the introductory statement of v. 12, the apostle rejects comparing himself with others who commend themselves after measuring themselves by one another (preferring the longer over the Western text). Certain background information assists our understanding.

Comparison was a fundamental tool of rhetoric in antiquity. Aristotle advocated comparison as a means of developing one's material in a speech of praise or blame. Compare your subject, he says, with illustrious persons if he can be shown to be better, or with ordinary persons if not, "since superiority is thought to indicate virtue" (*Rhetoric* 1368a). The *Rhetorica ad Alexandrum* supports comparison between that which one is praising and things in the same class, in order to magnify one's subject by the contrast (1426a). It should be no surprise, then, that the device was used by teachers to call attention to themselves and to gain followers thereby (cf. P Oxy 2190). For example, Lucian has the professor say to the new student, "Do not expect to see something that you can compare with So-and-so, or So-and-so; no, you will consider the achievement far too prodigious and amazing even for Tityus or Ephialtes. Indeed, as far as the others are concerned, you will find out that I drown them out as effectively as trumpets drown flutes." The teacher goes on to suggest that his pupil cultivate the same methods of advertisement: "if anyone accosts you, make marvellous assertions about yourself, be extravagant in your self-praise" ("A Professor of Public Speaking" 13.21). Excesses in this practice led both to cautions and to disavowals of the practice. Theon in *Preliminary Exercises* cautions that comparisons are not to be drawn between things that are vastly different from each other, as Paul felt the visiting apostles in Corinth were doing when they compared themselves with him (2 Cor 11:12). Others eschewed the practice altogether. Plutarch contends that it is most unstatesmanlike to pit oneself against the praise and fame of others (*On Praising Oneself Inoffensively* 545D). He advocates self-comparison (*On the Tranquil Life* 470C). Epictetus also rejects comparison with others (3.22.60). The danger was that one would become a boaster, a pretentious man. Aristotle put it, "To speak at great length about oneself, and to make all kinds of professions; and to take the credit for what another has done . . . this is a sign of pretentiousness" (*Rhetoric* 1384a) (C. Forbes, "Comparison, Self-Praise and Irony: Paul's Boasting and the Conventions of Hellenistic Rhetoric," *NTS* 32[1986]:1–30). Paul's apostolic competitors in Corinth were obviously people who used the rhetorical technique of comparison of themselves with their peers, claiming superiority as a way of gaining followers. Paul rejects this procedure in v. 12.

The first of the two corresponding parts of 10:12–18 is vv.13–14: "we will not boast beyond limit" (v. 13a). It continues, "but will keep to the limits God has apportioned us" (v. 13b). The limits prescribed by God for Paul's ministry were twofold. First, he was to evangelize the Gentiles. That was his task (Gal 2:9; Rom 1:5). Second, he was to preach in places where Christ was not already known. He was to be a pioneer church planter (Rom 15:20). It is the latter that is in view here. Given his limits, Paul was right in coming to Corinth: "we were the first to come all the way to you with the gospel of Christ" (v. 14b). The second of the two parts is vv. 15–18, which repeats the assertion, "we do not boast beyond limit," and adds, "in other men's labors" (v. 15a). It continues, "but our hope is . . . that we may preach the gospel in lands beyond you" (v. 16a). Again, Paul is staying within his limits. The subsection ends with an exhortation: "Let him who boasts, boast of the Lord" (Jer 9:24 LXX). The reason is given: "For it is not the man who commends himself that is accepted, but the man whom the Lord commends." In this context, the implication is that since the Corinthians became Christians when Paul preached to them, the Lord has validated or commended Paul's ministry (1 Cor 2:1–5). If Paul boasts, it is in the Lord who poured out his Spirit on the Corinthians at their conversion. When the visiting apostles compare themselves to Paul, they are boasting beyond limit because they are not pioneer apostles. Proper boasting is not a claim to superiority over another but glorying in the task and authority one has been given by God and in one's commendation by God (cf. Prov 27:2; Jer 9:23–24; Judg 7:2; 1 Sam 2:3).

Having dealt briefly with proper boasting (10:12–18), Paul now turns to a lengthy exercise in foolish boasting (11:1–12:13). This section is held together by an inclusion (11:5, "not inferior to these superlative apostles"; 12:11, "not inferior to these superlative apostles") and by the repetition of the key words "fool" (11:16, 17, 19, 21; 12:6, 11), "foolish" (11:16), and "foolishness" (11:1). Before it is possible to trace the train of thought in this unit, several items of background information are necessary.

The first item of background information that needs to be supplied concerns the visiting apostles with whom Paul had been disparagingly compared by the Corinthian challenger and his sympathizers. Whereas 1 Corinthians dealt with problems that were indigenous to the church in

Corinth, in 2 Corinthians there is the additional matter of visiting apostles whose style was different enough from Paul's that, in the minds of some, he came off second best. The charges against Paul's apostolic authority, made because of his behavior on the intermediate visit, were not only that in person he was not a powerful apostle but also that by comparison to the interlopers he came off second best. This is why he faced the need to deal with the matter of the other apostles. Both Paul and his apostolic rivals are best understood in terms of the larger cultural context (D. Georgi, *Paul's Opponents in Second Corinthians* [Philadelphia: Fortress, 1986], chap. 2, "Missionary Activity in New Testament Times").

The period of the early empire witnessed a strong missionary impulse. The various philosophies and cults of the Greco-Roman world strove for converts. Philostratus's *Life of Apollonius of Tyana* tells of a wandering neo-Pythagorean philosopher so engaged. Lucian's *Alexander the False Prophet* speaks of a successful attempt to establish a new religious cult and oracle. Juvenal recounts the evangelistic techniques of the priests of Cybele (*Satires* 6.511–41). Apuleius speaks of wandering preachers from the Cynics and from the Oriental religions (*Metamorphoses* 8.24; 11.8). Strategies for evangelization involved both itinerant teaching/preaching/ miracle working and the public display of certain dimensions of the cult.

Ancient Judaism shared this missionary zeal. At Antioch the Jews made converts of a great number of Greeks perpetually (Josephus *War* 7.3.3 §45); at Damascus the wives of almost all were addicted to the Jewish religion (Josephus *War* 2.20.2 §561); at Alexandria Jews needed the emperor's reminder to keep their own laws and not show contempt for the observances of others (Josephus *Antiquities* 19.5.3 §290); in Rome Jewish men (Josephus *Antiquities* 18.3.5 §81) and women (Juvenal *Satires* 6.541–47) alike strove for converts. Jewish legend told not only of the last king of Babylon, Nabonidus, being evangelized through a healing and pardoning of sins by a Jewish exorcist of the exile (*Prayer of Nabonidus* 1.4), but also of the conversion of queen Helena of Adiabene and her son Izates by at least three different Jews (Josephus *Antiquities* 20.2.3–4 §142) and of the conversion of Aseneth, daughter of a prominent pagan family of Egypt (*Joseph and Aseneth*). With these witnesses one may compare Matt 23:15. The strategies for evangelization included not only itinerant miracle workers (Josephus *Antiquities* 8.2.5 §45–49; Acts 19:13–16), teachers (Juvenal *Satires* 6.542–47), and merchants (Josephus *Antiquities* 20.2.3–4 §142), but also the synagogue service (Philo *Moses* 2.17–25).

The early Christians also shared the missionary impulse. Traveling evangelists were everywhere present. Matt 10, Luke 10, and Mark 6 all contain instructions for such missionaries. The Acts of the Apostles presents us with a narrative of evangelistic outreach. 2 John 10, 3 John 5–8, 10, Didache 11–12 also attest the itinerant Christian evangelist. Luke 10:9; Mark 6:12–13; Acts 6:8–10; 8:6–8; 14:8–18 link miracle and proclamation in this itinerant ministry. Paul himself was such a traveling missionary (Rom 15:18–32), as were his rivals in 2 Corinthians. Like pagans and Jews, the early Christians also used certain dimensions of their public worship to evangelize (cf. 1 Cor 14:23–25). The implication of this evidence for our understanding of 2 Corinthians is that neither Paul nor his apostolic rivals in Corinth were singular figures in antiquity but were typical not only of a large number of missionaries in the early church but also were Christian examples of a general cultural phenomenon in Greco-Roman and Jewish antiquity—the itinerant evangelist-missionary.

In the case of both Paul (1 Cor 1:1; 2 Cor 1:1; 12:12) and the visitors to Corinth (2 Cor 11:5, 13; 12:11), one of their self-designations was apostle. Again there is nothing distinctive about this in Christian circles. In early Christianity, apostle was the designation for a large circle without numerical limits (e.g., Rom 16:17; 2 Cor 11:13; 8:23; Phil 2:25, for the time of Paul; Rev 2:2; Didache 11.3–6, for just before and after A.D. 100). Some tried to set limits on the circle. Paul's limit was temporal. According to 1 Cor 15:7–8, he was the last. A generation after Paul, Luke-Acts also tried to set a limit that was both numerical and temporal. According to Acts 1:21–22, the apostles were twelve in number and were made up of those who had been with Jesus from the baptism of John until Jesus' ascension. Rev 2:2 and Didache 11.3–6 testify to the immediate ineffectiveness of such limits. There were many traveling missionaries/apostles in antiquity. Paul and his Corinthian rivals were different examples of the Christian variety.

Given the diversity of early Christianity, it is not surprising that different types of apostles should exist. One obvious difference between Paul and the interlopers was that Paul worked where no one else had yet gone (Rom 15:20; 2 Cor 10:15–16), while the subsequent visitors to Corinth worked where churches had already been established (cf. similar apostles in Didache 11). Another difference, as will be seen, is that Paul did not accept money from the Corinthians for his ministry while the visitors did (2 Cor 12:11–13). A more difficult difference to clarify is theological. Yet Paul felt it was so great that he called the interlopers preachers of another gospel (11:4). They were, he believed, false apostles (11:13). This difference can only be clarified as one reads through 2 Corinthians. The one thing that can be said at this point is negative. Contra Georgi, the difference was not that the visitors were miracle workers while Paul was a suffering speaker of the word. In any case, these visiting apostles were being held up by one member of the Corinthian church and his sympathizers as the model for true apostleship. By comparison, Paul allegedly came off second best.

The second item of background information that may facilitate one's understanding of 2 Cor 11:1–12:13 concerns its literary form, self-praise. Self-praise was the stock-in-trade of many ancient teachers. It was viewed negatively by the Old Testament (e.g., 1 Kings 20:11; Prov 27:2; Jer 9:23–24) and by certain philosophical circles (e.g., Philostratus apologizes for inserting the philosopher's defense speech before Domitian because it made him sound like a rhetorician [*Life of Apollonius* 8.7]). It was this tradition partially reflected by Paul in 2 Cor 10:12–18. But by the time of the New Testament period certain self-praise was considered all right. Plutarch says self-praise is permissible when defending one's good name, when on trial, and when one is wronged or slandered (*On Inoffensive Self-Praise*). Given his circumstances in 2 Cor 10–13 (e.g., 12:11; 10:1–11), Paul would have received Plutarch's permission to engage in self-praise.

Plutarch says certain rules are to be followed when engaging in self-praise. (*a*) One should mix in with one's self-praise certain shortcomings or blemishes in order to temper with shade the blaze of one's glory (*On Inoffensive Self-Praise* 13). 2 Cor 11:30–33 and 12:8–9 fit this criterion. (*b*) One may boast of one's care and worry over others (14). 2 Cor 11:1–4; 11:28–29; and 12:19 satisfy this rule. (*c*) One's self-praise should be coupled with exhortation so that some advantage to the hearer may be gained (15). 2 Cor 11:1–12:13 is followed by a series of exhortations (e.g., 13:5, 11a) and preceded by others (e.g., 10:2, 6). (*d*) Where mistaken praise of others injures or corrupts by arousing emulation of evil and adoption of unsound policy, it is no disservice to counteract it by pointing out the difference between oneself and the other (17). 2 Cor 10:13–18; 11:12–15; 11:23–29 meet the requirements of this test. It is difficult, in light of the remarkable correspondences between 2 Cor 10–13 and Plutarch's statement of general custom, to deny that in these chapters Paul is engaging in what was called inoffensive self-praise. At the same time, it is clear that the apostle is very uncomfortable with his use of this literary technique (11:1, "bear with me in a little foolishness"; 11:17, "what I am saying I say not with the Lord's authority but as a fool"; 11:21, "I am speaking as a fool"; 11:23, "I am talking like a madman"; 12:1, "I must boast; there is nothing to be gained by it"; 12:11, "I have been a fool! You forced me to it, for I ought to have been commended by you"), as someone with a Hebraic value system would be. That he uses this rhetorical device is testimony to the straits he is in (E. A. Judge, "Paul's Boasting in Relation to Contemporary Professional Practice," *ABR* 16 [1968]: 37–50; H.D. Betz, *Paul's Apology 2 Cor 10–13 and the Socratic Tradition* [Berkeley, Cal.:Center for Hermeneutical Studies, 1970]; S. H. Travis, "Paul's Boasting in 2 Cor 10–12," *Studia Evangelica VI* [Berlin: Akademie Verlag, 1973], pp. 527–32).

Although in 11:1 Paul asks his readers to put up with a little foolishness, it is not until v. 16 that this actually occurs. Between 11:1 and 11:16 is a digression giving Paul's reason for his foolish boasting, namely, his fear that the Corinthians will be deceived. 2 Cor 11:2–15 is a unit held together by an inclusion (11:3–4, the serpent and Paul's opponents; 11:14–15, Satan and Paul's opponents). The boundaries of the section are also signaled by v. 1 ("I wish you would bear with me in a little foolishness") and v. 16 ("I repeat, let no one think me foolish"). Within the inclusion are four claims made by Paul's Corinthian opponents, together with the apostle's responses.

As he sets forth his reason for boasting foolishly, Paul compares himself to the father of the bride who has arranged a betrothal (i.e., the founding of the Corinthian church) and who watches jealously over the bride's conduct before the wedding which is to take place when Christ returns at the parousia (11:2). Between betrothal and marriage, the father (Paul) fears lest the church, like Eve, be deceived by the enemy's cunning and led astray (v. 3). According to Jewish law, the violation of a betrothed virgin was no less serious than if the marriage had already been consummated (Deut 22:23–27; Philo *Special Laws* 1.107; 3.72). (For marriage language used for the relation between Christ and the church, cf. Eph 5:23–32; Rev 19:7–9; 21:2, 9.)

Ancient Judaism's speculations about the origins of evil encompassed existential, historical, and metaphysical theories. (1) Existentially, evil arose from the evil *yetzer* (Gen 6:5; 8:21; 2 Esd 3:21–22; 4:30; rabbinic literature, passim). (2) Historically, evil was believed to have originated as described in Gen 3 (Adam and Eve). Sometimes blame was placed upon Adam's shoulders (e.g., 2 Esd 7:118; 2 Baruch 54.15; 48.42–43); sometimes it was levelled at Eve (e.g., Ecclus 25:24; Life of Adam and Eve 44.2–5; Jubilees 3.17–35; 4 Macc 18:8). Occasionally Eve's sin is understood as sexual seduction (Apocalypse of Abraham 23; 2 Enoch 31.6). (3) Metaphysically, evil's origin was believed to lie either with the watchers of Gen 6 (1 Enoch 6–11, 85–90) or with Satan (Wisd of Sol 2:23) or with the evil spirits that struggle in the hearts of humans (1 QS 3.17–21; 3.21–24; 4.15–17, 23).

Paul's views on the matter also require these three dimensions. (1) Existentially, sin originates in human perversion of divine revelation by Gentile idolatry (Rom 1:18–32) and Jewish disobedience (Rom 2:17–29). (2) Historically, Gen 3 furnishes an explanation for the presence of evil, whether through Adam's act (Rom 5:12–21) or Eve's deception (2 Cor 11:3). (3) Metaphysically, evil originates with Satan and the evil spirits (2 Cor 11:3; 4:4; 2:11; 1 Cor 7:5). In 2 Cor 11:3, Paul appropriates the motif of Eve's deception because it fits the particular case he is arguing. It is significant that when the apostle is focusing on sin's origin as such (Rom 5:12–21), he speaks of Adam's disobedience.

In the period after Paul, (1) an existential origin of evil is found in the two *yetzers* theory of Hermas "Command" 12, and Justin *1 Apology* 10; (2) the historical origin of sin is expressed in 1 Tim 2:11–14; Justin *Dialogue* 100 (Eve) and 88 (Adam); and (3) the metaphysical origin of evil is found in the appropriation of the legend of the watchers by Jude 6–7 and 2 Peter 1:4; 2:4, and belief in Satan's power by the Epistle of Barnabas 12.5.

Many of the early fathers, appealing almost exclusively to 1 Tim 2:14, cast Eve in a negative light as the first sinner (Irenaeus *Against Heresies* 3.22.4; Tertullian *On the Dress of Women* 1.1–2; Ambrose *On Paradise* 4.24; Augustine *Literal Commentary on Genesis* 11.42; 12.56; Chrysostom *Homily 26 on 1 Corinthians* 2; *Discourse 4 on Genesis* 1). She loosed trouble on the world by her disobedience in part because of her inferiority (Tertullian *On the Dress of Women* 1.1–2; Augustine *Literal Commentary on Genesis* 11.42). It is difficult to escape the impression that at this point the Greek traditions about Pandora (Hesiod *Theogony* 11.570– 612; *Works and Days* 11.55–105) have affected the Christian perspective (John A. Phillips, *Eve; The History of an Idea* [San Francisco: Harper & Row, 1984]).

In the context of 2 Cor 11, it is not certain whether or not Eve's deception by the serpent is simply being led astray (as in Ecclus 25:24) or is understood in sexual terms as being seduced by the snake so that she lost her virginity in unfaithfulness (e.g., 2 Enoch 31.6; Apocalypse of Abraham 23), although the latter fits Paul's image better. In any case, Paul feels that Corinthian allegiance to these interlopers runs the risk of spiritual adultery. For this reason he will boast, inoffensively, of course.

But first there are four more assertions that must be challenged. (1) V.

5 echoes someone's sentiment that Paul is inferior to the superlative apostles from outside. The designation of them as "superlative" is sarcastic because of their exaggerated claims for themselves. Paul's reply in vv. 5–6 ("Even if I am unskilled in speaking, I am not in knowledge") is similar to that of philosophers in the Socratic tradition who disdained the pretentiousness of the Sophists: for example, Dio Chrysostom in such a context denies trying to equal such men in their speech ("For they are clever persons, mighty sophists, wonder workers; but I am quite ordinary and prosaic in my utterance, though not ordinary in my theme" [*Discourse* 32.39]). Paul's words drip with irony. (2) V. 7 implies that Paul acknowledged his inferiority as an apostle by not taking money from the Corinthians (cf. 1 Cor 9:4–5). In vv. 8–10 the apostle replies that his not accepting money from Corinth was to avoid burdening them. (3) V. 11a suggests that another reason for Paul's unwillingness to accept aid from Corinth was his lack of love for them. After all, he accepted assistance from Macedonia. The reply in v. 11b reaffirms Paul's love for the Corinthians. (4) The assertion that most agitates Paul is the interlopers' claim that they work on equal footing with him (v. 12). To this Paul responds, "No. They are false apostles" (vv. 13–15).

Having responded to the series of four assertions by opponents (11:5–15), Paul now returns to the foolishness promised in v. 1. Vv. 16–21 serve as an introduction. Although what he is about to say is not with the Lord's authority (v. 17), "since many boast of worldly things, I too will boast" (v. 18). It is the activity of a fool, but that is all right, since the Corinthians bear with fools (v. 19a). For example, "if anyone makes slaves of you, or preys upon you, or puts on airs, or strikes you in the face" (v. 20), you bear it. The interlopers are depicted in terms usually reserved for arrogant sophists. For example, Philostratus says of the sophist Polemon that he "used to talk to cities as a superior, to kings as not inferior, and to gods as an equal" (*Lives of the Sophists* 1.25.4). This was the spirit of Paul's opponents. With another touch of sarcasm, Paul apologizes for not having had the nerve for such behavior (v. 21a). Nevertheless, speaking as a fool, he says: "whatever any one dares to boast of . . . I also dare to boast of that" (v. 21b).

There follow sections of foolish boasting (1) about background (11:22), (2) about accomplishments (11:23–33), (3) about visions and revelations (12:1–10), and (4) about miracles (12:11–13). Each section deserves separate attention.

(1) "Are they Hebrews? So am I (Phil 3:5). Are they Israelites? So am I (Phil 3:5). Are they descendants of Abraham? So am I (Rom 11:1)." The

threefold claim about background means that the visiting apostles claimed to be full-blooded Jews, racially, culturally, religiously. Paul responds, I am too (Gal 1:14). The matter of one's "good breeding" was a standard topic in Hellenistic rhetoric. Theon says that in comparing people one first juxtaposes their status, education, offspring, positions held, prestige, and physique (*Preliminary Exercises*). Paul's opponents appealed to "breeding," and Paul countered.

(2) Theon goes on to say that next after "breeding" in comparison comes actions, especially those things done with effort rather than ease. The visiting apostles bragged about what they had suffered for Christ. Paul countered, "Are they servants of Christ? I am a better one" (v. 23a). Like them, he appeals to what his service of Christ has cost him (cf. 1 Clement 5.5–7). "With far greater labors, far more imprisonments [e.g., Acts 16:23–37], with countless beatings [e.g., Acts 16:22–23, 37], and often near death. Five times I have received at the hands of the Jews the forty lashes less one [Deut 25:2–3; m Makkoth 3:1–10; Josephus *Antiquities* 4.8.21 §238, 248]. Three times I have been beaten with rods [e.g., Acts 16:22–23, 37; Cicero says although it was not allowed to beat a Roman citizen, sometimes ruthless magistrates did (*In Verrem* 5.62, 66); Josephus claims Albinus did it, ignoring the rights of Romans (*War* 2.14.9 §308); cf. Acts 22:25, 29]; once I was stoned [Acts 14:19; 1 Clement 5.6]. Three times I have been shipwrecked; a night and a day I have been adrift at sea [not the events of Acts 27, because 2 Cor 10–13 recounts events prior to that time; however, Acts 27 is typical of what must have happened on other occasions]; on frequent journeys [cf. Acts 13–28], in danger from rivers, danger from robbers, danger from my own people [e.g., Acts 9:23, 29; 13:8, 45; 14:2, 19; 17:5; 18:6, 12; 20:3, 19; 21:11, 27], danger from Gentiles [e.g., Acts 16:20; 19:23–41], danger in the city, danger in the wilderness, danger at sea, danger from false brethren; in toil and hardship, through many a sleepless night, in hunger and thirst, often without food, in cold and exposure [1 Cor 4:11]." Over and beyond these physical sufferings (Acts 15:25–26) there has been the psychological strain. "And apart from other things, there is the daily pressure upon me of my anxiety for all the churches" (v. 28). This stress comes in part because of Paul's emotional identification with his Christian children! "Who is weak, and I am not weak? Who is made to fall, and I am not indignant?" (v. 29). As Plutarch had said, self-praise is all right if it involves boasting of one's care and worry over others (*On Inoffensive Self-Praise* 14).

The outburst of vv. 23–29 is followed by a slight narrative in vv. 30–33.

There are at least three reasons for its presence. First, it is an illustration of a danger in the city mentioned in v. 26. Second, as Augustine observed, to follow the outburst of vv. 23–29 with the brief narrative (vv. 30–33) functions to rest the author and his readers (*On Christian Doctrine* 4.7.12). Third, Plutarch called for one to mix in with self-praise some mention of personal flaws to temper the eulogy (*On Inoffensive Self-Praise* 13). Vv. 30–33 do that. The incident mentioned here is one also recorded in Acts 9:23–25 but with a different function. The story is told in Acts in order to show how God delivers his servant; here it reflects personal humiliation. Everyone in antiquity knew that the finest military award for valor was the *corona muralis* (wall crown), given to the man who was first up the wall in the face of the enemy (Polybius 6.39.5; Livy 6.20.8; 10.46.3; 26.48.5; Allus Gellius *Attic Nights* 5.6.16). Paul's point is that he was the first one down. Physical sufferings, psychological stresses, and personally humiliating experiences were, for Paul, marks of a servant of Christ. His opponents could not surpass him in this area either.

(3) "I must boast; there is nothing to be gained by it, but I will go on to visions and revelations of the Lord" (12:1): that is, since the interlopers bragged about their experiences (5:12–13), Paul will too. What follows consists of two parallel units (v. 2 and vv. 3–4), each one beginning "I know a/this man." As in occasional rabbinic usage, "this man" is a circumlocution for "I." It is of his own experience that Paul writes. Moreover, the two stanzas describe only one experience. It took place fourteen years before the writing of this letter. Although we hear elsewhere of visions (Gal 1:12; 1 Cor 9:1; 15:8; Acts 9:1–11, 12; 16:8–9; 18:9; 22:17; 23:11; 27:23) and revelations (Gal 2:1) that Paul experienced, the event of 2 Cor 12:2–4 cannot be identified with any event known otherwise. The experience was involuntary ("I was caught up," i.e., by God). It was a Paradise experience (v. 3). Paradise could refer either to the realm, already existing, entered upon death (Apocalypse of Moses 37.5; Testament of Abraham 20; 1 Enoch 60.7, 23; 61.12; 70.4; 2 Enoch 9.1–42.3; Apocalypse of Abraham 21.6; Luke 23:43) or to the final consummation at or after the resurrection (Testament of Levi 18:10; Testament of Dan 5:12; 1 Enoch 25.4; 2 Enoch 65.9; 2 Esd 7:36, 123; 8:52; Apocalypse of Moses 13; Rev 2:7). In this context, Paradise is the former, as in Luke 23:43. It is located in the third heaven (as 2 Enoch 8–9, where Enoch is brought up to the third heaven to Paradise; 3 Baruch 4:8; Testament of Levi 2–3, 5; Apocalypse of Moses, 37.5; 40.2; cf. Lucian, who, when caricaturing Christians, spoke of the Galilean "who went by

air into the third heaven" [*Philopatris* 12]). Paul could not be sure whether the experience was in the body (as 1 Enoch 12.1 has the preflood hero disappear with his body, to reappear in 81.5) or out of the body (as Philo says Moses laid aside his body for forty days and nights [*On Dreams* 1.36]; cf. Plato for the myth of Er, who leaves his body, his soul going on a journey [*Republic* 10.614-21]). This would seem to imply a solitary experience. What Paul heard in Paradise is too sacred to relate (v. 4; cf. Rev 10:2-4, where the seer has such a prohibition laid on him; cf. also Dan 12:9). This, then, was a mystical experience similar to that shared by some Jews (e.g., t Hagigah 2:1; j Hagigah 2:1-77a; b Hagigah 14b, where at least some form of the story of the four rabbis caught up to Paradise speaks of a mystical experience), by some pagans (e.g., Porphyry tells that, while he was with him, Plotinus attained to oneness with God four times [*Life of Plotinus* 2.23]), and by other early Christians (e.g., Odes of Solomon 11.16-24; 21.6-9; 36.1-2; 38.1-5). Its benefits were not social but for Paul alone. The benefit for Paul was not soteriological (i.e., it was not his conversion) nor vocational (i.e., it was not his call to be an apostle). Like tongues (1 Cor 14:18), such mystical experiences' benefits are for the private, devotional life of the believer. In this case, however, when confronted by the boasting of rival apostles, Paul could appeal to it, reluctantly, as part of his self-praise (A. T. Lincoln, "Paul the Visionary: The Setting and Significance of the Rapture to Paradise in 2 Cor 12:1-10," *NTS* 25[1979]:204-20).

This experience of vv. 2-4 was but one of many Paul had (v. 7, "abundance of revelations"). In order to keep him from "being too elated," there was given him a thorn in the flesh (v. 7). Of the various options of what this thorn might be (physical illness, so Tertullian *De Puducitia* 13; Irenaeus *Against Heresies* 5.3.1; opposition of adversaries, so Chrysostom *Homilies on 2 Cor* 26; cf. Num 33:55 LXX, where the Canaanites will be as thorns in the Israelites' sides; temptations of the flesh, so the Vulgate rendering, *stimulus carnis*; spiritual trials such as faintheartedness in his ministerial duties, temptation to despair and doubt, so Luther *Table Talk* 24.7), physical illness seems best to satisfy the requirements (cf. Gal 4:13-14, which mentions an occasion of sickness). It was given to him (v. 7). By whom? It is clear that it was a messenger of Satan (cf. Job, an Old Testament example of Satan's agency in afflicting a godly person's body; cf. T. Asher 6:4; Matt 25:41; Rev 12:7, 9; Barnabas 18.1, for angels of Satan). It is not clear whether, in addition, God is understood as the giver. Even if God is not the giver but rather Satan alone is, still, as in Job, God must have permitted it. When faced with serious illness, Paul prayed for healing: "Three times I besought the Lord about this, that it should leave me" (v. 8). Like Jesus in Gethsemane, Paul was no masochist who enjoyed getting hurt or who loved being abused. Like Jesus in Gethsemane, Paul believed God was able to do what he asked. Like Jesus in Gethsemane, Paul knew the meaning of an unanswered prayer of petition. Like Jesus' prayer in Gethsemane, Paul's prayer was not answered positively, not because God was unable, but because God willed something to be accomplished by means of the suffering ("to keep me from being too elated" [v. 7c]). This is similar to Philo, who says of the affliction of Jacob (Gen 32:25) that when the soul attains power and perfection, it must be saved from conceit by a certain disablement (*Dreams* 1.130–31). Moreover, God paid the bill ("My grace is sufficient for you, for my power is made perfect in weakness," v. 9a). There was compensation for the thorn that stayed. This is similar to the Jewish midrash on Deut 3:26, interpreting God's refusal to allow Moses to cross over the Jordan. "Be content that the evil impulse has no power over you, yea rather that I will not deliver you into the hand of the angel of death, but will myself be with you" (*TDNT*, 1:466). Grace is understood as the power of Christ resting on Paul (v. 9b) (Neil Gregor Smith, "The Thorn That Stayed: An Exposition of 2 Cor 12:7–9," *Int* 13[1959]:409–16; J. B. Lightfoot, *St. Paul's Epistle to the Galatians*, 5th ed. [London: Macmillan, 1876], pp. 186–91). "For the sake of Christ, then, I am content with weaknesses, insults, hardships, persecutions, and calamities; for when I am weak, then I am strong" (v. 10). Paul's weakness or vulnerability is the showplace of God's might.

(4) Paul has been forced to act the fool by engaging in self-praise. The Corinthians are responsible. Instead of commending Paul, they were silent in the face of the visiting apostles and their boasts of superiority (12:11). As Plutarch put it, those who praise themselves are blameless because they are doing what others should do (*On Inoffensive Self-Praise* 1). There remains yet one more dimension about which Paul must boast, that of miracles: "The signs of the apostle were performed among you in all patience, with signs and wonders and mighty works" (v. 12). It will not do to depict the historical Paul merely as a suffering proclaimer of the word and the Paul of Acts only as a miracle worker (Jacob Jervell, "Der schwache Charismaticker," in *Rechtsfertigung: Festschrift für Ernst Käsemann,* ed. J. Friedrich et al. [Tübingen:Mohr, 1976], pp. 183–98; "The Signs of an Apostle: Paul's Miracles," *The Unknown Paul*

[Minneapolis:Augsburg, 1984], pp. 77–95). Although the gift of working miracles is not specifically apostolic (1 Cor 12:28), Paul does speak of miracles accompanying his ministry of the word (Rom 15:18–19), "For I will not venture to speak of anything except what Christ has wrought through me to win obedience from the Gentiles, by word and deed, by the power of signs and wonders, by the power of the Holy Spirit"). Indeed, from passages like 1 Thess 1:5; Gal 3:1–5; 1 Cor 2:1–5, it seems that when Paul preached, the Holy Spirit was given, often in miraculous ways, and faith resulted (cf. Heb 2:4). Insofar as churches were founded by the word and deed of Paul, his apostleship was legitimated; he was commended by God. The same miraculous displays of God's power were witnessed in Corinth in connection with Paul's ministry that had been observed in the other churches (2 Cor 12:12–13a). Paul, then, does not reject miracle as a legitimate part of his apostolic ministry. At the same time, he was aware of the ambiguity of such mighty works, even as he was aware of the ambiguity of ethical activity (1 Cor 13:3). They could be used merely as a means of gaining status (1 Cor 12–14), as could moral effort, rather than as expressions of love; they could be expressions of the triumphalism of seeing as a possession what is gift, as with his opponents in 2 Cor 10–13, and so take the spotlight off who God is and focus it instead on his alleged servants. These errors the apostle opposed. What he neither opposed nor ignored were the signs and wonders that accompanied his ministry as a testimony to the lordship of Jesus and the presence of the Holy Spirit. (See C. H. Talbert, *Reading Luke*, [N.Y. Crossroad, 1984], pp. 135–37, for the biblical understanding of the causes and cure of illness.) His apostolic ministry consisted of both word and deed (Rom 15:18–19). With a sarcastic follow-through, Paul says, "For in what way were you less favored than the rest of the churches, except that I myself did not burden you? Forgive me this wrong!" (v. 13).

In the Mediterranean region the practice of accepting payment for one's teaching was a matter of debate. In the Greek world, from the time of Socrates there was a tradition of opposition to receiving such payment: (1) Socrates (Plato *Apology* 19D-E; Xenophon *Memorabilia* 1.2.6–7; (2) Plato *Protagoras* 313CD; *Gorgias* 520; *Apology* 20; (3) Aristotle *Ethics* 9.1–7; *Politics* 1.9.2; (4) The Cynic Epistles: "I generally do not regard it as right to make money from philosophy, and that goes for me especially, since I have taken up philosophy on account of the command of God" (Pseudo-Socrates *Epistle* 1.1–2); (5) Philostratus *Life of Apollonius* 1.13; (6) Lucian *Hermotimus* 59; *Peregrinus* 13. To this position the sophists responded negatively. For example, Philostratus says Protagoras of Abdera, at the time of Xerxes, was the first to introduce the custom of charging a fee for lectures. Philostratus comments that this practice is not to be despised, since the pursuits on which one spends money are prized more than those for which no money is charged (*Lives of the Sophists* 1.10). Also, Antiphon says to Socrates: "If you set any value on your society, you would insist on getting the proper price for that too. It may well be that you are a just man because you do not cheat people through avarice; but wise you cannot be, since your knowledge is not worth anything" (Xenophon *Memorabilia* 1.6.12).

The Jewish world reflected a similar disagreement. According to Hillel, it is forbidden for the scholar to make a profit out of the Torah or one's knowledge of it (m Aboth 1:13; 4:5). This was a rule followed by Judah ha-Nasi (b Ketuboth 104a). At the same time, Josephus tells of a Palestinian Jew in Rome who instructed people in the wisdom of the laws of Moses for payment (*Antiquities* 18.3.5 §81). Juvenal also tells of a Jewish woman who offered interpretations of the laws of Judaism and of dreams for a price (*Satires* 6.542–47). So Jewish appropriation of the sophists' position was to be found.

The differences in early Christianity are more subtle than those in the pagan and Jewish worlds. On the one hand, the general practice was for the churches to support various Christian missionaries (e.g., Matt 10:10; Luke 10:7; 1 Cor 9:3–14; 1 Tim 5:18; Didache 11). On the other hand, there was a concern to protect against abuses of this practice. Although Matt 10:10 says, "the laborer deserves his food," the two preceding verses say, "Heal the sick, raise the dead, cleanse lepers, cast out demons. You received without pay, give without pay." That is, a fee system for healing is ruled out. All a missionary gets is his food and lodging. Didache 11 grants the right of an apostle to bread and lodging but nothing more. If he says in the Spirit, "Give me money or something else," do not listen to him. He is a false prophet. Hermas condemns those who not only accept pay for prophesying but also will not prophesy without being paid ("Command" 11.12).

Against this background, Paul's practice may be understood. Like a Jewish rabbi he had a trade to support his daily needs (1 Thess 2:9; cf. 2 Thess 3:7–9; Acts 18:3; 20:34). Yet he sometimes received gifts from at least one of his churches (Phil 4:15–16; 2 Cor 11:9). In Corinth he argued both for his right to food and drink (1 Cor 9) and for his freedom to refuse it (2 Cor 11:9–10). Not receiving any money from the Corinthians functioned as a moral argument that he disinterestedly served the gospel and his people. It is difficult to escape the conclusion that Paul was, in the Greek world, aligning himself with the philosophic tradition of Socrates, Plato, and Aristotle and avoiding any seeming identification with the practice of the disreputable sophists.

The interlopers of 2 Corinthians went beyond the common Christian practice of accepting room and board. They seemed to embody the sophistic practice of performing for a fee on the grounds that the more they could charge, the more important they were (11:19). In the next generation, the Pauline school remembered the apostle Paul's freedom from love of money and institutionalized it in their requirements for bishops (1 Tim 3:3; Titus 1:7); these Paulinists also depicted their heretical opponents as sophists who taught for base gain (Titus 1:11; 1 Tim 6:5).

The third major subsection of 2 Corinthians 10–13 is 12:14–13:10, (A'), Looking Forward to His Presence with Them. Here, as in (A), 10:1–11, the apostle's concern is that the Corinthians' obedience be complete before his arrival. This unit is composed of two parallel parts, 12:14–21 and 13:1–10, each beginning with a reference to Paul's coming (12:14, "Here for the third time I am ready to come to you"; 13:1, "This is the third time I am coming to you"). If the (B) section, 10:12–12:13, ended with a reference to Paul's past refusal to accept money for his ministry in Corinth, this unit, (A'), 12:14–13:10, begins with a statement about Paul's future refusal: "I will not be a burden, for I seek not what is yours but you. . . . I will most gladly spend and be spent for your souls" (vv. 14–15). Vv. 16–18, however, must face and answer yet another issue related to Paul's practice of refusing monetary payment: "But granting that I myself did not burden you, I was crafty, you say, and got the better of you by guile" (12:16). The allegation was that all the while Paul had made a great show of asking for no money for himself, he had instituted a collection allegedly for the poor saints in Jerusalem and was likely to pocket the proceeds for himself. Such things had been known to happen. Josephus tells of a Palestinian Jew in Rome who, with three partners, professed to instruct people in the laws of Moses. The four persuaded Fulvia, a distinguished Roman convert to Judaism, to send purple and gold to the temple at Jerusalem. Once in their possession, the gifts and gold were sold and the money expended upon themselves. So great was the scandal arising out of it that Tiberius ordered all the Jews to be banished from Rome (*Antiquities* 18.3.5 §81). If it happened once, it could happen again! Vv. 17–18 ask, "Did I take advantage of you through any of those whom I sent to you? I urged Titus to go and sent the brother with him. Did Titus take advantage of you? Did we not act in the same spirit? Did we not take the same steps?" This particular trip of Titus to Corinth is not the same one as that mentioned in 2 Cor 8. This trip involves Titus and one brother; the one in 8:6, 16–18, 22, involves Titus and at least two others. This trip of Titus, then, poses no problem to 2 Cor 10–13's being earlier than 2 Cor 1–9. Paul is so concerned about being circumspect in his management of the collection that he works out an administrative plan to protect against such a charge as has been leveled against him (2 Cor 8:20–21).

What has been said so far has not been said because Paul is defensive but in order to build the Corinthians up (v. 19). Two fears have fueled this attempt. First, "I fear that perhaps I may come and find you not what I wish, and that you may not find me what you wish" (v. 20). Second, "I fear that when I come again . . . I may have to mourn over many of those who sinned before and have not repented of the impurity, immorality, and licentiousness which they have practiced" (v. 21). Some of the sexual libertinism dealt with in 1 Corinthians has apparently persisted (cf. 2 Cor 6:14–7:1).

The second part of 12:14–13:10 begins at 3:1a: "This is the third time I am coming to you." Following Deut 19:15 ("Any charge must be sustained by the evidence of two or three witnesses," v. 1b; cf. Matt 18:16; 1 Tim 5:19; Heb 10:28; 1 John 5:8), Paul will carry out a thorough investigation. Then comes the warning: "if I come again I will not spare them" (v. 2). Why? "Since you desire proof that Christ is speaking in me . . . in dealing with you we shall live with him by the power of God" (vv. 3–4).

The Corinthians have been questioning whether or not Christ speaks and lives in Paul. Now he asks whether Jesus Christ is in them. "Examine yourselves [the emphasis is on *yourselves*]. . . . Test yourselves. . . . I hope you will find out that we have not failed" (vv. 5–6). The foremost of Apollo's commandments, "know yourself" (Dio Chrysostom 4.57), offered cultural support to the apostle's demand. Paul hopes for their improvement (v. 9b) and not just so that he will not have failed (vv. 7–8). The reason for writing this is so that when he comes he will not have to use the authority given him for building up in severity (v. 10). In this statement, one finds the hortatory purpose of the whole of 2 Cor 10–13.

What follows is the briefest of paraeneses ("mend your ways, heed my appeal, agree with one another, live in peace," v. 11a) and the conclusion of the letter: the peace (v. 11b); the holy kiss (v. 12; cf. Rom 16:16; 1 Cor 16:20; 1 Thess 5:26; 1 Pet 5:14; Justin *1 Apology* 65; *Apostolic Constitutions* 2.7.57; 8.2.11). In antiquity a kiss functioned not only erotically and within friendship but also on occasion as a sign of reception into a closed group, as in Apuleius *Metamorphoses* 7.9; on initiation into a mystery cult, one kissed the mystagogue, so *Metamorphoses* 11.25, and members of the group were known as "those within the kiss," misunderstood by Lucian *Alexander* 41); greetings (v. 13); and the benediction (v. 14; cf. Rom 16:20b; 1 Cor 16:23; Gal 6:18; Phil 4:23; 1 Thess 5:28; Philem 25).

The argument in 2 Cor 10–13 is cast throughout in the form of a reputable philosopher's response to disreputable sophists. At virtually every point the positions of the participants are described by Paul with conventional means. This raises the question of whether or not it is possible to move behind the rhetoric to the theological issues involved.

The easiest conclusion to draw at the theological level is negative. The consensus for nearly a generation has regarded the issue as "good suffering" (Paul) versus "bad miracle" (the interlopers). But this has been shown to be exegetically impossible. Both the ministry of Paul and that of the visiting apostles encompassed preaching, miracle, and suffering service on behalf of Christ. If so, then where did the difference lie?

Using categories that are not explicitly Paul's (motive and consequences), it may be possible to define the differences in at least general terms. Paul regards the other apostles as acting out of self-centered motives (2 Cor 10:12; 11:12; cf. a similar problem in Phil 1:15–17). In promoting themselves, they are without understanding. Paul also thinks the consequences of their ministry to be largely self-magnification (2 Cor 11:20) instead of God's glory (2 Cor 10:17; 12:9–10) and the church's edification (2 Cor 10:8). His rejection of their ministry on these grounds is akin to his critique of the Corinthian spirituals in 1 Cor 12–14. In manifestations of spiritual power, the motive must be right (1 Cor 13, i.e., for others) and the consequences as well (1 Cor 14:26, i.e., for edification of the church; 14:25, i.e., for God's glory). The Jesus preached by Paul is one who calls us to die with him to sin. For one who has died to sin, the motive of self-interest is not viable, any more than the objective sought can be self-aggrandizement. If the love of Christ constrains us (2 Cor 5:14), then we seek God's glory (2 Cor 5:15) and the church's edification.

LAYING
A FOUNDATION FOR
FUTURE REQUESTS

OF MOTIVES AND CIRCUMSTANCES

2 Corinthians 1:1–2:13 and 7:4–16

2 Cor 1–9 is treated as a unity in this commentary. It consists of two parts, chapters 1–7 and chapters 8–9, the former mainly apology, the latter largely requests. A careful reading of 2 Cor 1–7 reveals two sections of itinerary (1:18–2:13 and 7:4–16) that frame the entire unit (cf. Rom 1:10–15 and 15:14–32, where an itinerary also forms a frame around a letter). Within the frame one encounters a fourfold repetition of "commend ourselves" (3:1; 4:2; 5:12; 6:4). At the end of the first two subsections that begin with "commend ourselves" is the same refrain: "we do not lose heart" (4:1b; 4:16a). If one takes the phrase "commend ourselves" as a repeated signal of the beginning of a thought unit and the repetition of "we do not lose heart" as a sign of the close of the two first subsections, then the material within the frame falls into five units: (1) 2:14–4:1; (2) 4:2–16a; (3) 4:16b–5:10; (4) 5:11–6:2; and (5) 6:3–7:4. The dominant theme throughout is Paul's ministry. The Pauline ministry is discussed in such a way as to lay the foundation for the requests that will come in 2 Cor 8–9. After a discussion of the two itinerary sections that frame 2 Cor 1–7 (1:8–2:13 and 7:4–16), each of the five subunits will be discussed in order.

In 2 Cor 1:1–2:13 and 7:4–16 there are three components lumped together: (1) the introduction to the letter, A to B, greeting, plus a prayer (1:1–7); (2) the first part of the itinerary that frames the body of the letter that is 2 Cor 1–9 (1:8–2:13); and (3) the second half of the itinerary (7:4–16).

(1) The introduction to the letter includes Timothy (1 Cor 4:17; 16:10; 2 Cor 1:19; cf. Acts 18:5) alongside Paul as the author (cf. 1 Thess 1:1; Phil 1:1). The recipients are specified not only as the church of God at Corinth (1 Thess 2:14; 2 Thess 1:4; 1 Cor 1:2; 10:32; 11:16, 22: 15:9; Gal 1:13) but all the saints in the whole of Achaia (2 Cor 9:2; Rom 16:1; cf. Acts 17:16–34). The greeting is the normal one for Paul, "grace to you and peace" (1 Cor 1:3; Rom 1:7; Gal 1:3; Phil 1:2; 1 Thess 1:1b;

2 Thess 1:2). Instead of the usual prayer form (thanksgiving, Rom 1:8; 1 Cor 1:4; Phil 1:3; 1 Thess 1:2; 2:13; 3:9; 2 Thess 1:3; petition, Rom 1:10; Phil 1:9; 1 Thess 3:11; 2 Thess 1:11), Paul uses a *berakah*, a blessing form (1 Kings 8:14; Ps 72:18–19; 2 Macc 1:17; Luke 1:68; Eph 1:3; 1 Pet 1:3): "Blessed be the God and Father of our Lord Jesus Christ." To speak this way does not mean to confer blessings on God but to praise or thank him for his blessings. V. 4a gives the ground for the praise, "who continually comforts us in all our afflictions"; V. 4b offers the purpose of the divine comfort, "so that we may be able to comfort those who are in any affliction." V. 5 is an explanation of v. 4a (cf. Phil 3:10–11; Col 1:24); vv. 6–7 are the explanation of v 4b. In Paul, affliction can refer both to external, objective suffering (Rom 8:35; 1 Cor 7:28) and to mental anguish (Phil 1:17). The general reference here, "in all our affliction" (v. 3), would encompass both. In them all, it is God's comfort that enables the Christian to endure.

(2) As a request or disclosure formula ("I beseech you" or "I would not have you ignorant") normally serves as the threshold of the body of a letter, so here: "For we do not want you to be ignorant, brethren" (v. 8). This section, 1:8–2:13, is the first part of the itinerary that frames the body of the letter (cf. Rom 1:10–15 and 15:14–32). This half of the itinerary falls into an ABA' pattern:

A. Paul's afflictions in Asia (1:8–11)
  B. Paul's justification of his changed travel plans (1:12–2:2)
A'. Paul's afflictions in Macedonia and Troas (2:3–13).

The function of the section is to respond to two criticisms of Paul: first, that the apostle does not really care for the Corinthians, as his hostile letter shows, and second, that Paul is an undependable flatterer, as his change in travel plans demonstrates. 2 Cor 1:8–11 plus 2:3–13 constitute an answer to the first; 1:12–14 and 1:15–2:2 formulate the apostle's reply to the second. Paul's great distress (affliction) proves his concern for the Corinthians. His motivation in changing his travel plans reveals that he is faithful to the relationship with the Corinthians. In beginning his letter this way, Paul follows the guidance of Aristotle, who says a defendant must first clear away all prejudice against himself, removing all obstacles, in introducing himself (*Rhetoric* 3.14.7).

(A), 1:8–11, treats Paul's affliction in Asia. Of the various options for the nature of the "affliction we experienced in Asia" (the Ephesian riot of Acts 19:23–20:1; an Ephesian imprisonment; a serious illness; the psychological anguish caused by the Corinthian rebellion and by regret at having sent the painful letter mentioned in 2:3; so 7:8, "though I did not regret it"), the last seems most probable. In 2 Cor 1–7 Paul speaks about "affliction" (1:8; 2:4; 7:5) and "absence of rest" (2:13; 7:5) which he experienced first in Macedonia, then in Asia, then in Troas, and finally again in Macedonia. In all four cases, the problem was his distress over the situation in Corinth. To speak about how seriously he took the feared estrangement from the Corinthians ("we were so utterly, unbearably crushed that we despaired of life itself," v. 8) shows Paul's concern for them. There was no better strategy with which to begin. As Epictetus said, "There is nothing more effective in the style for exhortation than when the speaker makes clear to his audience that he has need of them" (3.23.37). The deliverance from "so deadly a peril" (v. 10) was the reconciliation effected and mentioned later in 2:6–11 and 7:4–16. The experience of God's power to deliver in this occasion built confidence in God's ability to deliver in the future: "on him we have set our hope that he will deliver us again" (v. 10b).

(B), 1:12–2:2, gives Paul's justification for his changed travel plans. This subunit consists of a general affirmation (1:12–14) followed by an explanation (1:15–2:2). 2 Cor 1:12–14 is a general affirmation by Paul of a clear conscience about his dealings with Corinth. It is an expression of self-confidence typical of Greco-Roman arguments used to commend oneself as a credible teacher for the addresses (e.g., Pericles in Thucydides 2.60.5; Dio Chrysostom *Oration* 41.1). For example, Isocrates in *Cyprians*, written for Nicocles, the new king of Cyprus, to admonish his subjects to proper behavior, ends a long section of self-commendation (29–47) by having Nicocles say, "the reason why I have spoken at some length about myself . . . is that I might leave you no excuse for not doing willingly whatever I counsel and command" (47) (Stanley N. Olson, "Epistolary Uses of Expressions of Self-Confidence," *JBL* 103 [1984]: 585–97). Paul has written clearly to Corinth, so if they understand fully (v. 13b), they will grasp the apostle's motives as well as his actions and will be proud of him at the parousia (v. 14).

2 Cor 1:15–2:2 aims to explain Paul's motives in the change of his travel plans. The apostle's intention is stated in 1:15–16: "I wanted to visit you on my way to Macedonia, and to come back to you from Macedonia." This intent was not be realized. After coming to Corinth on an intermediate visit, Paul left for Macedonia and did not return. Instead

he sent a stinging letter (2:3–4). This raised the issue of personal dependability. Paul had agreed to a double visit to try to win friends by flattery, it was said, but he had no intention of carrying out his promise. This is the typical charge brought against flatterers by Greco-Roman authors. For example, Cicero cites a passage from Terence, (*The Eunuch* 251–53), when he describes the kind of flattery that undermines true friendship. In the passage, the rogue, Gnatho, describes himself in this way: "Whatever they say I praise; if again they say the opposite, I praise that too. If one says no, I say no; if one says yes, I say yes. In fact I have given orders to myself to agree with them in everything" (*On Friendship* 25.93). Plutarch says the flatterer "is not simple, not one, but variable and many in one, and like water that is poured into one receptacle after another, he ... changes his shape to fit his receiver" ("How to Tell a Flatterer from a Friend" 52b–53d). Paul belongs to this category, so some thought.

What was the cause of Paul's change in plans? The answer is twofold: a negative (1:17–22) supported by an oath (v. 18), and a positive (1:23–2:2) also supported by an oath (1:23). It was not that Paul was vacillating, making plans like a worldly man, "ready to say Yes and No at once" (v. 17). The apostle's behavior towards the Corinthians reflected the faithfulness of God as seen in Jesus Christ (vv. 18–22). It was rather "to spare you that I refrained from coming to Corinth" (1:23). "For I made up my mind not to make you another painful visit" (2:1). The intermediate visit had been painful. Paul did not want a repeat of that. He, therefore, not only withdrew, he did not return. Paul's behavior might have reflected the words of Jesus ("Do not resist one who is evil," Matt 5:39a), but there is no appeal to them here. It might have been shaped by the vision of the Stoic sage as expressed by Seneca: "Does a man get angry? Do you on the contrary challenge him with kindness. Animosity, if abandoned by one side, forthwith dies; it takes two to make a fight. But if anger shall be rife on both sides, if the conflict comes, he is the better man who first withdraws; the vanquished is the one who wins. If some one strikes you, step back" (*De Ira* 2.34.5). Although throughout 2 Corinthians Paul portrays himself as a sage and the interlopers as sophists, there is no explicit claim to that model here. Rather, it is the apostle's concern for the community to which appeal is made (1:24, "we work with you for your joy"; 2:2, "For if I cause you pain, who is there to make me glad?"). He hopes that the Corinthians now understand fully the motives behind the change of plans (1:13b).

(A'), 2:3–13, focuses on Paul's afflictions in Macedonia and Troas. Having explained in 1:15–2:2 why a projected visit to Corinth had been canceled, Paul proceeds in 2:3–13 to describe his afflictions in Macedonia and Troas. The reasons for his afflictions were two. There was first the matter of the "letter of tears" (2:3–4). "I wrote you out of much affliction and anguish of heart and with many tears" (v. 4a). "I wrote as I did, so that when I came I might not be pained by those who should have made me rejoice" (v. 3a). This letter was likely written from Macedonia after Paul's departure from Corinth after the intermediate visit.

The occasion for the changed travel plans and the painful letter (2 Cor 10–13, according to this commentary) was an incident that took place on Paul's intermediate visit to Corinth. A single individual (2 Cor 2:5; 7:7, 8, 10, 12) had acted in a way to injure Paul and, by derivation, the whole community (2:5; cf. 1 Cor 12:26a). Its gravity had not been recognized by a part of the Corinthian church (2:5–6). Because of the dissident minority, Paul wrote the "letter of tears" (2 Cor 10–13) to test the obedience of the whole group (2:9; cf. 10:6). Apparently, as a result of the painful letter the majority had disciplined the offender (2:6). A similar situation earlier (1 Cor 5) had involved excommunication. It may have been the punishment here. At Qumran we hear that one who has slandered his companion shall be excluded from the congregation's meal for a year and do penance; whoever has murmured against the authority of the community shall be expelled from the group and shall not return (1 QS 7.15–18). Unlike Qumran, however, Paul did not call for permanent expulsion. He now asked for forgiveness (2:7) and love (2:8) to be shown to the offender, lest the punishment be only punitive and not redemptive (Gal 6:1). "Anyone whom you forgive, I forgive. . . . to keep Satan [4:4, the god of this age; 6:15, Beliar; 11:3, the serpent] from gaining the advantage over us" (2:10–11) (C. K. Barrett, "*Ho Adikēsas*," in *Essays on Paul* [Philadelphia:Westminster Press, 1982], pp. 108–17, heavily dependent on Allo).

The second reason for Paul's afflictions had to do with his experience in Troas. "When I came to Troas to preach the gospel of Christ, a door was opened for me in the Lord" (v. 12, i.e., an opportunity was given for evangelism). Paul's mind could not rest "because I did not find my brother Titus there" (v. 13, i.e., Titus had not yet returned from Corinth with news of the results of Paul's painful letter). Without news from Corinth, the apostle was so preoccupied that he could not evangelize. Prompted by his obsession with matters at Corinth, he went on to Mace-

donia, hoping to meet Titus there. Vv. 12–13 conclude the section, 1:8–
2:13, by making yet another attempt to let the Corinthians know that
Paul really does care for them.

(3) The second part of the itinerary that frames the body of 2 Cor 1–9
comes at 7:4–16. This section is held together by an inclusion (7:4, "I
have great confidence in you, I have great pride in you . . . I am overjoyed"; 7:16, "I rejoice, because I have perfect confidence in you," together with 7:14, "pride in you"). It is an exposition of the statement in
7:4, "with all our affliction, I am overjoyed," v. 5 being the commentary
on "affliction," vv. 6–16 the elaboration of "overjoyed."

V. 5 resumes the thread of 2:12–13: "Even when we came into Macedonia, our bodies had no rest but we were afflicted at every turn—fight-
ing without and fear within." The distress experienced at Troas continues even in Macedonia until Titus arrives with the long-awaited
news. If v. 5 is related formally to v. 4 by the link terms "affliction" and
"afflicted," vv. 6, 7, 13a, b are formally tied to v. 4 by the key word
"comfort."

2 Cor 7:6–16 elaborates the theme of joy stated in v. 4: "I am overjoyed." The reasons for this joy are four, the last being a general summary. First, Paul rejoices because of Titus's arrival with news that comforted him (vv. 6–7): "he told us of your longing, your mourning, your
zeal for me" (v. 7b). The Corinthians affirmed their solidarity with the
apostle. Second, Paul rejoices because of the Corinthians' repentance
(vv. 8–13a). Although at one time after sending the letter Paul had re-
gretted sending it (v. 8b), now he is very glad he did. He is glad because
the grief the congregation had felt on hearing it was a "godly grief" that
produced a repentance that leads to salvation and brings no regret, unlike worldly grief that results in despair and death (vv. 9–10): "For see
what earnestness this godly grief has produced in you, what eagerness to
clear yourselves, what indignation, what alarm, what longing, what
zeal, what punishment!" (v. 11). The godly sorrow which leads to repentance and salvation is contrasted with worldly sorrow which leads to
death. Already in 2:7 Paul had expressed concern over one's being overwhelmed with excessive sorrow that would lead to despair or bitterness
(e.g., Judas, Matt 27:3–5; Esau, Heb 12:16–17). Godly sorrow is that
which produces not anger or self-condemnation or despondency but
rather a change for the better. The repentance spoken of here is not that
which is the conversion from paganism to Christianity (e.g., Rom 2:4)
but rather that of a Christian who has taken a wrong path and now

returns to the right way (cf. 12:21). The letter was written with the intent of revealing to the Corinthians their solidarity with Paul. This had been accomplished, so the apostle was comforted (vv 12–13a). Third, Paul rejoices at Titus's joy (vv. 13b–15). The reason is that Paul had boasted to him about the Corinthians and so is relieved to learn that he has not misled Titus about what he would find in Corinth: "so our boasting before Titus has proved true" (v. 14b). The Corinthian church is now obedient (v. 15). Fourth, Paul rejoices because "I have perfect confidence in you" (v. 16). This summary statement echoes v. 4: "I have great confidence in you." Paul's joy is based on his confidence in the Corinthians' obedience to his apostolic leadership. As such it reflects a cultural convention. In Hellenistic culture, expressions of confidence in the addressee's compliance functioned to undergird the letter's requests by creating a sense of obligation through praise (Stanley N. Olson, "Pauline Expressions of Confidence in His Addressees," *CBQ* 47 [1985]: 282–95).

Such expressions of confidence are most frequently found in the closing section of a letter, often adjacent to the letter's request (as 7:4, 16 stand next to 2 Cor 8–9). An example from Pseudo-Demetrius illustrates the technique:

> (*a*) For I can never forget you nor our indisputable comradeship from childhood on. Knowing that I myself am kindly disposed toward your affairs, and that I worked unhesitatingly for what is most advantageous to you,
> (*b*) I have assumed that you, too, have the same opinion of me and will refuse me in nothing.
> (*c*) You will do well, therefore, to give close attention to members of my household.... (*Typoi* 1, quoted in Olson, *CBQ*, p. 286).

With (*a*) compare 2 Cor 6:11; 7:2b; with (*b*) compare 2 Cor 6:12–13; 7:2a and 7:4, 16; and with (*c*) compare 2 Cor 8–9. Whereas in 2 Cor 1:12–14 Paul used an expression of self-confidence to legitimate his right to be heard by the Corinthians, in 2 Cor 7:4, 16 he uses an expression of confidence in his addressees to lay the foundation for his requests of them to follow in chapters 8–9. This expression of confidence in his addressees is but one of the links that ties chapters 1–7 together with chapters 8–9.

THE MINISTER OF
A NEW COVENANT

2 Corinthians 2:14–4:1

2 Cor 2:14–4:1 is a large thought unit whose opening is signalled by "commend ourselves" (3:1; cf. 4:2; 5:12; 6:4) and whose closing is marked by "we do not lose heart" (4:1; cf. 4:16). It is built around three components: two images of Paul's apostolic ministry (the triumph, 2:14–16a, and the new covenant, 3:7–18) with a question and answer sequence sandwiched between (2:16b–3:6). Its functions are two: first, through the use of another expression of self-confidence (3:4; remember 1:12–14) to lay the foundation for his right to advise the Corinthians; second, through an exposition of the glory of his ministry to present the grounds for his not losing heart in the midst of adversity (remember 1:8–9; 2:4; 2:12–13; 7:5). The theme throughout is Paul's apostolic ministry.

In 2:14–16a, the first image used for Paul's ministry is that of the Roman triumph. Polybius says that the Senate could add glory even to the successes of generals by bringing their achievements before the eyes of the Roman citizens in tangible form in what are called triumphs (6.15.8). It was the highest mark of honor that could be conferred on a Roman citizen (Livy 30.15.12). According to Orosius, no fewer than three hundred triumphs were celebrated during the period between the founding of Rome and the reign of Vespasian (*History* 7.9.8). Triumphs continued to be celebrated at least until A.D. 403. That known best by Christians and Jews is the one commemorated by the Arch of Titus at the Colosseum end of the Roman Forum, whose art depicts the Roman victory over the Jews in A.D. 70. In such a triumph, the victorious general entered the city through the Porta Triumphalis and, amid the cheers of the people, made his way in his chariot to the Capitoline Hill, where a solemn offering was presented to Jupiter (Tacitus *Histories* 4.58.6) (H. S. Versnel, *Triumphus: An Inquiry into the Origin, Development and Meaning of the Roman Triumph* [Leiden: Brill, 1970]).

140

Paul uses the image of the Roman triumph in two ways: (*a*) to depict himself as the one who makes the knowledge of God known throughout the world and (*b*) to portray himself as the one who attests to God the efficacy of Christ's sacrifice. On the one hand, in v. 14 the image reflects the practice of incense being offered up in the streets of the city as the procession moved along (Horace *Odes* 4.2.50–51; Appian *Punic Wars* 66). Here the fragrance goes *out*. Paul is depicted as the one in the triumphal procession who is responsible for the incense: that is, he spreads the knowledge of Christ everywhere. On the other hand, in vv. 15–16a the aroma of the sacrifice offered to God is in view. Here the fragrance goes *up*. Paul is portrayed as the aroma arising from Christ's sacrifice to God, spreading as it ascends the knowledge of God communicated in the cross. The fragrance of the triumphal sacrifice had two different effects on those present. For the crowds who welcomed their general, it was the aroma of victory; for the hapless captives being dragged along in the procession, it was the smell of doom. Just so is the preaching of the gospel by the apostle (cf. 1 Cor 1:22–24). Whatever the image, the apostle is the one who makes the knowledge of God known abroad.

What follows is a question and answer sequence (2:16b–3:6) held together by an inclusion ("sufficient," 2:16b; "sufficient," "sufficiency," 3:5). It consists of two questions (2:16b; 3:1) and two answers (2:17; 3:2–3) followed by a clarification (3:4–6). This awesome task of an apostle (2:14–16a) prompts the first question: "Who is sufficient for these things?" (2:16b). V. 17 gives the answer, stated both negatively and positively. Negatively, an adequate minister is not a peddler of God's word. The allusion is to the interlopers who have come to Corinth and worked on a fee system (remember 11:7–11; 12:13, 16). Paul depicts them as disreputable sophists, long discredited by the respected philosophic tradition. For example, Plato expresses dismay that the sophist sells his wares like the merchant who hawks his (*Protagoras* 313 CDE). Dio Chrysostom decries the huckstering of both wares and ideas at the time of the Isthmian Games (*Oration* 8.9). Philostratus has the hero criticize a certain Euphrates for huckstering his wisdom (*Life of Apollonius* 1.13). Lucian attacks philosophers who sell their wines, most of whom adulterate and cheat, giving false measure (*Hermotimus* 59). Paul, then, regards those who teach for their own gain as insufficient for the task of spreading the knowledge of God. Positively, an apostle who is sufficient for the task is one who speaks (*a*) sincerely (i.e., without secret faults), (*b*) from God (i.e., says what God wants said), (*c*) in the presence of God (i.e., with God as judge), and (*d*) in Christ (i.e., as one identified with Christ). This is how Paul sees himself.

Paul's positive appraisal of himself in 2:17b leads to the second question: "Are we beginning to commend ourselves again?" (3:1a). Remember in chapters 10–13, part of the painful letter (2:4; 7:8), Paul had been forced by circumstances to commend himself (inoffensive self-praise). Is he reverting to that again? The implied answer is "No." "Or do we need, as some do, letters of recommendation to you, or from you?" (3:1b). Behind this question is an ancient convention, the letter of recommendation. From the Greek world, Pseudo-Demetrius's *Typoi* contains descriptions of twenty-one types of private letters, with examples of each. Of the letter of introduction, he says that it is one we write to one person for the sake of another, inserting words of praise, and speaking of those previously unacquainted as if they were acquainted. The example offered of this type reads:

> X, who is conveying the letter to you, is a man who has been well tested by us, and who is loved on account of his trustworthiness. Kindly grant him hospitality both for my sake and for his, and indeed for your own. For you will not be sorry if you entrust to him, in any matter you wish, either words or deeds of a confidential nature. Indeed, you yourself will praise him to others when you have learned how useful he can be in everything.

> (This letter is one of more than forty examples given by Clinton W. Keyes, "The Greek Letter of Introduction," *AJP* 56[1935]:28–44. Cf. Hannah Cotton, *Documentary Letters of Recommendation in Latin from the Roman Empire* [Koenigstein: Anton Hain, 1981]; Chan-Hie Kim, *Form and Structure of the Familiar Greek Letter of Recommendation* [Missoula, Mont.: Scholars Press, 1972].)

Jewish appropriation of this practice is echoed in Acts 9:2 and 22:5. An example of a Jewish letter of recommendation is found embedded in the Palestinian Talmud. The Prince writes on behalf of Hiyya ben Abba, "Here we are sending you a great man, our emissary and like us until he comes back to our place" (p Neadarim 10:10, 42b).

Early Christians also used this form, for example, Acts 15:23–29, especially vv. 23–27; 18:27; Rom 16:1–2; 1 Cor 16:10–11; Col 4:7–11; Phil 2:25–30. One reason why its use was so widespread in early Christianity was the Christian practice of offering hospitality to visiting Christians (Rom 12:13; Heb 13:2; 1 Pet 4:9; 1 Clement 1.2; Hermas "Command" 8.10; Justin *1 Apology* 14 and 67.6; Ignatius of Antioch's six letters thanking Christians for hospitality; Lucian, who satirizes Christian hospitality [*Peregrinus* 11–13]) and the need to protect against abuse. Such hospitality figured in early Christian missions. It became the right of traveling Christians to expect entertainment from fellow Christians where they stopped en route (e.g., Mark 6:7–11; Matt 10:5–42; Luke 10:1–16; Didache 11.1–3; 12) (D. W. Riddle, "Early Christian Hospitality: A Factor in the Gospel Transmission," *JBL* 57[1938]:141–54).

Apparently the visiting apostles, with whom Paul was disparagingly compared by one Corinthian and his sympathizers (cf. 2 Cor 10–13), came with letters of recommendation and asked such of the Corinthians on their departure (3:2, "letters of recommendation to you, or from you"). When Paul asked his second question ("Do we need . . . letters of recommendation?"), it was to accomplish the same thing as his first (2:16b) and its answer (2:17). It aimed to distinguish Paul's relationship to the Corinthians from that of the other apostles who had just come through with their letters of recommendation. Such letters were advantageous only where there are already established churches. Paul, however, worked where no one else had yet gone with the gospel (remember 10:13–18). For a pioneer apostle who worked only in virgin territory (Rom 15:20), the very existence of Christian churches was his recommendation. So Paul says, "You are yourselves our letter of recommendation" (v. 2a). The author of the letter is Christ (v. 3a; for the notion of a letter written by a god to humans, see Ezek 2:9; Rev 2–3; Hermas "Vision" 2.1–2; Odes of Solomon 23); the writing instrument is the Spirit (v. 3b; Exod 31:18 says the commandments were written by God's finger; Luke 11:20//Matt 12:28 show that finger of God and Spirit of God were interchangeable expressions); the material on which the writing was done is "your hearts" (v. 2b), "tablets of human hearts" (v. 3b). The idiom is a common Greek one: Plato says a good teacher writes his words on a congenial soul (*Phaedrus* 276 C–E); Thucydides speaks of memorials of famous men written in the hearts of people rather than on stone (2.43.2). The specific background in this context is Jer 31:33, where God says of the new covenant, "I will write it upon their hearts." The one who delivers the letter is Paul (v. 3a); those who read it are "all men" (v. 2b). The existence of the Corinthian church is Paul's letter of recommendation for all people, including the Corinthians, to read. Paul was not, like Diogenes (Epictetus 2.3.1), condemning letters of recommendation but rather seeking to clarify the difference between himself as founder of the Corinthian community and the visiting apostles who worked in a church already established (remember 11:12; 10:15–16).

A clarification follows (3:4–6). It begins by declaring Paul's self-confidence rests upon the existence of the Corinthian community, his letter of recommendation (v. 4). This serves as a conclusion to question two and its answer (3:1–3). It continues by emphasizing that the Pauline sufficiency for the apostolic tasks is not of himself but from God (v. 5). This functions as a conclusion to question one and its answer (2:16b–17). It ends by defining the nature of Paul's role as apostle. He is a minister of a new covenant (v. 6), one that is not heteronomous ("not in a written code") but rather theonomous ("but in the Spirit"). This marks the transition to the next subunit (3:7–18). V. 6, then, is both the conclusion to what comes before and the lead-in to what follows. Because this is a conventional technique in the Hellenistic world and because Paul makes use of it repeatedly in 2 Corinthians, it deserves some comment. Lucian verbalizes the principle: "One thing should not only lie adjacent to the next, but be related to it and overlap at the edges" (*On the Writing of History* 55). The proper way for sections to be related is like a chain, interlocking, or like a hinge, allowing parts to swing both ways. This principle is used in v. 6; it also is used in 4:1 where "we do not lose heart" concludes the section 2:14–4:1, even though in Greek it is the beginning of a sentence whose second half (v. 2) functions as the opening of the next section (4:2–16a). The same phenomenon occurs again in 4:16a,b. It has already been seen in 1:8–11, where the paragraph served both as the end of the letter opening and as the beginning of the itinerary.

The second image used for Paul's ministry in 2:14–4:1 is that of "minister of a new covenant" (3:7–18). The entire subsection is an exegesis of this phrase in 3:6. The passage falls into two parts: vv. 7–11 and vv. 12–18. Vv. 7–11's theme is that the new covenant's splendor/glory surpasses that of the old. Following the established rabbinic exegetical principle of arguing from the lesser to the greater (*qal wā-hômer*, as in Rom 5:9, 10, 15, 17; 11:12, 24), he argues that if the old dispensation of the law which is characterized by death, which is external, which is fading/is being annulled, and which results in condemnation came with a splendor so great that the Israelites could not look on Moses' face (Exod 34:29–35; Philo *Moses* 2.69–70), how much more will the new dispensation characterized by life, by inwardness, by permanency, and by righteousness possess a surpassing splendor. In other words, the new covenant surpasses the old. "When the sun is risen, lamps cease to be of use" (Plummer, *2 Corinthians*, p. 91).

If the new covenant's splendor surpasses that of the old (vv. 7–11), then, by derivation, the new covenant's ministry surpasses that of the old (3:12–18). It is upon this fact that Paul's boldness is based (v. 12), in contrast to Moses, whose act of veiling himself was because the splendor of his ministry was destined to pass away (v. 13). This subsection involves an interpretation (midrash) of Exod 34:29–35. Two texts are cited, each followed by an interpretation:

Text One. "Moses put a veil over his face" (3:13a; Exod 34:33, 35)
Interpretation One. The purpose of this act was to conceal the temporary character of the splendor of the old covenant (v. 13b); the result of this was the hardening of the hearts of Israel to this day (vv. 14–15).

Text Two. "Whenever he [Moses] will turn to the Lord, the veil is removed" (v. 16; Exod 34:34; cf. NEB, TEV).
Interpretation Two. The Lord in this text means the Spirit of Christian experience (v. 17a). Where the Spirit of the Lord referred to is, there is freedom (v. 17b). All of us Christians who have turned to the Lord referred to and have no veils on our faces contemplate the divine glory and as a result are being transformed into his likeness. Just as (was said above, this comes) from the Spirit of the Lord (referred to).

(James Dunn, "2 Cor 3:17—'The Lord Is the Spirit,'" *JTS* 21[1970]: 309–20)

Over against the diminishing splendor of Moses' ministry, Paul emphasizes both the permanence and the increase of the Christians' splendor. It was a common belief in the Hellenistic world that the beholding of a deity could have a transformative effect on a worshiper. Seneca speaks for the Greco-Roman world when he says, "Pythagoras declares that our souls experience a change when we enter a temple and behold the images of the gods face to face, and await the utterances of an oracle" (*Epistle* 94.42; cf. *Corpus Hermeticum* 10.6). A similar theme of transformation by vision may be found at Qumran (1 QH 4.5–6; 3.3; 4.27–29; 1 QSb 4.24–28; 1 QS 2.2–4). Paul, therefore, is very bold (v. 12) because of the permanency of the new covenant, which covenant results in human transformation.

The entire section, 2:14–4:1, comes to an end with Paul's concluding statement in 4:1: "Therefore, having this ministry [which surpasses that of Moses] by the mercy of God [from whom our sufficiency comes], we do not lose heart" [although beset by affliction at every turn]. This thought unit raises acutely the issue of Paul's understanding of Christianity's relation to Judaism. To this matter we now turn. The issue may be stated in terms of the apostle's view of the covenants.

What is Paul's view of the covenants? To which covenants do we refer? In Paul's Bible, the LXX, covenant (*diathēkē*) refers to a structured relationship between two parties dependent upon an oath or promise for its existence (cf. Aristophanes *Birds* 440ff., for a similar usage in the Greek world). Covenant is used in a legal way of relationships between humans, for example, the covenant between Isaac and Abimelech, Gen 26:26–33; that between Jacob and Laban, Gen 31:44–54; that between Jonathan and David, 1 Sam 18:3; 20:8; 23:18. It is used in a theological way of relationships between humans and God. When employed theologically, covenant can describe two very different types of relationships. On the one hand, there are covenants in which God binds himself: for example, the covenant with Noah, Gen 9:8–17; that with Abraham, Gen 12; 15; 17; that with Phinehas, Num 25:10–13; Jer 23:17–22; that with David, 2 Sam 23:5; 1 Kings 8:23–26; Ps 89:3–4; Jer 33:17–22. When talking about such promissory types, covenant and oath are often synonymous (Testament of Moses 1.9; 3.9; 11.17; 12.13), as are covenant and promise (1 Kings 8:25). Such covenants are not conditional. On the other hand, there are covenants in which Israel is bound, for example, the Mosaic covenant, Exod 24; that at Shechem under Joshua, Josh 24; that under Josiah, 2 Kings 23; that under Ezra, Ezra 9–10; Neh 9–10. When talking about such obligatory types, covenant and law are often synonymous (Deut 4:12–13; Lev 26:46; Ecclus 28:7; 45:5; 1 Macc 2:20–21, 27, 50; 2 Esd 4:23; 7:24). Such covenants are conditional on the people's obedience.

The new covenant of Jer 31:31–34 requires separate treatment because it is like both the promissory and the obligatory types of covenant in the Bible used by Paul. It is like the obligatory covenant of Moses in that it refers to law and to the people's acceptance of God as suzerain and of the stipulations as binding ("they shall all *know* me"—"know" being used in ancient suzerainty treaties of recognition of the suzerain and acceptance of the stipulations). It is like the promissory types of covenant in that it depends for its existence and its effectiveness on God's promise or oath. In the new covenant promised through Jeremiah, God will assume responsibility for the people's obedience. It is based on God's oath to enable his people's faithfulness to the covenant. Unlike the rest of Israel's canonical spokesman, in this passage Jeremiah sees the old Mosaic covenant as a thing of the past. He does not call for a return to it. "My covenant which they broke" (31:32) dismisses the old order with finality. The prophet, in this instance, awaits a new order. If the very concept of covenant used theologically points to an understanding of God as personal, the notion of a new covenant signals a God who learns from his mistakes and makes new beginnings. A new covenant, God has learned, must be one of divine enablement because of human faithlessness (Delbert R. Hillers, *Covenant: The History of a Biblical Idea* [Baltimore: Johns Hopkins Press, 1969]).

Of some of these covenants Paul makes no mention: Noah, Phinehas, Joshua, Josiah, Ezra. The covenant with David is not central to Paul's thought, though it is apparently echoed in the oral tradition taken up in Rom 1:3–4 ("descended from David according to the flesh") and in the quotation from Isa 11:10 in Rom 15:12 ("The root of Jesse shall come, he who rises to rule the Gentiles; in him shall the Gentiles hope"). If so, then Paul would see the promise to David fulfilled in the reign of Jesus after the resurrection (1 Cor 15:20–28), much as Luke-Acts does (Luke 1:68–69; Acts 2:30–36; 13:33–37). Three of the covenants of his Bible receive significant attention in Paul's letters: (1) the covenant with Abraham, (2) the covenant through Moses, and (3) the new covenant of Jer 31.

Of the three covenants that play significant roles in Paul's letters, two are highly valued, the third's importance is minimized by the apostle. The construct that seems to make the most sense out of the various things Paul says about the covenants may be summarized as follows. (*a*) The covenant with Abraham furnishes Paul a scriptural way to argue that justification through faith has been God's plan all along for Jew and Gentile alike. (*b*) The Law (Mosaic covenant) was a temporary phase in God's dealings with his people. In spite of its just requirements, it was impotent because of human sin. Hence, it functioned only to expose sin. With the coming of Christ, the Law has come to an end as a part of ongoing salvation history. (*c*) The Mosaic covenant has been replaced by the prophesied new covenant of Jer 31, in which God himself enables his people's faithfulness to the relationship (i.e., their righteousness is from God). A survey of Galatians and Romans will confirm this construct.

In Galatians the issue is whether or not Gentiles who had already received the Spirit/been justified (i.e., had been granted the life of the New Age and God's eschatological inclusion in his people of the Eschaton) were incomplete in their relation to God without circumcision (Gal

5:2; 6:12) and observance of certain special days of Judaism, like the Sabbath and some festivals (4:10). Paul is arguing not with Jews but with other Christians (1:6–9) who contend that the Gentiles' status as sons of Abraham was not complete (*epiteleisthe*, 3:3) without observance of certain Jewish practices.

The apostle's point of orientation is Christian experience (3:1–5). The Gentile converts received the Spirit as a gift in connection with their hearing with faith (3:2, past tense, apparently referring to their conversion). They continue to experience the gift of the Spirit in the same way (3:5, present tense, pointing to an ongoing experience). Since they have this foretaste of the life of the New Age, there is, in Paul's opinion, no need to add anything to their hearing with faith. On the basis of this starting point, Paul then produces a midrash, showing that scripture agrees with their experience. Scripture, he argues, shows that the Abrahamic covenant of promise, not the Mosaic covenant of obligation, defines the essential relationship between God and the Gentiles.

The argument may be summarized something like this. The Gentile, Abraham, was justified through faith (3:6). His seed, Christ, was also a man of faith (2:16; 3:22). The promise of the land (the New Age) made to Abraham and to his seed (Christ) was fulfilled in the resurrection of Jesus and the outpouring of the Spirit. Gentiles who, like Abraham, are people of faith (are in Christ and have Christ in them) are likewise justified/receive the blessing of the Spirit (3:14). In other words, scripture testifies that God's plan all along, as revealed in the Abrahamic covenant, was to justify the Gentiles through faith (3:8–9). In Paul's opinion, this plan of God was not limited to Gentiles only. Out of his own experience as a Jew, he could say that Jews as well as Gentiles were justified through the faith of Christ Jesus (2:15–16).

If God's plan for the history of salvation is known through the covenant with Abraham, what is the place of the Mosaic covenant of obligation? In Gal 3:15–18 the apostle says the Law (the Mosaic covenant) does not annul the covenant of promise, the latter being chronologically prior. The Law was rather a temporary phase in salvation history. Its function was to keep us from harm by restraint, as a *paidagōgos* functioned in relation to an underage child in the Greek household, until the time of Christ when it was God's plan to justify *all* through faith (3:23–26). Once justified through faith, we are no longer under the Law (3:25). We are then Abraham's offspring, heirs according to promise (3:29).

In an allegorical play on the Abraham story, Paul characterizes the two covenants as that of freedom and that of slavery (4:21–31). The allegorical meaning of the story of Abraham's son (Ishmael) by the slave woman (Hagar) is the Mosaic covenant of obligation characteristic of the Judaism of Paul's time. The allegorical meaning of the story of Abraham's son (Isaac) by the free woman (Sarah) is the fulfilled covenant of promise characterized by freedom. The gift of the Spirit and justification (the inheritance/the life of the New Age) come not in connection with satisfying the Law but in the context of hearing with faith.

Paul's positions in Galatians may be summarized with three assertions. (*a*) Paul's position is rooted in experience. The experience of Jews, like Paul, showed the Spirit was not given (i.e., they did not receive the life of the New Age) in connection with obedience within the Mosaic covenant. The Spirit was given objectively as a result of Jesus' faithfulness and subjectively in connection with their faith in him. The experience of Gentiles, like the Galatians, showed that the Spirit was given (i.e., they were deemed righteous in God's eschatological judgment) in the context of their hearing with faith. Having already received the life of the New Age, they did not need to add anything to their faith. (*b*) Paul's midrash reflects the dual experiential reality described in (*a*). His view of the covenant with Abraham as basic and as prototypical for both Jew and Gentile after Jesus' resurrection and his vision of the Mosaic covenant as temporary discipline until Christ both grew out of his experiential data. He says that the Law is unnecessary in light of the Spirit. (*c*) Paul's aim throughout is to guard against a view of the Christian life that says one begins with faith but comes to maturity through law. The apostle's posture is that one grows as a Christian the way one becomes a Christian, through faith.

In Romans, addressed to a church made up of both Jews and Gentiles, the issue is whether or not Jews and Gentiles are deemed righteous by God in the same way, that is, on the basis of the faith of Christ and by one's faith in him. The apostle is writing to a church he did not found, one that is not within his orbit of influence. He wants to enlist this church in support of his projected mission to Spain and so needs their approval of his gospel. When he writes Romans, Paul is seeking to demonstrate that the gospel he preaches is in full accord with the divine plan. He aims to show a grand continuity between God's initial dealings with his chosen people and what he was bringing to pass in the last days. To do this, Paul goes back to Abraham and argues that, in the new realities of the present,

God is bringing to completion the promise he made to the father of us all, Abraham.

Tracing the line of thought in Romans will assist us. The theme of Romans is the righteousness of God (Rom 1:16–17). In this epistle the righteousness of God refers to God's faithfulness in keeping his promises to Abraham. Paul begins by showing that Gentile and Jew alike are sinful (1:18–3:20). God remains faithful (3:3–4) and through the faithfulness of Christ (3:22) has acted to fulfill his promise to Abraham. God is making Abraham, who believed God and was reckoned righteous (4:3) before his circumcision (4:10), the father of all who believe (4:11–12), both Gentile and Jew. Through the resurrection of Jesus (4:24), his spiritual descendants are given a pledge that the promise to inherit the world (New Age, 4:13) will be fulfilled. If this is so, then why have so few Jews believed? Does this mean God's word has failed (9:6)?

Rom 9–11 struggles with this issue. (*a*) In 9:6–29 the point is that Israel has always been divided into those who belong only by birth and those who belong according to promise. God 's promises were meant only for the latter. It is this ancient division that now is apparent in the decision for or against Jesus. (*b*) In 9:30–10:21 Paul argues that the righteousness through faith which applies to Jew and Gentile alike without distinction has been made known to all Israel, not just the elect. If after God has gone this extra mile they refuse to believe, that is their fault, not God's. (*c*) In 11:1–32 the apostle says God's faithfulness goes even further. Even after being rejected, God does not reject his people. On the contrary, he will save all. Even the unbelieving Jews serve a function, that of the spread of salvation among the Gentiles. When the full number of Gentiles have entered, then the whole of Israel will be included. When this happens, the general resurrection will occur (11:15). Although this vision of the future may be stated with a degree of tentativeness (11:33–34), Paul uses it to climax his claim that God can be trusted without reservation. He has revealed his fidelity to Israel over and beyond his promises. His fulfillment is more marvellous than his oath to Abraham. Near the end of Romans (15:8–9), the theme of the letter is heard again: the promises to the patriarchs are fulfilled through Christ. In Romans, as in Galatians, it is the covenant with Abraham that supplies the basic structure for Paul's soteriology. If so, how does he view the Mosaic covenant in Romans?

In Romans, as in Galatians, the Law is viewed as a temporary phase in God's plan (5:20, "law came in to increase the trespass"). Its primary function is to give a knowledge of sin (3:20; 7:7). Its just requirements (8:4) are good (7:13). These requirements, however, are impotent in the face of radical evil which resides in the self (7:7–25). Only the Spirit enables victory over this "sin" and thereby the fulfillment of the just requirement of the Law (8:3–4; 13:8–10). With Christ, the Law's era ends (10:4).

One can say, in summary, that Romans agrees with Galatians in asserting the priority of the covenant with Abraham over the Mosaic covenant, which is viewed as a temporary phase in God's history of salvation. There is also agreement in the contention that Jew and Gentile alike receive the inheritance/land (life of the New Age) through faith. Romans is unique in sketching a vision of the future in which unbelieving Israel will turn to Christ at the time of the Eschaton.

2 Cor 3 uses the term "fading" in two different ways. First, the glory on Moses' face was fading (3:7, 13). This is in contrast to Christians, who are being changed from one degree of glory to another (3:18). Second, the old covenant faded away (3:11). This is in contrast to the new covenant, which is permanent (3:11). This evidence indicates that Paul thought the new covenant not only surpassed the old but also replaced it, though this reality could only be seen by those from whose eyes the Spirit had taken away the veil (3:14–17). This conclusion agrees with the evidence of Galatians and Romans in which Paul contended the Mosaic covenant was temporary.

In summary, one may say that Paul's concerns about the covenants with Abraham and Moses and the new covenant is primarily soteriological. When he wants to make the point that Christian soteriological reality has been a part of God's plan from the very beginning, he works with the Abrahamic covenant and its relation to the Mosaic Law. When he wants to emphasize the soteriological reality that human faithfulness to God in the covenant relationship depends upon God, he works with the new covenant of Jer 31.

Comparison of Paul with his context enables further clarification of his position. The first thing to note is that Paul's perspective has nothing in common with the various varieties of pagan prejudice. Cultural prejudice against the northern barbarians existed in the Roman mind from Caesar to Tacitus, focusing on details of character, physique, and customs. There is no similarity between this cultural prejudice and the apostolic stance on the covenants. National prejudice is expressed in the second century A.D. in Greek attitudes towards Romans (e.g., Lucian

Nigrinus and *De Mercede Conductis*) and in Roman feelings about Greeks (e.g., Juvenal *Satires* 3). This is far from what is manifest in Paul's theology of the covenants. The Roman hostility towards Greeks was often based not only on the difference between them but on the jealousy felt by the native for his too successful foreign rival. Anti-Judaic feelings in the Hellenistic world had the same two roots. Such hostility was not based on a racial theory, as in modern times, but rather on a combination of dissimilarity and competition. On the one hand, Jews were disliked because they refused to mingle with the Gentiles, choosing instead to remain aloof from ancient society (e.g., Esther 3:8; 2 Macc 14:38; Diodorus 34. fragments 1–4; 40. fragments 3 and 5; Josephus *Apion* 2.10 §121; Juvenal *Satires* 14.96–106; Tacitus *Histories* 5.5.2; Philostratus *Life of Apollonius* 5.33). The same type of hostility was directed at early Christians for similar reasons (e.g., 1 Pet 4:3–4). On the other hand, Jews were objects of hostility because of sensed competition. They penetrated the pagans' position by religious proselytism on a large scale (e.g., Josephus says that at Antioch "the Jews made converts of a great number of Greeks perpetually, and thus after a sort brought them to be a portion of their own body" [*War* 7.3.3 §45]; at Damascus "yet did the Damascenes distrust their wives, which were almost all addicted to the Jewish religion" [*War* 2.20.2 §561]; Juvenal *Satires* 6.541–47, for Rome). Some of this acquisition of proselytes was done by active recruiting (e.g., Horace *Satire* 1.4.142–43; Tacitus *Histories* 5.5; Josephus *Antiquities* 20.1.3–4 §34–43; 19.5.3 §290; Matt 23:15; Rom 2:17–21; Rabbi Eleazar: "if one brings a proselyte to God, it is as though he created him" [Genesis Rabbah 84.4]). It ought to be obvious that this anti-Judaic attitude of Hellenistic people is not what one finds in Paul (A. N. Sherwin-White, *Racial Prejudice in Imperial Rome* [Cambridge: Cambridge University Press, 1967]; J. N. Sevenster, *The Roots of Pagan Anti-Semitism in the Ancient World* [Leiden: Brill, 1975]).

The second thing to note is that Paul's position towards Judaism is not analogous to Judaism's posture towards the pagan world. Jewish polemic against pagan polytheism was direct and harsh (e.g., Letter of Jeremiah; Wisd of Sol 13–14; Jubilees 15.31ff.; 22:16; Philo *Laws* 163; *Moses* 2.196; m Aboda Zarah). Nothing redemptive was to be found in pagan religion. It was a fraud to be opposed only. Neither the pagan antipathy towards Judaism nor the Jewish hostility towards pagan religion and mores offers any parallel to what one finds in Paul's attitude towards the covenants.

The closest analogy to the Pauline posture is to be found in Qumran.

Like Paul, Qumran believed something new was taking place in history under divine guidance. A separation was also occuring in the Jewish community, the faithful from the unfaithful. Mainline Judaism, unwilling to follow the lead of Qumran, was considered in a state of apostasy. Unlike Qumran, which anticipated the destruction of apostate Judaism, Paul held out a hope for the ultimate salvation of all Israel. In spite of their differences, Paul and Qumran both represent intra-Jewish debates over who is the true people of God in the present in light of the new thing God is doing. Both describe the new circumstances in terms of a new covenant (CD 6.19; 18.21; 1 QpHab 2.3, so Qumran). Both develop a midrash that differs significantly from what we now recognize as mainstream Judaism. It is in terms of an intra-Jewish debate that we may now move to a comparison of Paul with Pharisaic-rabbinic Judaism.

Paul was a Jew. He believed in the same God as the non-Christian Jew. He used more or less the same scriptures as the Pharisaic Jew. The basic difference between the Christian Jew, Paul, and the Pharisaic-rabbinic variety of Judaism was eschatology. Paul believed the New Age had been inaugurated with the resurrection of Jesus and the resulting gift of the Spirit, which signals God's eschatological justification of the recipients. Non-Christian Jews did not accept the claim about inaugurated eschatology. Given the different starting points, each variety of ancient Judaism (Christian and Pharisaic) developed a different reading (midrash) of scripture.

The Pauline midrash is different from the Pharisaic-rabbinic reading at a number of key points. (1) On the one hand, the covenant with Abraham and Jeremiah's promised new covenant are central for Paul. The Mosaic covenant is regarded as temporary, being replaced by the new covenant. When he argues that the Mosaic covenant was temporary, Paul does not deny that Israel as a sociological reality for whom the Mosaic covenant is constitutive continues to exist. What he says is that such a sociological reality has ceased to have positive soteriological significance in God's plan because it has not recognized and responded positively to the new thing God is doing since Jesus. If and when this sociological reality does recognize and respond positively to God's new developments, then it will again have soteriological significance and the Eschaton will occur. On the other hand, Pharisaic Judaism saw the Mosaic covenant as both permanent and central. The Abrahamic covenant was viewed eschatologically.

(2) On the one hand, the land is interpreted by Paul to mean the New

Age. On the other hand, Pharisaic Judaism continued to understand the land to mean Palestine.

(3) On the one hand, ethnicity is relativized by Paul. Within Israel only the children of promise are a part of salvation history up to Christ. Since Jesus, only those who have faith in him are a part of the divine plan. Gentiles have access to the Abrahamic covenant in the same way Jews do, but without having to become Jews. On the other hand, according to Pharisaic Judaism one is a member of the covenant by birth, unless drastic steps are taken to exclude oneself. Gentiles can become Jews through proselytism.

(4) On the one hand, human nature is assumed by Paul to be in bondage to sin, a bondage from which only God can deliver one. Humans are, as a result of their sin, faithless in any relation with God, a faithlessness from which only God can deliver. On the other hand, Pharisaic Judaism recognized both the good and the evil impulses within a human being but believed that one is able to conquer the evil *yetzer* through proper spiritual discipline. It is possible to be faithful to God within the covenant without extraordinary measures on God's part.

(5) On the one hand, evangelism is central to Paul. He was concerned to win both Jews and Gentiles to Jesus. On the other hand, there was also a strong proselytizing movement in Pharisaic Judaism to win Gentiles to Judaism in antiquity. The synagogue, however, resisted Christian missionary efforts (e.g., Gal 1:13; 1 Thess 2:14–16; 2 Cor 11:24, 26; Rom 15:31; Acts 13:44–50; 14:2, 5, 19; 17:5–7, 13; 18:12–17).

THE TREASURE AND TRIBULATIONS
OF THE MINISTRY

2 Corinthians 4:2–16a

This panel, like 2:14–4:1, begins with "commend ourselves" (3:1; 4:2) in conjunction with a denial ("not peddlers of God's word," 2:17; "refuse to tamper with God's word," 4:2). Just as in the case of 2:14–4:1, 2 Cor 4:2–16a ends with an expression of hope ("we do not lose heart," 4:1; 4:16a). This section is composed of two main thought units, 4:2–6 and 4:7–16a. Each must be examined in turn.

In 2 Cor 4:2–6, the first subsection, Paul says that his open preaching, based on his own conversion experience, is what commends him. The material is organized around two assertions (vv. 2 and 5). The first assertion contains both a negative and a positive side. On the one side, there are three negatives: "we have renounced disgraceful, underhanded ways; we refuse to practice cunning or to tamper with God's word" (v. 2a; remember 2:17a). Again, Paul distances himself from teachers who adulterate their word. The criticism is typical of Hellenistic critiques of dishonest philosophers. For example, Lucian says, "I certainly cannot say how in your view philosophy and wine are comparable, except perhaps at this one point, that philosophers sell their lessons as wine merchants their wines—most of them adulterating and cheating and giving false measure" (*Hermotinus* 59). The allusion is certainly to the visiting apostles who worked on a fee system in Corinth. On the other side, there is the positive assertion: "by an open statement of the truth we would commend ourselves to every man's conscience in the sight of God" (v. 2b). A defense follows the assertion (vv. 3–4; cf. 11:5–6). "And even if our gospel [1 Thess 1:5; Rom 2:16; Gal 1:11; 2:1] is veiled, it is veiled only to those who are perishing" (3:13–16). Why do some reject Paul's preaching? "In their case the god of this world [Eph 2:2; John 12:31; 14:30; 16:11; T. Judah 19:4] has blinded the minds of the unbelievers" (v. 4).

155

In the second assertion, Paul tells what it is that he preaches, again with a negative and a positive: "For what we preach is not ourselves, but Jesus Christ as Lord" (v. 5). Once again, the apostle's negative echoes the cultural critique of sophists. For example, Dio Chrysostom says, "Now the great majority of those styled philosophers proclaim themselves such, just as the Olympian heralds proclaim the victors" (*Oration* 13.11; remember 2 Cor 10:12). Paul's focus is not on himself but on Christ. Why is this so? The ground of Paul's proclamation is his own experience of conversion or call (v. 6): "For it is the God who said, 'Let light shine out of darkness,' who has shown in our hearts to give the light of the knowledge of the glory of God in the face of Christ." The parallel between the creation of the world (Gen 1:3) and the Pauline experience of grace (Gal 1:16; 1 Cor 9:1; 15:8) portrays Paul's conversion as an act of God's new creation (5:17). This experience was the basis for his focus on Christ as Lord (Segoon Kim, *The Origin of Paul's Gospel* [Tübingen: Mohr-Siebeck, 1981], pp. 5–11).

The second subsection, 4:7–16a, deals with the suffering that is a part of Paul's apostolic ministry described so forcefully in the two assertions of 4:2–6. He begins with a statement of the fact: "But we have this treasure [his apostolic ministry grounded in his religious experience] in earthen vessels." The term "earthen vessel" was often a metaphor of a human being in the Old Testament (Isa 29:16; 30:14; 45:9; 64:8; Jer 18:6; Lam 4:2; Job 10:9; 2 Esd 4:11). The connotation was sometimes on the frailty of such pots (Jer 22:28; Ps 31:12). The contrast here is between the container which is fragile and expendable and the contents that are precious. The image was common. In the East, treasure was often stored in earthen jars. Plutarch tells how, during the celebration of the Macedonian victory of Aemilius Paulus in 167 B.C., 3,000 men, following the wagons, carried silver coin in 750 earthen vessels ("Aemilius" 32). The treasure of apostleship is carried within the life of a vulnerable human being. This is a fact. The purpose of such an arrangement is "to show that the transcendent power belongs to God and not to us" (v. 7b; remember 12:9). How does Paul endure his sufferings? The tribulation list in vv. 8–10 tells us in its five components:

> We are afflicted in every way, but not crushed;
>> perplexed, but not driven to despair;
>> persecuted, but not forsaken;
>> struck down, but not destroyed;
> always carrying in the body the death of Jesus,
> so that the life of Jesus may be manifested in our bodies.

So, although the apostle knows the oppressive forces of life in the world, he is not overwhelmed because of the power of God that upholds him. Whereas as an apostle Paul is always in danger of being killed because of his proclamation of the gospel, the fact that he is still alive testifies to the resurrection life of Jesus (v. 11). There are benefits for the Corinthians as recipients of the apostolic ministry in Paul's sufferings: "So death is at work in us, but life [salvation] in you" (v. 12).

The fact that Paul uses a traditional tribulation list in vv. 8–10 is significant. It becomes yet one more means by which he attempts to gain the Corinthians' approval and to solidify their obedience to him. Catalogues of hardships were passages where a speaker enumerated the different circumstances, often negative, over which he boasts the victory. One type of such catalogues of hardships was that of the wise man's hardships. The common man of the Greco-Roman world felt only flux and had no assurance that the flux was benevolent. The answer to this problem was an internal one, a mental or emotional state free from disturbance. To achieve this state, one adapted an indifferent attitude towards things that are indifferent. Philosophy furnished the rational capacity to prefer adversity when necessary and to turn it to one's advantage. The person who could do this was the Sage. Seneca says the Sage remains unperturbed because he is "not harmed by poverty, or by pain, or by any other of life's storms" (*Epistle* 85.37). Epictetus argues that external things like a tyrant, disease, poverty, or an obstacle are not legitimate grounds for being disturbed (4.12.9). He says the true Sage is the man "who though sick is happy, though in danger is happy, though dying is happy, though condemned to exile is happy, though in disrepute is happy" (2.19.24). The Sage, according to Seneca, has "the weakness of a man and the serenity of a god" (*Epistle* 53.12). Although not immune to adversity, the wise man is not affected by it. So the ideal philosopher is revealed as such by his steadfast refusal to be bowed down under hardships. In this context, a tribulation list when used of a philosopher would serve as a literary foil in the depiction of his serenity and endurance. The catalogues of hardships become celebrations of the Sage's invincible virtue. By amplifying the hardships, the person is magnified because hardships reveal character.

Throughout 2 Corinthians 10–13 and 1–9 Paul depicts himself as the ideal philosopher over against opponents who are portrayed as despised sophists. The trial lists of 11:23–29, 4:8–10, and 6:4–10 function as an integral part of that image. For both Paul and the Sage, what enables the victory over adversity is power. Circumstances, like those in a catalogue of hardships, provide the occasion for the display of this power. In the case of the wise man, what is shown is the power of his mind or will, informed by philosophy. In the case of Paul, what is displayed is attributed to God (e.g., Phil 4:12–13; Rom 8:37; 2 Cor 4:7). Paul used such trial lists in 2 Corinthians because he was trying to show his converts that he is a person of integrity, one in whom they might have pride (2 Cor 1:13–14). Since the catalogues of hardships were a conventional way of demonstrating virtue, it was natural that the apostle would use them when needed. After all, according to Aristotle, character is the most powerful means of persuasion (*Rhetoric* 1.2; cf. Isocrates *Oration* 15.278) (John T. Fitzgerald, Jr., "Cracks in an Earthen Vessel: An Examination of the Catalogues of Hardships in the Corinthian Correspondence" [Ph.D. dissertation, Yale, 1984]; Robert Hodgson, "Paul the Apostle and First Century Tribulation Lists," *ZNW* 74[1983]:59–80).

If the apostolic vocation is so beset with suffering, why does Paul not lose heart? His answer is given in a quote from Ps 116:10 ("since we have the same spirit of faith as he who wrote, 'I believed, and so I spoke,' we too believe, and so we speak"), an appropriate choice, since Ps 116 is a hymn of thanksgiving for deliverance from death. That which is believed, which enables Paul to speak, is the traditional Christian affirmation: "he who raised the Lord Jesus will raise us also with Jesus and bring us with you into his presence" (v. 4; cf. Rom 8:11; 1 Thess 4:17). Again he returns to the benefits for the Corinthians: "it is all for your sake" (v. 15). Because of God's power that keeps him from being overwhelmed by his sufferings, the power that determines that death does not have final sway, the power that through Paul benefits the Corinthians, "we do not lose heart" (v. 16a). Whereas in 2:14–4:1 the emphasis was on the greatness of Paul's ministry, in 4:2–16a the focus is on the suffering that accompanies it. The basis of Paul's confidence set out in 4:13–14 leads very naturally to the next section, 4:16b–5:10, where the concern is the Christian hope.

THE COMFORT AND CHALLENGE
OF CHRISTIAN HOPE

2 Corinthians 4:16b–5:10

This section is related to 4:2–16a, where Paul says that although his ministry involves suffering, he does not lose heart (4:16a), because (1) the life of Jesus is manifested in his mortal flesh with benefits for the Corinthians (4:11–12) and (2) the God who raised Jesus will raise the apostle, a benefit to be shared by the Corinthians (4:14). 2 Cor 4:16–5:10 picks up on the theme of future glory as a basis for confidence amidst present suffering. It has the effect of saying that Paul's endurance of trials is due to God.

2 Cor 4:16–18 is the introduction: "this slight momentary affliction is preparing us for an eternal weight of glory beyond all comparison" (v. 17). In 5:1–10 there are two thought units, loosely corresponding to one another in their architecture:

We know that (5:1)	knowing that (5:6)
We groan, longing (5:2)	we would rather, we prefer (5:8)
For (5:4)	for (5:10)
So that (5:4)	so that (5:10).

These two paragraphs state respectively the two main components of early Christian eschatology: (1) the cosmic component (the parousia/ resurrection) and (2) the individual component (the inner person's being with the Lord). Just as in certain streams of ancient Judaism, when taken together they yield a pattern something like this. There will be a cosmic event at the end of history which will include the resurrection of the dead and the transformation of the living. Those Christians who die before this cosmic event go to be with the Lord, waiting for the End. Each of these segments deserves separate attention.

2 Cor 4:16–18 states the thesis: the contrast between present, momentary affliction and future, eternal glory is a ground for apostolic confidence. Life in the present, empirical world partakes of the character of

159

this age. It is transient ("wasting away," v. 16b—cf. 1 Cor 7:31; "transient," v. 18b; "momentary," v. 17a) and is characterized by affliction (v. 17a). Such "momentary affliction" for a Christian has its purpose. It prepares one for "an eternal weight of glory beyond all comparison" (v. 17b). It is because the coming glory is so great that the present affliction seems so "slight" (v. 17a). Paul is like the Sage of the philosophers, who can be "unterrified in the midst of dangers" and "happy in adversity" because he "passes through every experience as if it were of small account" (Seneca *Moral Epistles* 41.4–5). His basis, however, is akin to that of his Jewish roots (2 Baruch 48.50, "For surely, as you endured much labor in the short time in which you live in this passing world, so you will receive great light in that world which has no end").

What is this eternal hope which is the basis of the apostle's confidence? It has two components, which are treated in 5:1–5 and 5:6–10 respectively. 2 Cor 5:1–5 focuses on the cosmic dimension of eschatology that is rooted in present experience. What is said is a traditional Christian affirmation ("we know," 5:1a): "if the earthly tent we live in is destroyed, we have a building from God, a house not made with hands, eternal in the heavens" (5:1b). The expression "earthly tent" was a common idiom for earthly life in the body (Isa 38:12; Wisd of Sol 9:15; 2 Pet 1:13; Corpus Hermeticum 13.15). The destruction of the earthly tent is a reference to death. Although the "building from God" has sometimes been understood as the heavenly temple, the church, it most probably is a reference to the resurrection body. If so, how must "we have" be interpreted? If the expression is taken with the normal meaning of a present tense, then the meaning would be that one receives the resurrection body immediately upon death. If so, then it would be necessary to posit a development in Paul's thought from 1 Cor 15, where the resurrection body comes at the parousia, not at death (so also Phil 3:20–21; 1 Thess 4:16–17). If the present tense here is taken as akin to the prophetic perfect in Hebrew (cf. Rev 22:20; Rom 8:30 for analogies), then "we have" is a forceful way of stating the possession of something which is actually still future. If so, then the eschatology here is in continuity with that of the rest of Paul's letters. V. 1 says that if Christians die, they will have resurrection bodies.

The groaning of the creation (Rom 8:22–23) is matched by that of the Christian: "In this present body we do indeed groan; we yearn to have our heavenly habitation put on over this one—in the hope that, being thus clothed, we shall not find ourselves naked" (v. 2, NEB).

The translation "put on over" captures the meaning of the compound verb (*ependusasthai*). The picture here is that of a person wearing clothes who wishes to put on another garment over those already being worn. Another picture comes in v. 4: "For while we are still in this tent, we sigh with anxiety; not that we would be unclothed, but that we would be further clothed, so that what is mortal may be swallowed up by life." The image is that of a person living in a house or tent who wishes to put up another around the one already inhabited. Both pictures allow Paul to say that he wishes to receive the new clothes or tent without having to give up the old. He hopes not to have the old tent taken down by death but longs to live to the parousia, when he will receive the new dwelling in addition—"to put it on like an overcoat" (Barrett, *2 Corinthians*, p. 152; cf. 1 Cor 15:51). If this happens, Paul will not have to be "naked" (v. 3) or "unclothed" (v. 4), that is, without a body (cf. 1 Cor 15:37–38). Unlike Plato (*Phaedo* 67DE; 81C) and Philo (*Virtues* 76; *Allegorical Interpretation* 2.57, 59), Paul did not regard soul-nakedness as desirable. Implicit in this discussion is the apostle's belief that there are two routes to the resurrection body. For those who have died before the parousia, there will be resurrection (i.e., after a period of nakedness, they will be given their resurrection bodies). For those who live until the parousia, there will be transformation (i.e., without a period of nakedness, one will be changed from mortal into immortal, like a person putting one garment on over another). For all, there will be a spiritual body suitable for the new state of existence (1 Cor 15:51–52). Paul's longing for an imminent End is linked to his desire to avoid the "naked" state (vv. 2–4). He shared the average person's fear of the nakedness of the soul (Plato *Cratylus* 403B; *Gorgias* 523, 524; *Republic* 9.577B). The God who has prepared Christians for this resurrection life, moreover, has given a pledge or guarantee of its reality in the gift of the Spirit in the present (v. 5). The term *arrabōna* in v. 5 is a commercial term meaning a down payment in guarantee that the whole amount will be paid. The future, cosmic eschatology is thereby rooted in the Christians' present religious experience. The cosmic dimension of the future hope is one side of the basis for Paul's not losing heart.

2 Cor 5:6–10 focuses on the individual dimension of eschatology conditioned by the future hope. Another item of traditional Christian belief begins this unit ("we know," v. 6): "while we are at home in the body we are away from the Lord" (v. 6—cf. Phil 1:21–26; Philo speaks of this bodily life as a state of being away from home, a sojourning in a foreign

land [*Who Is the Heir of Divine Things?* 82, 267]). In v. 7, "for we walk by faith, not by sight," living by sight is the equivalent of being "with the Lord" (cf. 1 Cor 13:12, "then face to face"). Paul's preference is to be "with the Lord" (v. 8; Polycarp says Paul is in the place he deserved with the Lord [*To Philippians* 9.2]). Paul presupposes an intermediate state here, where the Christian dead who await the resurrection are in the presence of Christ, conscious of the Lord. His Jewish roots would have furnished him the concept. 1 Enoch 22 speaks about places for the spirits of the dead to gather until the day of their judgment. The righteous and sinners occupy separate places. 2 Esd 7:75 raises the question of an intermediate state in an explicit way; 7:32 says that at the Last Judgment "the chambers shall give up the souls which have been committed to them." 2 Baruch 21.23–24 reads, "let the treasuries of the souls restore those who are enclosed in them," while 30.2, says, "And it will happen at that time that those treasuries will be opened in which the number of the souls of the righteous were kept." Outside of Paul, Christian references to an intermediate state are few (e.g., Luke 16:22; 23:43; Heb 12:23; Rev 6:9) but are sufficient to show that Paul was not alone in his Christian appropriation of this Jewish background (Phil 1:23; 2 Cor 5:6–9) (George Ladd, *The Last Things* [Grand Rapids:Eerdmans, 1978], chap. 3; Karel Hanhart, *The Intermediate State in the New Testament* [Franeker: T. Wever, 1966]). Read in this way, 2 Cor 5:1–10 offers little support for a development in Pauline eschatology (Gerhardus Vos, *The Pauline Eschatology* [Grand Rapids: Baker, reprint 1979], chap. 7).

Paul is like the philosophic Sage who not only recognizes that "the body is not a permanent dwelling, but a sort of inn" for one's brief sojourn but also is ready to depart this temporary dwelling (Seneca *Epistle* 120.12–15). Because of his Christian hope, the apostle is "always of good courage" (vv. 6, 8).

Eschatology is not only a source of comfort for Paul (vv. 6–8), it is also a challenge to right conduct (vv. 9–10; cf. Rom 2:16; 14:10; 1 Cor 3:10–15): "So whether we are at home or away, we make it our aim to please him. For we must all appear before the judgment seat of Christ, so that each one may receive good or evil, according to what he has done in the body." The judgment referred to here is that of the Last Day (1 Cor 4:4–5; 5:5; Rom 2:16; 1 Thess 5:1–3; 2 Thess 1:9–10; cf. Acts 17:31). The idea would have been intelligible to Jews (2 Esd 7:113–15), to pagans (Lucian *Dialogues of the Dead* 10.13), and to non-Pauline Christians (Heb 9:27; Matt 25:31–46; Mark 8:38; 1 Pet 4:5; 2 Pet 3:10–12;

James 5:9; Rev 20:11–15). Paul's point is that it behooves the Christian to live always in the light of the Last Day.

Paul's ministry involves suffering. This, however, is but a temporary prelude to eternal glory. So Paul is of good courage (1) because of the Christian hope of the resurrection, which he wants to occur while he is still alive, and (2) because even if he dies, he goes to be with the Lord until the End. In the meantime, he is determind that he will please the one whose presence he longs for, because all (both those alive when the End comes and those who have died before it comes) will endure judgment.

THE MINISTER OF RECONCILIATION

2 Corinthians 5:11–6:2

This panel, like 2:14–4:1, 4:2–16a, and 6:3–7:4, opens with "commend ourselves" (5:12). The thought unit is held together by an inclusion (5:11, "we persuade men"; the two appeals of 5:20b and 6:1). It is built around two components: a promise to provide an answer (5:11–12) and the provision of the answer (5:13–6:2). Once again, it is Paul's apostolic ministry that is the focus of attention.

The promise is given in 5:11–12. Given the fact that all must stand before the judgment seat of Christ (5:10; 5:11, "knowing the fear of the Lord"), "we persuade men" (v. 11), that is, Paul pursues an evangelistic activity. The Lord knows his heart (v. 11b; cf. 1 Cor 4:4; 2 Cor 1:12); he hopes the Corinthians do, too. The apostle has no intent of repeating his self-praise of 2 Cor 10–13 (the letters of tears). What he wants to do is to give the Corinthians a basis for answering those who boast in external appearances (v. 12). In a sense this is the purpose of all of 2 Cor 1–9. Here the promise is specific and explicit: "We are . . . giving you cause to be proud of us, so that you may be able to answer those who pride themselves on a man's position and not on his heart" (cf. 1 Sam 16:7 for a similar contrast).

Paul fulfills his promise in 5:13–6:2. The answer that he provides falls into two parts: 5:13–17, which focuses on the apostle's motives, and 5:18–6:2, which concerns his ministry. 2 Cor 5:13–17 tells the readers that Paul's motives are rooted in the Christ-event, from which two consequences flow, one for Paul and the other for everyone else. There are three logical steps in the argument. (1) It is not externals but motives that are determinative (5:13), and Paul's life is controlled by Christ's love (v. 14a). The idiom is Greek (cf. Plato's contrast between the ecstatic and the sober-minded person [*Phaedrus* 244AB]). The point that is made utilizes the part of 1 Corinthians that deals with spiritual gifts (chaps. 12–14). Paul's behavior reflects the principles set forth there. "If we are beside ourselves, it is for God [1 Cor 14:2, "one who speaks in a tongue speaks . . . to God"]; if we are in our right mind, it is for you ["in church I would rather speak five words with my mind, in order to instruct others," 1 Cor 14:19]. For the love of Christ controls us" (1 Cor 12:31b, "I will show you a still more excellent way"; 14:1a, "make love your aim"). In other words, Paul is trying to clarify the motives behind certain dimensions of his behavior, like, why he always used rational speech in the church services instead of tongues. He is motivated by the love that comes from Christ.

(2) The love of Christ is defined in terms of his death for us, that death being looked at in terms of its necessity (v. 14c, "all have died") and its objective (v. 15b, "that those who live might live for him"). The statement "we are convinced that one has died for all" (v. 14b) is a variation on a traditional creedal formula ("Christ died for our sins," 1 Cor 15:3; "Christ died for us," Rom 5:8; 1 Thess 5:10). The "for all" makes it inclusive. The phrase that follows, "therefore all have died," may be understood in either of two ways. Either all have died to sin, potentially at least, in the death of their representative and await the actuality of their faith, or the fact that Christ died for all implies universal disobedience, all are dead in sin (Rom 5:12). The latter is the reading preferred here. The love of Christ is defined by the fact that when a universal need existed, Christ died to meet it. The objective of Christ's death was to reverse the problem (universal disobedience) and to insure that "those who live might live no longer for themselves but for him who for their sake died and was raised" (v. 15; cf. Rom 5:15-19; 6:10-11; 14:7-9). It is this kind of love that motivates the apostle. Would that this fact were known to the Corinthians' conscience (v. 11b).

(3) The consequences of living for Christ are twofold. For Paul, it means that he can no longer judge anyone in terms of externals: "From now on, therefore, we regard no one from a human point of view [v. 16a, in contrast to the others who pride themselves on a man's position, v. 12b]; even though we once regarded Christ from a human point of view, we regard him thus no longer" (v. 16b). Literally, v. 16b reads, "Even though we knew Christ according to the flesh, now we do not." The phrase "according to the flesh" may be taken adverbially as modifying the verb, "we know," or adjectivally as modifying the noun "Christ." The major translations correctly take it as referring to a way of knowing and not to the one known. Hence Paul contrasts his pre-Christian estimate of Christ by what was external with his Christian valuation of him. Just as his way of evaluation changed in his view of Christ after his conversion, so has his way of looking at all people. For Christians gener-

ally, the consequences of living for Christ mean a new creation: "there-fore, if anyone is in Christ, he is a new creation (Gal 6:15; Rev 21:1–5; 2 Pet 3:13; Isa 43:18–19; 65:17; 1 Enoch 72.1; 2 Baruch 32.6; Jubilees 4.26; 1 QS 4.25; 1 QH 11.10–14); the old has passed away, the new has come" (v. 17). The implication is, of course, that this radical change de-mands that all Christians, like Paul, judge by criteria that take motives into account. If the Corinthians understood the apostle's motives, they would be able to answer those who judge merely on the basis of surface data.

The second part of Paul's provision of an answer so that his Corinthian converts can respond to those who pride themselves on a man's position and not his heart (v. 12b) comes in 5:18–6:2. This subunit tells the readers that Paul's ministry was received from God, from whom two ap-peals follow, each with its basis given. Again, the argument unfolds in three logical steps. (1) The source of Paul's ministry of reconciliation is God: "All this is from God, who through Christ reconciled us to himself and gave us the ministry of reconciliation, that is, God was in Christ re-conciling the world to himself, not counting their trespasses against them, and entrusting to us the message of reconciliation" (vv. 18–19). Unlike 2 Macc 1:4–5; 5:20; 7:33; 8:29, where God is said to be recon-ciled to his people, Paul speaks of God as the reconciler of the world (Rom 5:10; contrast 1 Clement 48.1, "May God be reconciled to us"). Here the reconciliation is not of God, but is from God to God. The means of this reconciliation from God's side is variously described: "through Christ" (v. 18); "in Christ" (v. 19), which almost certainly is to be understood as parallel to v. 18, hence "by means of Christ"; "not counting their trespasses against them" (v. 19). How "not counting their trespasses against them" (v. 19) is related to "through Christ" and "by means of Christ" is here not spelled out. The object of God's reconciling activity is the world (v. 19a).

(2) The nature of Paul's ministry is that of being an ambassador for Christ through whom God makes his appeal (5:20a): "so we are ambas-sadors for Christ, God making his appeal through us" (1 Cor 1:17; Rom 10:15). The language is that used in the Greek East for the emperor's leg-ate. It is also reminiscent of the true Cynic who has been sent by Zeus as a messenger to humanity (Epictetus 3.22.23). Paul depicts himself as an ambassador sent to conclude a peace.

(3) Two illustrations of Paul's attempt to persuade people (5:11) are given next. The first appeal (v. 20b) is directed to the non-Christian

world: "We beseech you all on behalf of Christ, be reconciled to God." Given the divine initiative in the reconciling work (vv. 18–19), this must mean, allow God's reconciling work to be effective in you. The basis (v. 21) is the subject of a great debate. Literally translated, it reads, "the one not having known sin, on behalf of us he made sin, in order that we might become the righteousness of God in him." There is no dispute about the reference here to the sinlessness of Jesus (cf. 1 Pet 2:22; 1 John 3:5; Heb 4:15; 7:26; John 7:18; 8:46). The major problem concerns the meaning of the statement "he made *sin*" (*hamartian*). At least three different interpretations of this assertion are found in ancient Christian writers, interpretations that continue to this day. (*a*) "He made sin" may be understood to mean "God made him an offering for sin" (e.g., the Greek-speaking Cyril of Alexandria; the Latin-speaking Ambrosiaster and Augustine; the consensus of the Middle Ages). This reading is reflected in the NIV and NEB footnotes. (*b*) "He made sin" may be taken to mean "God caused him to assume our sinful nature" (e.g., Gregory of Nyssa). This is the tradition behind the NEB. (*c*) "He made sin" may be interpreted as "God allowed him to be condemned as a sinner" or "God treated him as a sinner" (e.g., Chrysostom, Luther, Calvin). Commentaries like those of Bultmann (*2 Corinthians*, p. 165) and Barrett (*2 Corinthians*, p. 180) echo this tradition in the present (Stanislas Lyonnet and Leopold Sabourin, *Sin, Redemption, and Sacrifice: A Biblical and Patristic Study* [Rome:Biblical Institute Press, 1970], Part III; William Hulitt Gloer, "*An Historical, Exegetical, and Theological Study of 2 Corinthians 5:14-21*" [unpublished Ph.D. dissertation, Southern Baptist Theological Seminary, 1981], chap. 1).

In favor of the first interpretative tradition several arguments may be advanced. (*a*) It is an ancient tradition, the dominant reading up to the time of the Reformation. (*b*) It is compatible with the use of language in the LXX. The LXX speaks about two types of sacrifice, using the term *hamartia* (sin): the sacrifice for sin (Hebrew, *hattā't*) and the sacrifice of reparation (Hebrew, *'āsām*). The former is rendered by the LXX either *peri hamartias* (Lev 5:9; 6:18–25) or *hamartia* (Exod 29:14; Lev 4:24; 5:12; Num 6:14). The latter may also be rendered in the LXX by *peri hamartias* (Lev 7:1–10; Isa 53:10) or *hamartia* (Num 18:9). It is linguistically possible, then, to read 2 Cor 5:21 as "he made a sacrifice for sin." This meaning is also possible in Rom 8:3, where *peri hamartias* is also used (so NEB, "sacrifice for sin"; NIV, "sin offering"; RSV footnote, "sin offering"). (*c*) The common objection that this would require two different meanings for the one word *hamartia* in the same verse and so be impossible is a specious argument. The LXX uses *hamartia* in the same verse with the same two different meanings proposed for 2 Cor 5:21: e.g., Lev 4:3, "let him offer for *sin* [*hamartias*] which he has committed a young bull without blemish to the Lord *for a sin-offering* [*peri hamartias*]." (*d*) If a choice had to be made between the sin offering and the sacrifice of reparation for 2 Cor 5:21, the latter would fit this context better. The sin offering was used for cleansing, for example, to cleanse the sanctuary of impurity. The guilt offering's purpose was the reparation of damages (*HBD*, p. 1144). The apostle, acting as an ambassador charged with concluding a peace, issues an appeal: "We beseech you . . . be reconciled to God" (5:20b). The basis for the appeal is given: "For our sake he [God] made him who knew no sin [Christ] a sacrifice for sins [a sacrifice of reparation]." That is, reparations have already been made by God, the wounded party. Nothing stands in the way of reconciliation except the human will. (*e*) Such a reading of "he made sin" would fit the context admirably. In 5:19 Paul had just said God, by means of Christ (in an unspecified way), was reconciling the world to himself, "not counting their trespasses against them." In v. 21 the apostle says explicitly how "not counting their trespasses against them" and "by means of Christ" are related. Christ's death is a sacrifice of reparation offered by God himself. The appeal to the non-Christian world is, Be reconciled to God because in Christ's death God has already borne the cost of any debt owed him.

The object of the sacrifice offered by God is "so that we might become the righteousness of God in him." Righteousness in the Bible is first and foremost faithfulness to the covenant relationship. It may refer to God's faithfulness to the relation with his people (Neh 9:7–8, 33; Rom 1:17), or it may point to the desired faithfulness of humans to the relation with God. It is Paul's conviction that history has shown that human beings are incapable of righteousness/faithfulness (Rom 3:20//Ps 143:2; Rom 9:30–31). The good news is that God has acted in Jesus to assume responsibility for the righteousness/faithfulness of his creatures. Christ, who was faithful unto death, now indwells the believer, living out in the Christian that same faithfulness he displayed in the days of his flesh (Gal 2:15–20). In this sense, righteousness is a gift from God (Phil 3:9). Our faithfulness to the relationship derives from God. Paul's picture in 5:21 seems to be that of a sacrifice of reparation having been offered by God, the offended party. To identify with that offering is to participate once again in the relationship with God with a faithfulness/righteousness God himself makes possible. If this is a correct reading of 2 Cor 5:21, then in his letters Paul uses references to at least three different Jewish sacrifices in his exposition of Jesus' death: the sacrifice of reparation here, the Passover sacrifice (1 Cor 5:7), and the sacrifice on the Day of Atonement (Rom 3:25). Because of analogies in the Greek and Roman worlds, this language would have been intelligible to the pagan as well as the Jewish hearer (Martin Hengel, *The Atonement: The Origins of the Doctrine in the New Testament* [Philadelphia: Fortress, 1981]).

The second appeal illustrative of Paul's attempt to persuade people comes in 6:1–2. This appeal is linked to the previous one in 5:20b–21 by the repetition of *parakalountes* (we beseech, 5:20b) and *parakaloumen* (we entreat, 6:1). This appeal is addressed to those who are already Christians: "Do not accept the grace of God in vain" (6:1b). This kind of language is used in two different ways by Paul. In 1 Cor 15:2 ("unless you believed in vain"); 15:14 ("if Christ has not been raised, then our preaching is in vain and your faith is in vain"); and 15:58 ("knowing that in the Lord your labor is not in vain"), the reference is to the emptiness of Christian confession if the resurrection of Jesus and of Christians is not a reality. In Gal 3:4 ("Did you experience so many things in vain?—if it really is in vain?") the reference is to Christians acting in a way contrary to their experience of grace. It is the latter usage that is appropriate for 2 Cor 6:1. The Corinthian Christians have received the grace of God (1 Cor 1:4). Now the question is whether or not they will act in ways contrary to their experience and fail to meet the test (2 Cor 13:5). In this context "not to accept the grace of God in vain" means to act as a new creation (v. 17) and regard no one from a human point of view (v. 16) but rather discern the realities of a person's heart (vv. 11–12). It means to recognize Paul's apostleship for what it is—a mission of God's ambassador aimed at effecting a reconciliation between earth and heaven. The basis for Paul's appeal comes from Isa 49:8 LXX. It reminds the Corinthians of their experience of God's grace: "At the accepted time I have listened to you, and helped you on the day of salvation" (6:2). The implication is that this foundational experience is to be worked out into their discernment of the realities of who Paul is.

RIGHTEOUSNESS IS
A REQUIREMENT FOR
PEOPLE AS WELL AS PASTOR

2 Corinthians 6:3–7:4

2 Cor 6:3–7:4 is a thought unit which, like 2:14–4:1, 4:2–16a, and 5:11–6:2, begins with "commend ourselves" (6:4). It is held together by an inclusion (6:3, "we put no obstacle in any one's way"; 7:2, "we have wronged no one, we have corrupted no one, we have taken advantage of no one"). It falls into two parts (6:3–12 and 6:13–7:4), the first being assertion, the second appeal.

Before tracing the train of thought in 6:3–7:4, it is necessary to clarify the position being taken on the relation of 6:3–10 to 6:1–2. Although traditionally it has been held that 6:3–10 is syntactically dependent on the finite verb of 6:1 ("we entreat"), the two participles of vv. 3 and 4 ("putting," v. 3; "commending," v. 4) being subordinated to it, it is grammatically possible that the participles of vv. 3–4 may be simply another instance of Paul's use of a participle instead of a finite verb and thus may be independent of 6:1 (Furnish, *2 Corinthians*, p. 342; also on 5:12, see p. 307, citing Plummer, *2 Corinthians*, p. 170). To have a sentence with a participle and no finite verb is not an un-Pauline construction (e.g., Rom 5:11; cf. *BDF*, sect. 468, 2). Numerous modern translations begin a new paragraph with 6:3 (e.g., RSV, NIV, NEB, TEV). This is the way the organization of the materials is understood in this commentary. With v. 3 a new thought unit begins.

In 2 Cor 6:3–12, the subunit focusing on assertion, Paul says, Given my actions, if there are any problems between us, they are due to you, Corinthians. This is made explicit in three assertions. (1) The first assertion comes at v. 3a: "We put no obstacle in any one's way." The motivation for such behavior is given in v. 3b: "so that no fault may be found with our ministry" (cf. 1 Cor 9:19–23; 10:32–33). Paul avoids scandalizing people so as not to expose his ministry to criticism. Here again Paul's position sounds remarkably like that of the true Cynic (ideal philosopher) as depicted by Epictetus. The true Cynic is the messenger and herald of the gods (3.22.69), sent by god to show people the truth (3.22.23). Because it is the work of Zeus he is engaged in, the Cynic takes care not to do anything that would invalidate the testimony he gives (4.8.32).

(2) The second assertion is offered in v. 4a: "as servants of God we commend ourselves in every way." What follows in vv. 4b–10 is an illustration of his self-commendation in the form of a brief resumé of his credentials. It is a mixture of hardships and virtues in a catalogue (cf. 2 Enoch 66.6 and Dio Chrysostom *Oration* 8.15–16, for a similar mixture) whose structure has four strophes (vv. 4b–5; vv. 6–7a; vv. 7b–8a; vv. 8b–10). There are (*a*) ten hardships, (*b*) eight virtues, (*c*) three combinations introduced by *dia* (RSV, with, in, in), and (*d*) seven antitheses contrasting the visible appearance and the essential reality of the apostle's life. Such conduct illustrates the worthiness of his character and commends him as an apostle (cf. 2 Thess 1:3–4). Again, the figure of the ideal philosopher seems to stand in the background. Of the true Cynic, Epictetus says that he takes upon himself hardships and bears them serenely as he undertakes his task (3.22.45–46). "Show me someone who is sick and happy, in danger and happy, dying and happy, exiled and happy, disgraced and happy. Show me, by the gods, I want to see a Stoic" (2.19.24).

(3) The third assertion concludes this part of the thought unit. "Our mouth is open to you, Corinthians" (a Hebraic circumlocution for "speaking," here meaning, "we have spoken frankly to you," TEV); "our heart is wide" (a sign of affection). "You are not restricted by us, but you are restricted in your own affections." If there is any lack of openness between the apostle and the Corinthians, it is the fault of the latter.

2 Cor 6:13–7:4 shifts from assertion to appeal. Here Paul appeals to the Corinthians to relate openly to him as he does to them, with the obvious result of their following his admonitions. Of the two appeals, the first is found at 6:13–14a. It consists of two seemingly unrelated parts: v. 13, "In return—I speak to you as to children [1 Cor 4:14; Gal 4:19; 1 Thess 2:7–8]—widen your hearts also," and v. 14a, "Do not be mismated with unbelievers." No interpretation can be ventured of the text as it stands until the problems of 6:14–7:1 are treated.

It is widely believed that 6:14–7:1 is an interpolation into 2 Corinthians. The reasoning runs thus: (*a*) it is a self-contained unit; (*b*) it interrupts the thought of its context; (*c*) if 6:14–7:1 is removed, then 6:13 joins easily to 7:2. An earlier generation of scholars often contended that 6:14–7:1 was a fragment of Paul's first letter to Corinth, a letter we hear about in 1 Cor 5:9. Today this theory is generally rejected because, whereas in 1 Cor 5:9 Paul says he wrote the former letter about not associating with the immoral among professing Christians not immoral pagans, in 2 Cor 6:14–7:1 he writes unambiguously about not being mismated with immoral and idolatrous pagans. Recent arguments have maintained that 6:14–7:1 is non-Pauline, even anti-Pauline (J. A. Fitzmyer, "Qumran and the Interpolated Paragraph in 2 Cor 6:14–7:1," *CBQ* 23[1961]:271–80; H. D. Betz, "2 Cor 6:14–7:1: An Anti-Pauline Fragment?" *JBL* 92[1973]:88–108).

The debate on this issue may be summarized as follows. (*a*) The material is non-Pauline because the contrast between "righteousness" and "iniquity" points to a Torah context for this pericope. However, the ethical use of righteousness is not un-Pauline (Rom 6:19), nor is the use of iniquity for sin (Rom 6:19). (*b*) The "light-darkness" contrast points to Qumran dualism. However, this is a Pauline metaphor (Rom 13:12; 2 Cor 4:6; 2 Cor 11:14; 1 Thess 5:5). The dualism of 2 Cor 6:14 is no different from that of Rom 13. (*c*) *Pistos* used in an absolute way to denote one who believes is a usage not found in Paul. However, Paul does use *apistos* elsewhere to mean unbeliever (1 Cor 6:6; 7:12; 10:27; 14:22–23; 2 Cor 4:4) just as in 2 Cor 6:14–15. Since the series of contrasting pairs demands it, the *pistos* (believer) in 6:15 derives from the *apistos* (unbeliever) there. (*d*) The use of "temple" for the community points to a Qumran setting. However, 1 Cor 3:16 uses temple in just this way of the community of Christians, and 1 Cor 6:19 uses temple of the individual Christian. (*e*) The citation formula "as God said" is not Paul's usual one, but it does appear in the Damascus Document of Qumran (6.13; 8.9; 19.22). However, Rom 9:15, 25; 2 Cor 4:6; 6:2 use basically the same formula. In 6:16 this formula is natural because it introduces the direct speech of God himself. (*f*) "Every pollution of body and spirit" points towards an ascetic tendency akin to that of Qumran. However, Paul can use flesh and spirit without giving them either their full theological meaning or without any ascetic tendency (2 Cor 7:5; 2:13; 1 Thess 5:23; 1 Cor 7:34). (*g*) "Make holiness perfect" points towards a non-Pauline perfectionism. However, in Paul sanctification/holiness is not only something God gives (1 Cor 1:30; 2 Thess 2:13) but also something which Christians strive to complete (1 Cor 7:34; 1 Thess 4:1–8; Rom 6:19) as well as something that ultimately God completes (1 Thess 3:13). The bottom line from such a debate is that this section, 6:14–7:1, is not alien to Paul's thought. All that is being asked for here is separation by Christians from idolatry and immorality, something Paul has already called for in 1 Corinthians.

At the same time, there are six key words that are not found elsewhere in the New Testament: "to be mismated," 6:14; "partnership," 6:14; "accord," 6:15; "agreement," 6:16; "Belial," 6:15; "defilement," 7:1. This argues for the traditional nature of 6:14–7:1. Since much of the language is characteristic of early Christian paraenesis, this may be the source of the tradition (so righteousness, iniquity, holiness/sanctification, uncleanness, cleanse, light, darkness; cf. Rom 6:19; 1 Thess 4:2–8; 5:5; Rom 13:12; Eph 5:8). This is supported by the fact that both Rom 6:19 and 1 Thess 4:1–8 refer to instruction given Christians in the midst of clusters of these terms. The case seems clinched by the fact that 1 Pet 2:4–11 is a section of Christian paraenesis containing the combination: (*a*) Christians as God's house (v. 5); (*b*) holiness (vv. 5, 9); (*c*) contrast between believers and unbelievers (v. 10); (*d*) contrast between light and darkness (v. 9); (*e*) combination of flesh and soul (v. 11). The hypothesis that seems to account for most of the facts is that 6:14–7:1 consists of a Pauline adaptation of early Christian paraenesis in order to call for abstinence from idolatry and immorality. If so, the question still remains as to whether 6:14–7:1 is integral to 2 Corinthians or is an interpolation into it.

The position taken in this commentary is that 6:14–7:1 is a digression, what Quintilian called an apostrophe (9.2.39–44). An apostrophe, he says, is the technique of turning aside from the main flow of the argument for a moment to address another aspect of the speech. For example, the speaker might attack the adversary directly. This device has already been observed in 2 Cor 11:2–15, which stands between 11:1 and 11:16–18. Vv. 2–15 are a digression that do attack the opponents' charges against Paul directly. In New Testament narrative, like the Gospel of Mark, an analogous procedure is usually called intercalation or a sandwiching technique. It is characteristic of Greco-Roman literature both before and after Paul. There is no reason, therefore, to think that the frame of 6:11–13 and 7:2 demands an interpolation theory.

The key issue is whether or not one can interpret 6:14–7:1 so as to make sense of its presence at this point in 2 Corinthians. What follows is an attempt to do so. 2 Cor 6:13–7:1 and 7:2–4 are the two parts of the appeal section of 6:3–7:4. The first appeal is given in 6:13–14a. It consists of two components: (*a*) "Widen your hearts also" (v. 13), which means the Corinthians are being asked to relate to Paul with the same openness that he has toward them; and (*b*) "Do not be mismated with unbelievers" (v. 14a), which means the Corinthians are not to become entangled with the world. They are related to one another in that if the Corinthians respond properly to Paul (i.e., as an authoritative apostle), they will then take his admonition against pagan influences seriously. This was the thrust of 2 Cor 10–13 and has been a thread throughout 2 Cor 1–7 so far. (Nils Dahl tries to read the two components together but erroneously takes the second to refer to the apostolic opponents of Paul ["A Fragment and Its Context: 2 Cor 6:14–7:1," in *Studies in Paul* (Minneapolis: Augsburg, 1977), pp. 62–69].)

This first appeal is followed up with two bases (6:14b–16a and 6:16b –18). The first basis for avoiding heathen influence is introduced by "For" (v. 14b). It consists of five rhetorical questions, each presupposing a negative answer (remember 9:1, 4–7): (*a*) "What partnership have righteousness and iniquity?" (v. 14b); (*b*) "What fellowship has light with darkness?" (v. 14c); (*c*) "What accord has Christ with Belial?" (v. 15a); (*d*) "What has a believer in common with an unbeliever?" (v. 15b); (*e*) "What agreement has the temple of God with idols?" (v. 16a). In antiquity it was common practice to use rhetorical questions to reinforce moral exhortation and instruction (e.g., Epictetus 3.23.16; Philo *On Drunkenness* 57; Ecclus 13:2b, 17, 18). Paul employed this strategy elsewhere (e.g., Rom 2:3–4, 21–23; 1 Cor 9:1–7) as well as here. The five questions have the effect of saying that there is a radical distinction between good and evil.

The second basis offered for the appeal comes in 6:16b–18. It also begins with "For" (v. 16b). It consists of a confession ("we are the temple of the living God," v. 16b) followed by a series of scripture quotations (vv. 16c–18) that function in three ways. First, v. 16c (Lev 26:12) aims to support the confession: "as God says, 'I will live in them and move among them, and I will be their God, and they shall be my people'" (cf. 1 Cor 3:16). Second, v. 17a,b (Isa 52:11) draws an implication from the church's character as temple: "Therefore, come out from them and be separate from them, says the Lord, and touch nothing unclean." Third, vv. 17c–18 (a combination of perhaps Ezek 20:34; Isa 43:6; and 2 Sam 7:14) give a promise: "I will welcome you, and I will be a father to you, and you shall be my sons and daughters, says the Lord Almighty" (cf. Rom 3:10–18 and 15:9–12 for similar use of the catenae principle). Since the Christians are God's temple and the locus of his presence, they are to live worthily. A similar line of thought is found in Epictetus:

> You carry God about with you, and know it not. You carry him within you, and perceive not that you are polluting him with unclean thoughts and filthy acts. In an image of God were present, you would not dare to do any of the things which you do. But when God himself is present within and sees all, you are not ashamed of thinking such things and doing such things. (2.3)

The cultural mind-set would reinforce Paul's point. Since there is a radical distinction between good and evil, and since Christians are God's temple, God calls them to separation from evil, promising to bless a separate people with his presence.

The first appeal closes with a final exhortation (7:1): "Since we have these promises, beloved, let us cleanse ourselves from every defilement of body and spirit, and make holiness perfect in the fear of God." Given what Paul had said in 1 Cor 5:9 ("since then you would have need to go out of the world"), the separation being called for is not so much spatial as spiritual (contrast Jubilees 22.16, where Abraham's final blessing of Jacob includes: "Separate yourself from the nations . . . for their works are unclean and all their ways are a pollution and an abomination and uncleanness"). Given the fact that we are dealing with traditional paraenesis, it is not clear what the specific behavior being designated "iniquity," "darkness," "idols" really is. Moreover, the concluding exhortation of 7:1 speaks generally of "every defilement of body and spirit." It is probably too specific to say the issue is "mixed marriages" or "association with pagans in their temples." It is safer to speak of Paul's concern with idolatry and immorality generally. (G. D. Fee rightly sees 6:14–7:1 as integral to 2 Corinthians but tries to be too specific about the problem against which it was directed ["2 Cor 6:14–7:1 and Food Offered to Idols," *NTS* 23(1977):140–61].) That such problems remained in the Corinthian church even after 1 Corinthians may be seen from the tearful letter (2 Cor 12:21, "I fear . . . I may have to mourn over *many* of those who sinned before and have not repented of the impurity, immorality, and licentiousness which they have practiced"; 13:2, "I warned those who sinned before . . . if I come again I will not spare them"). If problems remained after 1 Corinthians' admonitions, then when Paul had reestablished himself as an authoritative apostle in the Corinthians' eyes, he would want to see that these were remedied before he arrived. Understood in this way, 6:14–7:1 fits nicely into the argument of 2 Cor 1–9. That it comes in the section (2 Cor 1–7) which devotes most of its attention to laying a foundation for the requests that will follow in chapters 8–9 is no problem. Remember, it was a canon of Hellenistic style that adjacent sections should be related as a chain, with overlap at the edges. So, as Paul's apology for his authority in chapters 1–7 comes to an end, there is a request already present before the section concentrated on requests (chaps. 8–9).

There remains yet another, a second appeal, in 7:2a: "Open your hearts to us." The thought returns to that of 6:13. Unless this goal were achieved, the appeal for spiritual separation would not be heeded. So this second appeal is followed by its basis in 7:2b–3: "we have wronged no one, we have corrupted no one, we have taken advantage of no one (cf. 12:17–18). I do not say this to condemn you, for I said before that you are in our hearts, to die together and to live together" (cf. 2 Sam 15:21).

Following his assertion (6:3–12) and his appeal (6:13–7:3), Paul offers a concluding expression of hope (7:4, which according to ancient canons of style, functions both as the conclusion to what has come before and as the introduction to what follows in chap. 7): "I have great confidence in you; I have great pride in you; I am filled with comfort. With all our affliction, I am overjoyed."

Having traced the train of thought in 2 Cor 1–7, we shall now attempt to summarize the situation after the reception of the letter of tears in Corinth (2 Cor 10–13). As the result of 2 Cor 10–13, the church majority had disciplined the individual who had offended Paul (2:6) and had assured Titus of their identification with the apostle (7:7, 11). At the same time, certain problems remained. (1) There may have been lingering questions about Paul's apostleship in the minds of some. (2) There were resentments by some over Paul's change of travel plans (1:16–17; 1:23–2:1). (3) There were some who persisted in a life-style that was idolatrous and immoral (6:14–7:1). (4) There was still the need to complete the collection for the poor in Jerusalem (chaps. 8–9).

Faced with these issues, Paul began his letter (2 Cor 1–9) with an attempt to resolve complaints about his changed itinerary (1:15–2:4). He then gave an extensive apology for his apostleship (2:14–4:1; 4:2–16a; 5:11–6:2; 6:3–10). In 6:14–7:1 he returned to the need for the idolatrous and immoral within the community to cleanse themselves. In all of this, the apostle was attempting to lay a foundation for the requests that would follow in chapters 8–9, requests related to the completion of the collection.

REASONABLE REQUESTS OF AN ATTESTED APOSTLE

T hese two chapters are a thought unit held together by an inclusion (*charis*/grace/gift in 8:1 and 9:15). Their organization is that of an ABA' pattern:

    A. Why the Corinthians need to complete their collection (8:1–15)
      B. A commendation of the representatives (8:16–9:5)
    A'. Why the Corinthians need to give generously (9:6–14).

The subject matter is the collection already mentioned in 1 Cor 16:1–4. They are integrally related to chapter 7 and function as the concluding exhortations or advice for the body of the letter (2 Cor 1:8–7:16), in much the same way that Rom 14:1–15:13 functions. If 2 Cor 1–7 lays a foundation for the requests that are to come, 2 Cor 8–9 makes the requests on the basis of the foundation laid.

Before proceeding to the exposition of 2 Cor 8–9, it is necessary to justify briefly the position just stated. Such a justification comes in two logical stages. First, do chapters 8 and 9 belong together? Some suggest that chapter 9 is a separate letter (H. D. Betz, *2 Corinthians 8 and 9* [Philadelphia: Fortress, 1985]). The debate may be summarized in terms of five arguments. (*a*) Advocates of the position that chapter 9 is a separate letter contend that v. 1 uses the phrase employed in 1 Cor to introduce a new topic ("Now concerning"). However, critics note that it is not exactly the same phrase (1 Cor uses *peri de*, "now concerning," while 2 Cor 9:1 uses *peri men gar*, "for concerning"). (*b*) It is argued that 9:1 gives the full description of the collection already used in 8:4, "the offering for the saints." This would be unnecessary if chapters 8 and 9 were part of one letter. However, considering the amount of material that separates the two references, the repetition is not unusual. (*c*) It is claimed that 9:2 ("Achaia has been ready since last year") seems contradictory to 8:10

("complete what a year ago you began"). This would be understandable if chapters 8 and 9 were different letters. However, the verb in 9:2 could just as easily be translated "were ready to give" (so NIV) or "have been ready to help" since last year. If so, the implication is not that the collection is complete in Achaia but that the project was begun a year ago. (*d*) Critics point out that 9:2 is addressed to Achaia while chapter 8 seems intended for Corinth. However, 2 Cor 1:1b says the letter was for Corinth and Achaia. (*e*) Finally, it is argued that 9:3–5 gives a different reason for the coming of the brothers than that offered by 8:20. However, the two reasons are not incompatible. Moreover, it was typical of biblical and Pauline argument to repeat with variations.

Second, does chapter 8 go with chapter 7? Some have wanted to separate chapter 8 from chapter 7 (D. Georgi, "2 Corinthians," *IDBSuppl*, p. 184). The arguments are essentially two. (*a*) Critics contend that chapter 7 does nothing to prepare for the collection for the Jerusalem church which dominates chapter 8, and chapter 8 does not pick up the reconciliation theme of chapter 7. However, there are formal, thematic, and logical links between chapters 7 and 8. Formally, the two chapters are linked by the repetition of key terms: earnestness/zeal (*spoudē*), 8:7,8 and 7:11, and boasting (*kauchēseōs*), 8:24 and 7:14. Thematically, 6:11–13 and 7:2 speak of Paul's love for the Corinthians and his request for their affection in return, a theme picked up again in 8:7–8. Logically, chapter 7 contains the conventional technique, expressions of confidence in the addressees (7:4, 16), which functions to lay the basis for an appeal (Stanley N. Olson, "Pauline Expressions of Confidence in His Addressees," *CBQ* 47[1985]:282–95). So logically chapter 7 is the basis for chapter 8. (*b*) It is argued that in chapter 7 Titus seems to have just returned from Corinth, while in chapter 8 he seems on the brink of leaving for Corinth, taking chapter 8 with him. However, all this requires is that 2 Cor 1–8 (9) be Paul's letter to Corinth after Titus' return with good news (chap. 7) and that part of this response be to prepare for the collection before Paul's arrival. The sum of the matter is stated by Furnish: "No serious problem stands in the way of reading these chapters as a single, integrated discussion of the collection project, preceded by the preliminary assurances of confidence in 7:4–16" (*2 Corinthians*, p. 433).

In (A), Why the Corinthians Need to Complete their Collection (8:1–15), there are two subunits (8:1–9 and 8:10–15). 2 Cor 8:1–9 focuses on competition between Macedonia and Achaia. The question addressed is why Paul is sending Titus to Corinth this time (for previous visits, see 2 Cor 12:18; 2:13 and 7:13). In this complex sentence Paul speaks first of the presupposition of Titus's visit (8:1–5). It is the example of the Macedonians: "We want you to know about the *grace* that God has *given* the Macedonian churches" (v. 1, NIV). In the following verses the topic is the generosity of the Christians in Macedonia. Paul says this liberality in giving is a spiritual gift, just like other more unusual manifestations of the Holy Spirit (v. 7; cf. 1 Cor 12–14). The same position is set forth in Rom 12:6–8: "Having gifts that differ according to the *grace given* to us, let us use them: if prophecy, in proportion to our faith. . .; he who contributes, in liberality; he who gives aid, with zeal; he who does acts of mercy, with cheerfulness." In the midst of persecution and poverty the Macedonians have manifested the gift of liberality, giving "beyond their means, of their own free will" (v. 3). Behind this eagerness to participate in the collection for the saints by generous giving lay two other types of giving: "first they gave themselves to the Lord and to us" (v. 5b). The correlation between "to the Lord and to us" is crucial in 2 Corinthians, where the two allegiances are in danger of separation. The Macedonian Christians' gift of themselves to God and to Paul and gift of funds to their Christian brethren in Jerusalem are the presupposition of Titus's current visit to Corinth. The purpose of that visit is given in v. 6: "accordingly we have urged Titus that as he had already made a beginning (cf. 12:8), he should also complete among you this *gracious work*" (v. 6, literally "this gift"). Here the apostle utilizes the ancient technique of comparison to evoke competition between rivals. There is a definite tone of challenge running through vv. 1–6. The Macedonians are worse off than the Corinthians financially, and yet they have come through. The Macedonians are manifesting a spiritual gift that puts them ahead of the Corinthians. This is why Paul is now sending Titus to Corinth again. He is hoping the Corinthians will emulate the Macedonian Christians.

There are two dimensions of Macedonia's example to which Paul appeals. The first is their manifestation of the spiritual gift of generosity. Hence the apostle's appeal: "Now as you excel in everything—in faith, in utterance, in knowledge [1 Cor 13:1–2, 8; 1:5], in all earnestness [2 Cor 7:11–12], and in the love that we have for you [so P[46], B—cf. 2 Cor 6:11–13; 7:2]—see that you excel in this gracious work also [literally "in this gift"]". In other words, do not allow the Macedonians to surpass you in spiritual gifts.

The second dimension of Paul's appeal to the example of the Macedonians is their love for the Lord and for Paul ("they gave themselves to the Lord and to us," v. 5). Hence the apostle's words: "I say this not as a command, but to prove by the earnestness of others that your love also is genuine" (v. 8). The love referred to here is specified by the context. It is first of all a love of the Lord (v. 5, "they gave themselves to the Lord"). What it would mean to give oneself to the Lord is defined in v. 9 by the Lord's behavior: "For you know the grace [gift] of the Lord Jesus Christ, that though he was rich, yet for our sakes he became poor, so that by his poverty, you might become rich." This is also how the Macedonians acted (generously) after they had given themselves to the Lord. The love spoken of (v. 8) is in the second place a love of the apostle. The logic is the same here as in 6:11–13; 7:2. The Corinthians have received Paul's love (v. 7, our love for you); now they are to reciprocate and be like the Macedonians ("gave themselves . . . to us," v. 5). Do not let the Macedonians outdo you in love for the Lord and love for your apostle.

The second subunit in (A) (Why the Corinthians Need to Complete the Collection, 8:1–15) is 8:10–15, which consists of two parts: the advice and the motivation for following it. The advice comes in vv. 10–11: "And in this matter I give my advice: it is best for you now to complete what a year ago you began not only to do but to desire, so that your readiness in desiring it may be matched by your completing it out of what you have."

Paul's involvement in the collection had its roots in the agreement narrated in Gal 2:10. When Paul had worked out his accommodation with James and Peter and John, they had agreed about his mission to the Gentiles, "only they would have us remember the poor, which thing I was very eager to do." Paul seems to have understood the collection as having a threefold theological significance: (*a*) it would be the realization of Christian charity (Gal 2:10; 2 Cor 8:14; 9:12; Rom 15:25); (*b*) it would be an expression of Christian unity (2 Cor 9:13–14; Rom 15:27); and (*c*) it would be an anticipation of Christian eschatology (Rom 9–11, i.e., the delivery of the collection and the presentation of the representatives of the Gentile churches would serve as irrefutable evidence that God had included the Gentiles and so serve as a prod to unbelieving Jews to profess faith in Christ). Of course, Acts 24:17 depicts it as a delivery by Paul of traditional Jewish contributions from the Diaspora to Jerusalem in order to keep it within the bounds of legality for Romans. When 1 Corinthians was written, the collection of money at Corinth had hardly begun. In 16:1–4 the apostle responds to a question raised in a letter from the Corinthians about procedure for gathering the collection. If 2 Cor 10–13 was written before 2 Cor 1–9, as this commentary contends, then 12:18 doubtless refers to Titus's visit to Corinth after 1 Corinthians and before 2 Cor 10–13, during which time he dealt, in part at least, with the matter of the collection. Now in 2 Cor 8–9 Paul writes urging completion of the project before he arrives. From Rom 15:24–29 we learn that this appeal was successful and Paul went to Jerusalem with his project completed. If Acts is to be trusted, Acts 20:4–6 gives a list of those accompanying Paul to Jerusalem, although it is likely that some are not named (Keith F. Nickle, *The Collection* [Naperville, Ill.: Allenson, 1966]).

In vv. 10–11 Paul calls for completion of the collection by the Corinthians: Let your good will be matched by your actions. The motive given for such action in vv. 12–15 is equality: "as a matter of equality your abundance at the present time should supply their want, so that their abundance may supply your want, that there may be equality" (v. 14). In Rom 15:27 Paul's interpretation reads, "if the Gentiles have come to share in their spiritual blessings, they ought to be of service to them in material blessings." That is, the Jerusalem Christians had spiritual blessings to share with the Gentiles, and the Gentile Christians had material blessings to share with the Jewish Christians. The same type of argument was given by Hermas, who said that the rich have money to share with poor Christians, whereas poor Christians have power in prayer to benefit the rich Christians ("Parable" 2.5–7). If in 2 Cor 8:14, taken alone, such a meaning is not clear, taken together with 9:12–14, 8:14 seems to reflect the same mentality as Rom 15:27 and Hermas "Parable" 2.5–7. The argument from equality is reinforced by a quote from Exod 16:18 LXX.

Having given two arguments why the Corinthians needed to complete the collection (8:1–9, 10–15), Paul now turns to (B) (8:16–9:5), A Commendation of the Representatives. This carefully organized unit falls into an *aba'* pattern (*a*. 8:16–23; *b*. 8:24–9:2; *a'*. 9:3–5). The first component, (*a*) (8:16–23), states Paul's first aim in sending the representatives. The pattern here is concentric:

Titus (vv. 16–17)
  The first brother (vv. 18–19)
    Paul's aim (vv. 20–21)
  The second brother (v. 22)
Titus (v. 23).

There is a delegation of three (cf. 1 Cor 16–17): Titus, the brother who is famous for his preaching, and our brother who has often been tested and found earnest. Titus represents Paul, the two brethren represent (i.e., are apostles of, v. 23; cf. Phil 2:25, Epaphroditus, your representative/ apostle) the churches. Paul's aim is stated in vv. 20–21: "We intend that no one should blame us about this liberal gift which we are administering, for we aim at what is honorable not only in the Lord's sight but also in the sight of men." There was to be no room for suspecting underhanded dealing, as some had apparently claimed (cf. 12:16–18; 7:2). Paul's procedure reflected the best advice of pagan and Jew. Cicero said, "The chief thing in all public administration and public service is to avoid even the slightest suspicion of self-seeking" (*On Moral Obligations* 2.21.75). Philo, in discussing the logistics of getting the Jewish collection for the temple at Jerusalem from the Diaspora, said envoys were chosen from every city who were men of highest repute (*Special Laws* 1.78). Paul's first aim in sending the representatives is to avoid suspicion.

His second aim, (*a'*) (9:3–5), is "so that our boasting about you may not prove vain in this case, . . . lest if some Macedonians come with me and find that you are ready, we be humiliated—to say nothing of you— for being so confident." Paul does not want the Corinthians to be guilty of pledge dodging (v. 5, cf. Acts 5:1–11; Isaeus tells of a certain Dicaeogenes who pledged three hundred drachmas under pressure and then failed to make the payment [5.37–38]). This is clearly an appeal to self-esteem, to pride, to the Corinthians' self-respect. Surely they want to avoid being shamed.

The (*b*) component (8:24–9:2) offers an exhortation that, Paul says, is really unnecessary: "So give proof, before the churches, of your love [cf. v. 8] and of our boasting about you [cf. 7:14] to these men" (8:24). That is, complete the collection and show those who come with this letter that you love the Lord and me and that you are my obedient children, as I have boasted to them. Then, as if to anticipate the readers' reactions (oh no, not another tirade about this old subject!), Paul says, "Now it is superfluous for me to write to you about the offering for the saints, for I know your readiness" (9:1–2a). The reference to the Achaeans (v. 2) is an effort to include all those to whom the letter was addressed (1:1).

(A') (9:6–14) reverts to the theme of why the Corinthians and other Christians in Achaia need to give generously. The benefits will be for the Corinthians (vv. 6–11a, 14), for the poor in Jerusalem (v. 12a), and for God (vv. 11b, 12b, 13). Vv. 6–11a hang together and speak of benefits of generosity for the Corinthians. 2 Cor 9:6, "the one who sows bountifully will also reap bountifully," is a maxim of contemporary morality: "As you sow, so shall you reap" (Cicero *De Oratore* 2.65.261; cf. Job 4:8; Gal 6:7–8); "For those who have sown well will also harvest well" (2 Baruch 15.2; cf. Ps 126:5). V. 7 is a commentary on what "sows bountifully" means. It means one's giving must not be reluctantly or under compulsion but cheerfully (cf. Prov 22:8a LXX; Ecclus 35:9; Philo *Special Laws* 4.74; Seneca *On Benefits* 2.2.2). Vv. 8–11a are a commentary on "reap bountifully." It means liberality is beneficial to those who practice it (cf. Mal 3:10–11; Ecclus 35:10–11; Prov 11:24–25; 19:17). "God is able to provide you with every blessing in abundance, so that you may always have enough of everything and may provide in abundance for every good work" (v. 8). Here God's financial blessings are a gift (blessing, RSV), not a payment for services rendered, that enables one to provide for others ("This is why the Master has made you rich, that you may perform these services for him" [Hermas "Parable" 1.9]). V. 10 makes the same point, echoing Isa 55:10–11. If people are willing to give, God will make it possible for them to do so. V. 11a reiterates the same point: "You will be enriched in every way for great generosity." The attitude towards wealth underlying this section is that widespread at the time: wealth is good if it leads to generosity (cf. Matt 6:19–21, 24; 7:7–11; Hermas "Parable" 2.5–7; Clement of Alexandria *Can the Rich Man Be Saved?*).

Vv. 11b, 12b, and 13a speak of the benefits for God: "thanksgiving to God," "many thanksgivings to God," "glorify God." Just as in 1:11 and 4:15, the ultimate meaning of human activity is seen to be the praise of God. The collection will glorify God.

V. 12a tells of the benefits of the collection for the poor: "supplies the wants of the saints." V. 14 returns to the benefits of generosity for the giver: "while they [the poor whose needs have been met] long for you and pray for you." Here Paul reflects the belief that the prayers of the poor were especially efficacious (Hermas "Parable" 2.5–7; 1 Clement 38.2). Throughout the section, 9:6–14, the benefits of liberality for all concerned have been extolled in order to motivate the Corinthians to complete their part of the collection.

The thought unit ends with praise: "Thanks be to God for his inexpressible gift" (9:15). In a sense, this expression of thanks functions as yet another motive for generosity. Over and beyond the benefits to be received, there is the benefit already received, even our salvation through

Jesus Christ our Lord (cf. 8:9). If chapters 10–13 are part of another letter, then the ending of 2 Cor 1–9 has been lost, unless 13:11–14 was the
original ending.

Having laid his foundation in 2 Cor 1–7, the apostle turns in 2 Cor 8–9
to make the requests of the Corinthians necessary for the completion of
the collection. The motivations to which Paul appeals in chapters 8–9
are not always the highest, but they were apparently successful. The
Corinthians came through with at least something. Rom 15:25–27, written from Corinth during the visit anticipated in 2 Cor 8–9, indicates suc-
cess. "At present, however, I am going to Jerusalem with aid for the
saints. For Macedonia and Achaia have been pleased to make some contribution for the poor among the saints at Jerusalem; they were pleased
to do it, and indeed they are in debt to them, for if the Gentiles have
come to share in their spiritual blessings, they ought also to be of service
to them in material blessings."